FALLEN ANGELS
ANGELS
Among Us

ARCHANGEL MICHAEL

FALLEN ANGELS
Among Us

What You Need to Know

ELIZABETH
CLARE PROPHET

SUMMIT UNIVERSITY ✣ PRESS®

Gardiner, Montana

FALLEN ANGELS AMONG US: *What You Need to Know*
by Elizabeth Clare Prophet
Copyright © 2010 Summit Publications, Inc.
All rights reserved. Printed in the United States of America.

For information, contact Summit University Press
63 Summit Way, Gardiner, MT 59030.
Tel: 1-800-245-5445 or 406-848-9500
Web site: www.summituniversitypress.com
Library of Congress Control Number 2010932979
ISBN 978-1-932890-55-6

SUMMIT UNIVERSITY 🍂 PRESS®

Summit University Press, Science of the Spoken Word, and *Pearls of Wisdom* are trademarks registered in the U.S. Patent and Trademark Office and in other countries. All rights reserved.

Cover and interior design by Lynn M. Wilbert

Printed in the United States of America
14 13 12 11 10   1 2 3 4 5

Notes and Disclaimers: (1) No guarantee is made by Summit University Press that the meditation and visualization practices described in this book will yield successful results for anyone at any time. They are presented for informational purposes only, as the practice and proof of the Science of Being rests with the individual. (2) Because gender-neutral language can be cumbersome, we have often used he and him to refer to God or the individual. These terms are not intended to exclude women or the feminine aspect of the Godhead. The soul of man and woman is feminine in relation to the masculine, or spirit, portion of being. The soul is therefore often referred to as "she." (3) Commentary on current events has been added by the editors. (4) It is unwise to attempt to identify specific individuals as fallen angels, as only God knows the motives of the heart.

CONTENTS

ILLUSTRATIONS

One of Those Great Moments...

A timely book for this age, *Fallen Angels Among Us: What You Need to Know* takes a look back in cosmic and planetary history to reveal the forces behind the controllers and manipulators on the world scene today. The goal is to provide the background and context that will allow us to safely navigate the turbulent waters of our time.

This compilation of teachings given by spiritual teacher, mystic and author Elizabeth Clare Prophet is an eye-opening account that will answer many of your questions as to how planet earth has evolved to her perilous state in the twenty-first century.

This book is Mrs. Prophet's sequel to her bestseller, *Fallen Angels and the Origins of Evil: Why Church Fathers Suppressed the Book of Enoch and Its Startling Revelations*. In that book she examines the primordial drama of good and evil, when the first hint of corruption entered our pristine world, earth. Through a detailed analysis of scriptural and scholarly evidence, she offers compelling proof that two separate falls of angels took place long, long ago. She explains that some fell through pride with Lucifer and that others took human bodies to fulfill their lust for the "daughters of men." Both groups have reembodied through the ages.

In *Fallen Angels Among Us,* Mrs. Prophet shows that these fallen angels are still among us today and outlines specific strategies and lies that they have used to subjugate the people of earth for millennia. She also offers practical spiritual tools to meet the forces of darkness with the indomitable force of light.

TWO VIEWS OF THE FUTURE

There are two ways to view the future. First, the future is predestined and therefore happens to us. Second, we can change the future up until the very instant it becomes a reality.

We are at one of those great moments in history when those who have knowledge of earth's ancient past and their place in it can perceive more clearly the unique role they are to play today. We are at a moment of tremendous opportunity when we can make a difference in our own spiritual destiny as well as in the destiny of our planet and her people.

Our search for who we are, where we came from and where we are going takes us into the distant past, beyond the reckoning of historians—back to the lost continents of Atlantis and Lemuria,[1] back to the time when angels cast down from heavenly realms arrived on earth.

Planet earth has become home to many different evolutions. Some are loyal to the light and others are committed to darkness. Some are men. Some are fallen angels. Some are angels of light who volunteered to embody in order to assist God's children. Earth is indeed a crossroads in our galaxy. It is a complex tapestry.

ANCIENT MEMORIES OF PAST GOLDEN AGES

Many of us have a soul memory of Lemuria and Atlantis, an inner awareness of when, under the influence of fallen angels, we compromised the light and left off our spiritual path.

On Lemuria this compromise, along with the abuse of technology, contributed to the sinking of that continent over twelve thousand years ago. All that remains is the Ring of Fire, which traces the boundaries of the Pacific Ocean along the west coast of the Americas and the east coast of Asia. About a thousand years later Atlantis sank. The once-great continents of Lemuria and Atlantis now lie beneath the oceans, their triumphs and their failures covered by the shifting sands of time.

Since then, the ages have rolled by like cars on a great Ferris wheel. Civilizations have risen, flowered, declined and disappeared. And the people of Lemuria and Atlantis have reincarnated again and again—

ATLANTIS

interacting with each other, and with fallen angels—
making good and bad karma along the way.

It is against this backdrop that we are about to take
our place on the stage of cosmic history and discover
our role in making the Aquarian age a golden age.

A POTENT INDICATOR OF THE FUTURE

Before looking at some of the challenges and
opportunities we face in Aquarius, let us take a look
at one potent indicator of the future—astrology.

Astrology shows us the effects of causes that we

have set in motion in the past, the return to our doorstep of both our positive and negative karma. On the positive side, Aquarius has been seen as a gateway to the golden age. It has the potential to be an age of freedom, peace, brotherhood and spiritual enlightenment.

On the negative side of the karmic ledger, the cycles of the next decades, even the next two hundred years, portend wars, plagues, political tyranny, economic turmoil, even the sinking of continents. But this need not be. Roger Bacon, the first modern scientist, said the purpose of studying astrology is to avoid its negative portents. Bacon believed that it was possible to avoid wars through the study of astrology. He said that if leaders of the Church had read the astrological warnings—such as the comet of 1264, which preceded the battles that broke out all over Europe—they might have averted the wars of their times.[2]

The birth of the new millennium coincides approximately with the age of Aquarius. What exactly is the Aquarian age? There are twelve astrological ages, each about 2,150 years long. They take their names from the signs of the zodiac. The entire cycle of twelve ages spans about 25,800 years.

Ages are related to the precession of the equinoxes. In astronomy this is the slow movement of the earth's polar axis. As the axis moves, the point of the spring equinox moves through the signs of the zodiac, denoting which age we are in.

No one knows exactly when each age begins or ends, but we do know that we are in the waning days of the age of Pisces. Because of the precession, we move through the ages in reverse order. Prior to the age of Pisces, we were in the age of Aries and before that the age of Taurus, and so on.

In each age, we are destined to assimilate a certain attribute of God and develop it to its fullest potential. The age of Aries, for example, brought the awareness of God as the Father, the Lawgiver. That age was characterized by God's direct communion with Moses. Moses showed us that we, too, could walk and talk with the indwelling Presence, the I AM THAT I AM, the name of God he received on Mount Sinai.

MOVING FROM PISCES TO AQUARIUS

The opening of each astrological age is often accompanied by the birth of an avatar, or God-man, who embodies the spirit of the age that he inaugurates. The age of Pisces brought the awareness of God as the Son, revealed to us in the universal Christ personified in Jesus the Christ. Jesus' mission for the Piscean age was to be our mentor on the path of self-mastery.*

The conclusion of Pisces is the hour when, after

---

*Jesus came to show us how to walk the path of personal Christhood so that we could realize the fullness of the Son of God within ourselves. The word *Christ* is from the Greek *Christos,* which means "anointed." Jesus was referred to as the 'Christ' because he was fully anointed with the light of Almighty God. Christianity holds no exclusive right to the universal path of higher consciousness as two thousand years of Jesus' example, we are intended to display self-mastery over ourselves, our emotions, our thoughts, the environment and all aspects of our lives.

The dawning age of Aquarius brings us the awareness of God as the Holy Spirit and as the Divine Mother. In this age, both man and woman are intended to develop their feminine side—the creative, intuitive, nurturing and compassionate side of their soul. This can be a time of opportunity for renewed wholeness for our souls and for Mother Earth.

Some believe that a golden age will happen no matter what, but this is not the case. People have free will, and they can use it to either choose a path of freedom or to go the way of a civilization corrupted by fallen angels.

IMMORTAL TEACHERS

Some of us were there in the great golden-age civilizations of Lemuria and Atlantis, when we were guided by masters and advanced adepts. We knew and applied the laws of God, and we enjoyed a quality of life superior to what we have today.

Indelibly inscribed in the records of our own sub-

---

taught and demonstrated by Jesus Christ. John 1:9 gives scriptural confirmation that this is the birthright of every son of God: "That was the true light, which lighteth every man that cometh into the world" (John 1:9). Hence, to be the manifestation of the Christ means to be the light of that universal Christ consciousness, or universal Son of God.

conscious is the memory of an era when we walked and talked with these immortals. Today they are known as the ascended masters. They have been the wayshowers of our souls throughout our many lifetimes and have from the beginning held the vision of epochs of perfection we once knew. They are called ascended masters because they have mastered the circumstances of life, overcome the human ego, fulfilled their life's purpose, graduated from earth's schoolroom and ascended—that is, accelerated in consciousness—to become one with God. In the West we say they have entered heaven. In the East it is said that they have become enlightened or attained parinirvana.

These masters have come from all races and religions. They are the saints and sages of all ages who have risen from every walk of life and from every continent. Included among them are Gautama Buddha, Lao Tzu, Kuan Yin, Confucius and others from the Far East. In the West we have seen Enoch, Moses, Jesus the Christ, Mary the Mother and Saint Thérèse of Lisieux and many others. Included also are countless known and unknown devotees from all walks of life who have ascended after fulfilling lives of service and devotion. All offer perpetual assistance to the people of earth.

Collectively we know these spiritual beings, together with the archangels and the angelic host, as the Great White Brotherhood. This ancient name has nothing to do with race but refers to the one light out of which all races and religions have come, the white light that can be seen in the aura of the saints.

In this and in every age, the masters have sent their messengers as representatives to deliver their teachings to those who seek to reunite with their Source. These messengers are both spokesmen and scribes; empowered by the Holy Spirit, they speak or write down the master's teachings. Mark L. Prophet and Elizabeth Clare Prophet were messengers for the ascended masters. It is through their teachings that the presence of the fallen angels among us is revealed at this time.

AN AGE OF ENLIGHTENMENT IS POSSIBLE

As we move from Pisces into Aquarius, we are facing the karma of many past ages. This is a time when we are called to demonstrate our spiritual maturity. The end of the age of Pisces marks the day of personal and planetary reckoning.

The astrological indicators of oncoming karma show the darkness that can ensue if we do nothing. Astrology also shows the magnificent potential for a golden age should we choose to act.

How can we help bring in an age of enlightenment?

The ascended master Saint Germain, sponsor of the Aquarian age, brings a solution to the problem of our very ancient, complex karma. He brings a teaching and a way of life. Of greatest importance, he brings the gift of the violet flame. This spiritual energy, when

SAINT GERMAIN

used in accordance with the laws of alchemy, can transmute karma. (This will be discussed in detail in Part 5.)

It has been said that the best prophet of the future is the past. As we explore the potential for planet earth's future, it is essential to identify the events that have brought us to the present. The philosopher George Santayana said, "Those who cannot remember the past are condemned to repeat it."[3] While that is true, even those who do remember the past will repeat it if they do not have the awareness and means to transcend it. It is for this reason that *Fallen Angels Among Us: What You Need to Know* is being published at this time.

Stop a moment and ask yourself: "Where have I been for the past twelve thousand years? Who am I? Where have I come from? And where am I going?"

That is exactly what you are about to find out.

THE EDITORS

PART 1

FALLEN ANGELS
AMONG US

OUR FATHER ENOCH

CHAPTER 1

FORBIDDEN MYSTERIES OF ENOCH
THE UNTOLD STORY OF MEN AND ANGELS

With the incredibly fast pace of modern life, most of us don't take a lot of time to think about angels. But it was not always so. Back in the fourth century, for instance, when the warring Visigoths stormed the Roman Empire, when civil disorder and social corruption reached an all-time high, when a regulated economy triggered double-digit inflation—people were thinking about angels.

And it was more than quaint musings about how many angels could fit on the head of a pin. No, they were asking questions that had serious and far-reaching ramifications.

The hottest debate revolved around a single crucial issue: Were angels ever transformed into flesh-and-blood beings in order to perform earthly deeds? Though most of the debate seems to have escaped history's chronicling pen, we can, and should, reconstruct a few of its questions—for reasons that will soon become clear.

If angels ever did become fleshly beings that looked like ordinary men, what would they be like? How would you pick one out from among your neighbors? Would he be extra good, a sweet cherub of a person? Or extra evil, one of those fiendish fallen angels?

Regarding the latter, what began as a casual curiosity of the cloth has taken on the cloak of a Sherlock Holmes detective story, a probe into ancient cosmological history through fragmentary documents that piece together the missing links of much more than a mere theological dissertation on the nature and origin of evil.

EVIDENCE OF FALLEN ANGELS IN OUR MIDST

I believe that my investigations of the Book of Enoch, the texts of Origen, related scripture and apocrypha, mythological texts and ancient artifacts, though by no means complete, uncover the key to certain historical facts concerning the evolution of men and angels on this and other systems of worlds. I believe that these facts have been concealed from the children of light for thousands of years by deliberate design and that, once exposed and acted upon by dedicated hearts, they will be the essential ingredient in the turning of worlds toward a new age of peace and enlightenment.

Although space does not permit the full presentation of the facts at hand, it does afford me the opportunity to begin to unravel the forbidden mysteries of Enoch concerning the true nature of the fallen angels known as the Watchers. Enoch passed on these mysteries to his sons and their households to preserve for a far-distant generation.

Based on convincing evidence from a number of sources, our thesis confirms the Book of Enoch—that there are indeed fallen angels, that they have embodied on earth and corrupted the souls of her people, and that they will be judged by the Elect One in the day of the coming of his elect servants. By force of logic, our thesis must also put forth the corollary that these fallen ones (together with the progeny of the Nephilim who were cast out of heaven by Michael the Archangel) have continued to embody on earth without interruption for at least half a million years.

Therefore, I am prepared to prove and document that they are with us today in positions of power in Church and State as prime movers in matters of war and finance, sitting in the banking houses and on policymaking councils that determine the actual fate of mankind by population control and genetic engineering, the control of energy and commodities, education and the media, and by ideological and psychopolitical strategies of divide and conquer on all fronts.

The untold story of men and angels is a crack in the door of the full and final exposé of the manipulators and the manipulated, the oppressors and the oppressed. When I shall have penned the last word of the last volume of my ongoing essay, it will be clear, by the grace of God and his Spirit, that the embodied fallen angels, who are the main subject of Enoch's prophecy, have been from the beginning the spoilers of the dreams of God and man. At every hand, they are turning the best efforts of the noblest hearts to a mockery of the Word incarnate and setting in motion the relentless spirals of degeneration and death in both Western and Eastern civilization.

The question that has become the subject of my research is this: If evil angels used to be around on earth and, as scripture seems to indicate, wore the guise of common men, why couldn't they still be around? Given the state of affairs on planet earth, where would we find them today? Do they manipulate our government? Mismanage the economy?

Who are they anyway?

THE MATERIALITY OF ANGELS

Fourth-century men had some of the answers, preserved in little-known, hard-to-procure books, some of which have never been translated into English. A little digging into the archives of Christianity's early Church Fathers turns up the intriguing fact that they indeed knew something about the incarnation of angels—knowledge so dangerous it was banned as heresy.

Back in the first few centuries after Christ, the Church Fathers were philosophizing on the origin of evil in God's universe, especially on earth. All agreed that evil was rooted in the angels who fell from heaven, the familiar scriptural account about an archangel's rebellion against the Almighty and the angels who were cast out with him.[1]

Usually these angels were depicted as immaterial winged creatures, dark and shadowy demons tempting man to err, whispering wicked thoughts into his ear. But certain key passages in the holy books indicated that there might be more substance—literally and physically—to the fallen angels.

The materiality of angels seems to have been an age-old belief. There was the angel with whom Jacob wrestled—physical enough to cripple him at least temporarily, if not for life. So tangible was this angel that the author of the Book of Genesis calls him a man, although elsewhere scripture reveals that he was an angel.[2] The "angel" said to Jacob, "Let me go, for the day breaketh." How could Jacob have had hold upon an incorporeal angel?

The angels who came to visit Sodom had to be bolted indoors in Lot's house in order to protect them from an intended sexual assault by local townspeople, Sodomites who wanted to get to "know" the angels.[3] And Manoah offered to cook dinner for his guest—presumed to be an ordinary man until he ascended to heaven in the fire Manoah had lit. Only then did

JACOB WRESTLING WITH THE
ANGEL OF THE LORD

Manoah know that the "man of God" was "an angel
of the Lord."[4]

The bad angels, the fallen ones, were no less physical, according to certain religious scriptures of the
world. Zarathustra, the great Persian prophet, report-
edly dashed the angels' bodies to pieces because they
had used them to wreak evil. The angels (according to
the story) had instigated illicit love affairs with earthly
women—hard to accomplish without physical bodies,

especially since the tale attributed offspring to them.[5] The story of corporeal angels, despite its question-ability, at least made sense of scripture and legend.

THE BOOK OF ENOCH

And then there was the Book of Enoch. Once cherished by Jews and Christians alike, this book later fell into disfavor with powerful theologians—precisely because of its controversial statements on the nature and deeds of the fallen angels.

Its theme so infuriated the later Church Fathers that one, Filastrius, actually condemned it as heresy.[6] Nor did the rabbis deign to give credence to the book's teaching about angels. Rabbi Simeon ben Jochai in the second century A.D. pronounced a curse upon those who believed it.[7]

So the book was denounced, banned, cursed and no doubt burned—and last but not least, lost (and conveniently forgotten) for a thousand years. But with an uncanny persistence, the Book of Enoch found its way back into circulation two centuries ago.

In 1773, rumors of a surviving copy of the book drew Scottish explorer James Bruce to distant Ethiopia. True to hearsay, the Book of Enoch had been pre-served by the Ethiopic church, which put it right along-side the other books of the Bible.

Bruce secured not one, but three Ethiopic copies of the precious book and brought them back to Europe and Britain. When in 1821 Dr. Richard Laurence, a

Hebrew professor at Oxford, produced the first English translation of the work, the modern world gained its first glimpse of the forbidden mysteries of Enoch.[8]

The Book of Enoch speaks from that obscure realm where history and mythology overlap. Privy to those unfathomable founts of ancient lore, its author draws for the reader a brimming cup of secret wisdom.

A primordial drama of good and evil, light and dark, unfolds. The book tracks Enoch's footsteps back to antiquity's timelessness—back to the first hint of corruption upon a pristine world: earth.

THE FALL AND DESTRUCTION OF THE WATCHERS

The trouble began, according to the Book of Enoch, when the heavenly angels and their leader named Samyaza developed an insatiable lust for the "daughters of men" upon earth and an irrepressible desire to beget children by these women. Samyaza feared to descend alone to the daughters of men, and so he convinced two hundred angels called Watchers to accompany him on his mission of pleasure.

Then the angels took oaths and bound themselves to the undertaking by "mutual execrations"—curses. Once such a pact was sealed, betrayal was punishable by unnamed horrors.

In their gang-inspired bravado, the angels descended and took wives from among the daughters of men. They taught the women sorcery, incantations, and divination—twisted versions of the secrets of heaven.

The plot thickens like a science-fiction thriller, easier to take as fantasy than as fact. The women conceive children from these angels—evil giants. The giants devour all the food that the men of earth can produce. Nothing satiates their hunger. They kill and eat birds, beasts, reptiles and fish. To their gargantuan appetites, nothing is sacrosanct. Soon even Homo sapiens becomes a delicacy. (En. 7:1–15)

As the story goes, one spiteful angel named Azazyel taught men every species of iniquity, including the means for making swords, knives, shields, breastplates and other instruments of war. Thus, millennia ago, someone explained war not as a man-invented or God-sent plague, but as a vengeful act of a fallen angel barred from the planes of God's power. The implication is that man, through one form of manipulation or another, latched on to the war games of the fallen angels and allowed himself to commit genocide in defense of their archrivalries.

But there is more to Enoch's account of the Watchers. When the men of earth cry out against the atrocities heaped upon them, heaven hears their plea. The mighty archangels—Michael, Gabriel, Raphael, Suryal and Uriel—appeal on behalf of earth's people before the Most High, the King of kings. (En. 9:1–14)

The LORD orders Raphael to bind Azazyel hand and foot. Gabriel is sent to destroy the "children of fornication," the offspring of the Watchers, by inciting them to their own self-destruction in mutual slaughter. Michael is then authorized to bind Samyaza and his wicked offspring "for seventy generations underneath the earth, even to the day of judgment."[9] And God sends the Great Flood to wipe out the evil giants, the children of the Watchers.

RETURN OF THE WATCHERS

In succeeding generations, after the sinking of the continent of Atlantis, the giants return once again to haunt mankind. Likewise it seems that the Watchers will hold power over man (in some curiously undefined way) until the final judgment of these angels comes, which, the author implies, is long overdue.

There is also a most significant passage near the end of the Book of Enoch that speaks of the latter days upon earth:

> In those days will the angels return and hurl themselves upon the East,... to stir up the kings and provoke in them a spirit of unrest....
>
> And they will march up to and tread under foot the land of His elect ones....
>
> They will begin to fight amongst themselves... till the number of corpses through their slaughter is beyond count, and their punishment be no idle one.[10]

This seems a chilling prophecy of our own time—with wars and rumors of wars in "the East" and the countless corpses in a holy land. There is no date stamped on the prediction, but a few word changes in the right places would make it duplicate today's headlines.

The main theme of the Book of Enoch is the final judgment of these fallen angels, the Watchers, and their progeny, the evil spirits.[11]

ENOCH'S INFLUENCE ON JESUS

Most scholars say that the present form of the story in the Book of Enoch was penned sometime during the second century B.C. and was popular for at least five hundred years. The earliest Ethiopic text was apparently made from a Greek manuscript of the Book of Enoch, which itself was a copy of an earlier text. The original was apparently written in a Semitic language, now thought to be Aramaic.

Though it was once believed to be post-Christian (the similarities to Christian terminology and teachings are striking), discoveries of copies of the book among the Dead Sea Scrolls found at Qumran prove that the book was in existence before the time of Jesus Christ. But the date of the original writing upon which the Qumran copies of the second century B.C. were based is shrouded in obscurity. It is, in a word, old.

It has largely been the opinion of historians that the book does not really contain the authentic words of the ancient biblical patriarch Enoch, since he would have lived (according to the chronologies in the Book of Genesis) several thousand years earlier than the first known appearance of the book attributed to him.

But, of course, the contemporary historians' knowledge of Judaic scriptural history is by no means complete. As time progresses, new discoveries may help clarify the picture painted by the rabbinical tradition in the Zohar, which implies that Enoch's writings were passed faithfully from generation to generation.[12]

Despite its unknown origins, Christians once accepted the words of this Book of Enoch as authentic scripture, especially the part about the fallen angels and their prophesied judgment. In fact, many of the key concepts used by Jesus Christ himself seem directly connected to terms and ideas in the Book of Enoch.

Thus, it is hard to avoid the conclusion that Jesus had not only studied the book, but also respected it highly enough to adopt and elaborate on its specific descriptions of the coming kingdom and its theme of inevitable judgment descending upon "the wicked," the term most often used in the Old Testament to describe the Watchers.[13]

There is abundant proof that Christ approved of the Book of Enoch. Over a hundred phrases in the New Testament find precedents in the Book of Enoch. Our Lord's beatitude "Blessed are the meek: for they shall inherit the earth"[14] perhaps renders Enoch 6:9, "The elect shall possess light, joy, and peace; and they shall inherit the earth."

Likewise, Jesus' scolding "Woe unto that man by whom the Son of man is betrayed! it had been good for that man if he had not been born"[15] is reminiscent of Enoch's "Where [will be] the place of rest for those who have rejected the Lord of spirits? It would have been better for them, had they never been born."[16]

And the "woe unto you that are rich"[17] of Jesus Christ is found almost verbatim in Enoch: "Woe to you who are rich, for in your riches have you trusted; but from your riches you shall be removed; because you have not remembered the Most High in the days of your prosperity."[18]

ENOCH AND THE EPISTLE OF JUDE

There is other dramatic evidence of the early Christian acceptance of the Book of Enoch. The Epistle of Jude clearly discusses the content of the Book of Enoch, noting that

> there are certain men crept in unawares, who were before of old ordained to this condemnation, ungodly men, turning the grace of our God into lasciviousness....
>
> These are spots in your feasts of charity, when they feast with you, feeding themselves without fear: clouds they are without water, carried about of winds; trees whose fruit withereth, without fruit, twice dead, plucked up by the roots;
>
> Raging waves of the sea, foaming out their own shame; wandering stars, to whom is reserved the blackness of darkness for ever.[19]

Jude actually quotes Enoch directly and refers to him by name, saying:

> And Enoch also, the seventh from Adam, prophesied of these, saying, Behold, the Lord cometh with ten thousands of his saints,
>
> To execute judgment upon all, and to convince all that are ungodly among them of all their ungodly deeds which they have ungodly committed, and of all their hard speeches which ungodly sinners have spoken against him.[20]

Note that the entire premise and conclusion of the Book of Enoch—i.e., the judgment of the Watchers as the key to the liberation of the souls of light and as a necessary planetary purge prior to the LORD's kingdom come—is predicated to occur "in a generation which is to succeed at a distant period, on account of the elect." (En. 1:2)

Who are the elect? We define the elect as those who elect to be instruments of God's will, according to their calling from the Father and the Son to be bearers of the light of the Elect One.

We take Enoch 1:2 to mean that the judgment is a direct and inevitable consequence of the coming of the Elect One—the incarnate Word—and his chosen in this and succeeding centuries.

The judgment prophesied by Enoch will come through the Christ light that the Son has ignited in the hearts of his own. The light is of the "inner man," known to Paul as "Christ in you, the hope of glory."[21]

Enoch's prophecy on the judgment is quoted by Jude as acceptable scriptural evidence of "the ungodly." Jude based his entire epistle upon this Enochian theme. But when Enoch's book was later questioned, Jude himself also became suspect, his letter barely remaining among the canonical books of the Bible.

Another remarkable bit of evidence for the early Christians' acceptance of the Book of Enoch was for many years buried under the King James Bible's mistranslation of Luke 9:35, describing the transfiguration of Christ: "And there came a voice out of the cloud, saying, This is my beloved Son: hear him." Apparently the translator here wished to make this verse agree with a similar verse in Matthew and Mark. But Luke's verse in the original Greek reads: "This is my Son, the Elect One.[22] Hear him."

The Book of Enoch was also much loved by the Essenes, the new-age community that had a large monastery at Qumran on the Dead Sea at the time of Jesus Christ. "The motif of the fallen angels," Dr. Charles Francis Potter notes, "was a favorite legend among the Essenes."[23]

Fragments of ten Enoch manuscripts were found among the Dead Sea Scrolls. The famous scrolls actually comprise only one part of the total findings at Qumran. Much of the rest was Enochian literature, copies of the Book of Enoch, and other apocryphal works in the Enochian tradition, like the Book of Jubilees.

The Essenes were waiting for the coming Messiah to deliver them from the persecution they suffered, which they attributed to the "sons of Belial"[24]—undoubtedly the fallen angels. They awaited the coming of the Elect One; for as the Book of Enoch had prophesied, "You shall behold my Elect One, sitting upon the throne of my glory. And he shall judge Azazeel [Azazyel], all his associates, and all his hosts."[25]

In this same tradition, Jesus himself said, "Now is the judgment of this world [the world system of the Watchers]: now shall the prince of this world be cast out."[26]

Certainly his listeners, well versed as they were in the teachings of the Book of Enoch, would have caught Jesus' clear inference: that he came to implement the judgment of the fallen angels prophesied in the Book of Enoch.

In essence, Jesus revealed himself as the Messiah, the Elect One of the Book of Enoch, who came not only to fulfill the prophecies of the Old Testament but also to fulfill one very special prophecy in the Book of Enoch—namely, the judgment of the Watchers and their offspring.

LATER CHURCH FATHERS CHALLENGE THE BOOK OF ENOCH

Everybody loved and respected the Book of Enoch, at least for a time. The turning point of opinions came in the fourth century, during the era of the Church

Fathers. These highly respected interpreters of Christ's theology were the prominent leaders and teachers of the Christian Church who thrived from the first to the eighth centuries A.D.

At first the Fathers devoted much attention to the subject of the fall of the angel whom they knew as the biblical Satan. They also addressed the subject of the personalities of other fallen angels, the modus operandi of wicked spirits, and the nature of evil itself. Convinced that these ancient wicked ones were still quite active in the world, the early Fathers often quoted the Book of Enoch to make their case for good against evil.

Now let us examine how the later Church Fathers turned away from the concept of embodied angels and the Book of Enoch, thus playing into the hands of the fallen angels.

The later Church Fathers did indeed have difficulty with the Enoch viewpoint and sought another explanation for the fall of the angels. Perhaps they were uncomfortable with the implications of the story of some among us who are not of us—men who are not men but fallen angels. So they looked to the record of Lucifer's fall in Isaiah 14:12–15, which reads:

> How art thou fallen from heaven, O Lucifer, son of the morning! how art thou cut down to the ground, which didst weaken the nations!
>
> For thou hast said in thine heart, I will ascend into heaven, I will exalt my throne above the stars

of God: I will sit also upon the mount of the con-
gregation, in the sides of the north:

I will ascend above the heights of the clouds;
I will be like the most High. Yet thou shalt be
brought down to hell, to the sides of the pit.

Some Church Fathers saw in these verses of Isaiah
the story of the fall of an archangel and subsequently
that of his underlings, drawing by "his tail," according
to Revelation 12:4, "the third part of the stars [angels]
of heaven." They saw the fall as being through pride
rather than through lust, as in the Enoch account.

The Fathers, it seems, came up with an idea—an
easy way to avoid the troublesome tale of embodied
evil angels. They unanimously chose the version of the
fall of the angels through pride instead of the Enochian
version of the fall through lust, making it an either/or
equation.

The question is: Was their motivation in challenging the Book of Enoch to avoid the controversial doctrine of the corporeality of the wicked angels and their
bodily presence upon earth? And if so, why?

Perhaps we can reconstruct the logic of their argu-
ment. If the angels fell through lust, they must have
had (or gotten) physical bodies to outplay their physical desires. But if the angels merely fell through pride,
a corruption of mind and heart, they need not have had
bodies to consummate their sin. They could simply be
those bat-winged demons that whisper into men's ears,

inciting them to vanity of vanities.

The latter explanation was, in theological terms, less problematical. And to this very day—though the Genghis Khans, et al., have made their grandiose entrances and exits, parading their superhuman or subhuman vileness, as the case may be—that belief prevails.

I for one do not believe that the sin of pride does not require a physical body to outplay itself. The culture these fallen angels have created today, as I will show, is based in materialism and the pride of the eye, from all manner of fixations on the body to an obsession with fashion. They have created a civilization that is rooted in both pride and lust, that has become the proving ground for fallen egos vying for attention and acclaim through the success cult.

In fact, the sin of lust itself technically does not require a physical body to stain the soul and life record of men or angels. For did not Jesus teach that the sin of lust could be carried out mentally and spiritually through an impure heart? "Whosoever looketh on a woman to lust after her hath committed adultery with her already in his heart."[27]

It would seem that to dwell upon the flesh-and-blood aspects of sin should cause a digression from the fact that the state of sinfulness or virtue is a condition of the soul which may be carried to its logical conclusion in contempt of the Almighty on any plane of habitation by either men or angels, whether clothed with bodies earthly, astral or ethereal.[28]

THE INCARNATION OF FALLEN ANGELS

Notwithstanding, the Church Fathers who grasped at a few verses of Isaiah as salvation from their Enochian dilemma overlooked the most astounding story of all. The narrative, after detailing the fall of the archangel Lucifer, outlines the contemptuous deeds, the earthly deeds, of this ambitious "son of the morning," calling him outright "the man that made the earth to tremble."

> They that see thee shall narrowly look upon thee, and consider thee, saying, Is this the man that made the earth to tremble, that did shake kingdoms;
>
> That made the world as a wilderness, and destroyed the cities thereof; that opened not the house of his prisoners?
>
> All the kings of the nations, even all of them, lie in glory, every one in his own house.
>
> But thou art cast out of thy grave like an abominable branch, and as the raiment of those that are slain, thrust through with a sword, that go down to the stones of the pit; as a carcase trodden under feet.[29]

Isaiah called Lucifer a man—giving strong indication that he believed that the "cast down one" had walked the earth in the flesh, had moved among mortals as one of them.[30]

Cyprian, a third-century bishop of Carthage, noted the specific use of the word *man* and used it as proof that the Antichrist—Lucifer—would someday come as a man. Aphrahat, a fourth-century Christian theologian from Persia, believed that Lucifer had already incarnated—as Nebuchadnezzar, king of ancient Babylon.[31]

But this phenomenal piece of evidence for the incarnation of fallen angels was brushed aside by the other Church Fathers—if they ever recognized it for what it was—who instead used the Isaiah passage to launch another debate: the pride-versus-lust controversy.

Christian writer Julius Africanus (200–245) first opposed the traditional story of the fall of the angels through lust. He even tackled Genesis 6, verses 1–4, about the "sons of God," traditionally interpreted to be the Watchers, and the "daughters of men," i.e., the descendants of Cain—a parallel to the Book of Enoch in approved scripture. The pivotal verses read:

> And it came to pass, when men began to multiply on the face of the earth, and daughters were born unto them,
>
> That the sons of God saw the daughters of men that they were fair; and they took them wives of all which they chose.
>
> And the Lord said, My spirit shall not always strive with man, for that he also is flesh: yet his days shall be an hundred and twenty years.
>
> There were giants in the earth in those days; and also after that, when the sons of God came in unto the daughters of men, and they bare children to them, the same became mighty men which were of old, men of renown.

Julius Africanus preferred to believe that the "sons of God" in Genesis 6:2 who "saw the daughters of men" and "took them wives" didn't refer at all to angels, despite the fact that certain translations of the Bible in his day explicitly read "angels of God" rather than "sons of God."[32]

Julius Africanus thought that the verse referred instead to the righteous sons of Seth who "fell" (in the moral sense) by taking wives of the inferior daughters of Cain.[33] He formed his opinion in spite of the fact that both the Book of Enoch and the Book of Jude refer to angels who left their first (heavenly) estate,[34] which Julius should have known, and also in spite of the fact that the term "sons of God" is elsewhere used in the Old Testament to indicate angels,[35] which Julius also should have known.

The opinions of the Church Fathers soon flocked to this interpretation. In the early fourth century, the Syrian authority Ephraem also declared that Genesis 6 referred to the Sethites and Cainites—and therefore not to the fall of angels through lust.[36]

The controversy continued to rage among Church Fathers and scholars until finally Enoch was declared heresy.

And so the words of Enoch faded from the source books of civilization. It might not be irrelevant or irreverent to ask, Who made the deletions—men or angels? Who so wanted to keep the presence of fallen ones upon earth a guarded secret?

In the guise and garb of Christian and Jew, they—the fallen angels and those whom they had influenced—denounced and suppressed the Book of Enoch's record of the fall of angels through the lusts of the flesh. Their verdicts of heresy and blasphemy rested against Enoch for over fifteen hundred years.

WHICH CAME FIRST, GENESIS OR ENOCH?

The twentieth-century discovery of several Aramaic Enoch texts among the Dead Sea Scrolls prompted Catholic scholar J. T. Milik to compile a complete history of the Enoch legends, including translations of the Aramaic manuscripts.

Milik's 400-page book, published in 1976 by Oxford,[37] is a milestone in Enochian scholarship, and Milik himself is no doubt one of the world's finest experts on the subject. His opinions, based as they are on years of in-depth research, are highly respected.

Milik notes the obviously close interdependence of the story of the fallen angels in Enoch and the story of the "sons of God" in the Book of Genesis. But he does not draw the same conclusion as the Church Fathers, namely that the Book of Enoch misinterpreted the earlier Genesis account and was therefore irrelevant.

Milik, rather, arrives at a surprising yet well-justified conclusion: that not only is the history of the fallen angels in Enoch older than Genesis 6, but Genesis 6 is in fact a direct summary of the earlier Enoch account.[38]

This is what Milik calls the "ineluctable solution": It is Genesis 6 that is based on Enoch and not the other way around. Milik thinks that the text of Genesis 6, by its abridged and allusive formulation and direct quoting of two or three phrases of Enoch, must be the later of the two, making the Enoch legend earlier than the definitive chapters in Genesis.[39]

Milik has thus deftly turned the tables on the late Church Fathers who banned the records of fallen angels mating with daughters of men and who labeled Enoch's teaching a heretical misinterpretation of Genesis 6. For if Genesis 6 was really based on the Book of Enoch, then obviously Genesis 6 is retelling the same event as Enoch: the lusting of the fallen angels after the daughters of men. Enoch's account was in the Bible, right in the approved text of Genesis, all along.

If Milik is right—and the evidence leans in his favor— then the criteria upon which the Fathers based their judgments against the Book of Enoch are fully invalidated and their testimony against Enoch is refuted. Their arguments have no ground. Enoch's case must be reopened and retried.

TWO FALLS OF ANGELS

But the astute reader will ask, If Genesis 6 tells of the fall of the angels through lust, what about the other biblical fall of the archangel through pride, as told in Isaiah and as noted (or rather, used) by the later Church Fathers long ago? Here again, twentieth-century scholarship provides an answer that was unavailable in the patristic era.

In an unparalleled and detailed probing into the specific meaning of the passage, Hebrew scholar Julian Morgenstern discovered that tied up in the Genesis verses are traces of "two distinct and originally entirely unrelated myths dealing with gods or angels."[40]

In his remarkable exegesis (Hebrew Union College, 1939), Morgenstern proves that originally two accounts of separate falls of the angels were known: one, that of the archangel's rebellion against the authority of God and his subsequent fall through pride, in which he was followed by a multitude of lesser angels, biblically called the Nephilim (the "fallen ones"); and two, the other account, recorded faithfully in the Book of Enoch—the later fall of the angels, called Watchers, through inordinate lust for the daughters of men.[41] And so, Morgenstern concludes, the angels fell not once but twice.

Morgenstern explains that the very construction of Genesis 6:4, one of the most intricate and obscure Old Testament verses, implies that it is a synthesis of two different stories. In the literal English of the Jerusalem Bible, this verse reads:

> The Nephilim were on the earth at that time (and even afterward) when the sons of God resorted to the daughters of man, and had children by them.[42]

The text specifically sets side by side two facts: one, there used to be beings called Nephilim on earth; and two, they were still around when the sons of God came down and mated with the daughters of men. Clearly, says Morgenstern, the Nephilim are fallen angels who were already on the earth when the sons of God—the other angels which Enoch depicted—also fell through their own lust.

But how did the Nephilim fallen angels get to earth in the first place? That, states Morgenstern, is where the rebellious archangel and the fall through pride fits in. That is the earlier of two entirely separate celestial events.[43]

VALIDATION FOR ENOCH

The seeming contradiction between two falls of angels, eventually used by the Fathers against Enoch, disappears if there are separate stories of two falls.

Enoch's book, then, is a trustworthy preservation of the one fall, the one through lust, that would otherwise have been lost to posterity but for a few other brief apocryphal references.

The later Church Fathers' denial of the Book of Enoch thus clouded man's understanding of the fallen angels for centuries. Furthermore, the statements of the later Church Fathers against the idea of physical incarnation of angels are far from authoritative. Linguistic proof supports the theory that the Jews of ancient times believed the fallen angels physically incarnated in flesh bodies.

Morgenstern also hints that for the early Jews, the fallen angels were quite physical, noting that the crime of the "sons of God" was one which was characteristic of the human level of existence. He shows that God's punishment of these angels was that they take on the nature and quality of the human women with whom they had associated themselves carnally and that they become mortal. Morgenstern says, "No other conclusion is possible."[44] Sentenced to an earthly life, the angels thereafter became as mortal men.

One by one the arguments against the Book of Enoch fade away. The day may soon arrive when the final complaints about the Book of Enoch's lack of historicity and "late date" are also silenced by new evidence of the book's real antiquity.

Not only could the book be authentically the ancient story of the real Enoch; it could also be the answer to the philosophers' conundrum of the origin of evil in God's universe. According to Harvard's Dr. Paul D. Hanson, the myth of the fallen angels "offers an etiology of evil in the world: all of the evil in the world stems from a heavenly event, the rebellion of certain divine beings, and more immediately, from the resulting generation of their pernicious offspring in the world."[45]

CHAPTER 2

THE FALL OF LUCIFER, OF MAN AND THE COMING OF THE LAGGARDS

Today we look around at the confusion on the planet and wonder where it all started and how we got into this realm of twilight, of absence of vision and unity among people and nations. It wasn't always this way. Looking back in cosmic history, we find that the compromise began during the time of the biblical Adam and Eve, when the fallen angels entered the picture. Let's look at how and why these angels were in the Garden of Eden.

Among the angelic evolutions is the higher order of archangels. Many people today are familiar with Archangels Michael, Gabriel and Raphael. But there is one whom we might not recognize as an archangel, and that one is Lucifer, who was an archangel of great stature before he rebelled against God. His rebellion was prompted by his refusal to serve God's offspring—man.

THE FALL OF LUCIFER

There is a story in the apocrypha of the New Testament—religious writings that have been handed down from the early Christians but which have not become a part of our Bible—that when God created mankind in his image and likeness, he created sons and daughters. He sent forth Christed ones and said to his angels: "I have formed man out of my own image, out of my own likeness. This image is myself incarnate. Now, therefore, worship the image of God." Thus we see that in the hierarchy of the kingdoms of God, the angels occupy a position as ministering servants to the sons of God.

You might say that Lucifer became jealous that the LORD God did not require that the creation worship him, for he had been with God in the very creation of his offspring. And so he would not bow before the light of the offspring of the Most High.

The apocryphal Gospel of Bartholomew elaborates upon the reason for the archangel's fall, explaining that Lucifer revealed his pride when he refused to bend the knee before the Christ within the man made by the LORD: "I am fire of fire," boasts the archangel. "I was the first angel formed, and shall I worship clay and matter?"[1] His refusal to worship the Son of God within man was the beginning of the Great Rebellion.

It is sometimes difficult to understand how one so close to the heart of God, one who was such an exalted

Photograph by Luc Viatour

FALLEN LUCIFER

being—one who was called son of the morning and
Lucifer (meaning "lightbearer")—could rebel. I see
Lucifer's pride and egocentrism, the marks of his fall,
as an intellectual rationale that is devoid of God in the
center, an attitude of self-sufficiency that claims: "I
don't need God because I can do better than God."

When all of this took place in the consciousness of
Lucifer, he still had great light; and that great light was
the result of his momentum before his fall. So great
was his light that millions of angels were in his service,
and when he made the decision to separate from the
fiery core of God's being, the angelic hosts, so accus-
tomed to obedience to their leader, followed after him.

We read in the twelfth chapter of the Book of
Revelation:

> And there was war in heaven: Michael and his
> angels fought against the dragon; and the dragon
> fought and his angels, and prevailed not; neither
> was their place found any more in heaven. And the
> great dragon was cast out, that old serpent, called
> the Devil, and Satan, which deceiveth the whole
> world: he was cast out into the earth, and his angels
> were cast out with him.

Having put themselves out of harmony with their
point of origin, these rebellious angels were no longer
able to dwell in the higher realms of God's kingdom.
"Cast down into the earth" meant that they were cast
into the physical plane to take on physical bodies, such

as we wear, and that they would thereafter be subject to the laws of karma and reincarnation.

The Devil (also called Lucifer) and his angels did not want to be cast down. They wanted to have their rebellion and remain in heaven. It took a heavenly battle, a galactic Armageddon, for Archangel Michael

ANGELS CAST DOWN FROM HEAVEN

to force these angels out of heaven into the planes of the earth. Thus began the fallen angels' sojourn on earth.

One name listed in Revelation 12:9 for the "great dragon" is Satan. Let us understand who Satan is and what he represents. The word *satan* means "adversary." We speak of one devil named Satan, but in fact there is a band of fallen angels, called Satans [pronounced Seh-'tanz], who were cast out of heaven along with Lucifer and his angels. Satan is the original progenitor, or the highest ranking, of the Satans. We refer to them collectively as Satan and his seed.

Before the Great Rebellion, the Satans served as initiators who instructed and tested souls, assisting them to attain greater God-mastery. After their fall, the Satans became tempters, and their focus shifted to attempting to lure the sons of God into breaking their vows and violating God's laws.

The Book of Job describes Satan as an initiator, a tester. The first chapter records "a day when the sons of God came to present themselves before the LORD, and Satan came also among them." God spoke to Satan of Job's goodness, saying "there is none like him in the earth, a perfect and an upright man." Satan replied, "Doth Job fear God for nought?"

The LORD gave Satan permission to prove, or test, Job to see how intense and how great his love for God would be if he were stripped of all his worldly possessions and his family. Throughout Satan's testing of

**FALLEN SATAN YIELDS
TO THE ANGELS OF THE LORD**

him, Job remained steadfast in his love and worship
of God.

After the Satans were cast into physical embodiment on earth, they began to intermarry and procre-
ate. And to this day the seed of Satan are in embodiment among us. We see these spoilers in the media and

other arenas, including the churches and other religious bodies. Wherever they go, they take an adversarial position to God and his people, opposing the light and the truth.

THE FIRST ROOT RACES

Thousands and hundreds of thousands of years before the fall of Lucifer and the subsequent fall of the Watchers, the children of God on earth had enjoyed a long history of purity and perfection in several golden-age civilizations. The earliest of these civilizations existed on the continents of Africa, Asia and South America and in other areas now buried beneath oceans and desert sands. These golden ages antedated the more recent golden ages on Atlantis and Lemuria.

Just as we see great variety in the races of man today, so there is also great diversity in the origin and soul evolution of the lifewaves who have been, and still are, working out their destiny on earth. According to esoteric tradition, seven primary groups of souls— the first to seventh root races—are to embody on this planet.

A root race is a lifewave, an evolution of souls that comes forth from the heart of God in a certain epoch in cosmic history to ensoul a particular aspect of God's consciousness. The members of each root race share a unique archetypal pattern, divine plan and mission to fulfill on earth.

The first three root races lived in harmony with

each other and with the laws of God in three golden ages before the Fall of Adam and Eve. Like us, they had free will. Unlike us, they used it only to do the will of God. They had spiritual teachers from whom they received a knowledge of evil (the *energy veil*) and a forewarning of the consequences of choosing to experience evil directly. They never fell for the rationale that you have to experience evil in order to understand it, in order to distinguish it, in order to choose. For them, the analysis in the laboratory of the soul was enough.

Thus, the members of those first three root races did not depart from the ideal consciousness of constantly beholding the absolute perfection of God. They never experienced what has been called the Fall—the descent in consciousness from the planes of Spirit to the planes of Matter, the descent from the fiery core of God's consciousness to the plane of duality, of relative good and evil. Living as one and in harmony with God and nature, their bodies were far less dense, less physical than ours are today. At the conclusion of their cycles on earth, they reunited with God in Spirit without ever experiencing sin.

THE FALL OF MAN ON LEMURIA

It was during the time of the fourth root race that the allegorical Fall of man took place under the influence of the band of fallen angels known as Serpent. The biblical Adam and Eve were symbolic of man and woman living on the continent of Lemuria during that epoch, some tens of thousands of years ago.

Unlike those of the first three root races, an impersonal knowledge of evil did not satisfy the members of the fourth root race. Succumbing to the temptations and lies of the fallen angels, they decided to experiment with the energy veil firsthand, partaking of the forbidden fruit of the tree of knowledge of good and evil. This decision marked their departure from innocence and their descent into the world of duality—of unreality, or maya, as the Hindus call it.

We understand from this allegory that the knowledge of good and evil is not knowledge at all in the divine sense of the word, but the belief in an existence apart from God. It is the belief that God and man are two instead of one. This so-called knowledge immediately lowered the consciousness of man from the plane of oneness in God, or Spirit (the etheric plane), to that of duality in dense form (the physical plane). This knowledge produced, therefore, the synthetic image in place of the image of absolute perfection.

Originally, man's inclination was to outpicture only good; having been made in the image of God, he was inherently good. God had forbidden man to eat of the fruit of the tree of knowledge of good and evil because he knew that once man partook of duality, it would become an integral part of his self-awareness and he would lose the standard of absolute good, or oneness with God.

Prior to his descent into the consciousness of duality, man's attention and energies were God-centered: His life was God's life, and by the intelligent use of free will he dedicated God's energies to the lowering of the patterns made in the heavens into the patterns made in the earth.[2] The covenants between God and man had

ADAM AND EVE IN THE GARDEN

not been broken; therefore, as man surrendered his all to God, God surrendered his All to man.

As long as Adam and Eve communed with God face to face in the Garden in the cool of the day, as long as they were aware of the reality of only God, there was no sense of separation for them. It was when they could no longer commune with God that the Garden was closed to them. Thus, once they had entertained the idea of themselves as being outside of the consciousness of their Source—the divine image in which they were created—they felt naked and alone. Recognizing this, they symbolically clothed themselves with fig leaves, but to no avail, because it is the soul and not the flesh that suffers the pangs of a lost identity. That point of contact with the Infinite can only be found by returning to the unity of the eternal God Presence.

God had given man the freedom to choose from among the infinite virtues of good, but man used his freedom to choose from among the finite manifestations of the energy veil. He did not heed God's warning: "In the day that thou eatest thereof thou [the discriminating consciousness of good] shalt surely die."[3] He simply would not believe that his ability to distinguish between the Real (absolute good) and the unreal (relative good and evil) would be lost once his pure consciousness had absorbed the impure substance of the veil. Such was man's unfortunate misconception of free will.

Those who had succumbed to the influence of the

fallen angels became subject to mortality. When their reference point became dual and finite, they were no longer exempt from death, for death is the consequence of finitude. As Genesis tells the story, once man had partaken of the fruit, his creative powers were curtailed. He was driven out of paradise and denied

ADAM AND EVE BEING CAST OUT OF THE GARDEN

access to the fruit of the Tree of Life—this fruit being the essence of God's power, which endows both the being and the creation of those who partake of it with the infinite, creative energies of immortal life.

Just as Lucifer had been cast out of heaven into a state of mortality, so Adam and Eve, by their freewill choice, were excluded from an ongoing communion with God in a heavenly paradise, where only the laws of perfection had previously been outpictured by the first three root races.

REVENGE OF LUCIFER

From the hour of his fall, Lucifer was cut off from God, from the energies of his Source. He still had at his command, however, the energies of his prior momentum of attainment in God as well as the energies of the angels who were cast down with him. The same is true of all the angels who fell, including the Watchers at the time of their descent to earth.

In order to sustain that energy, the fallen angels have sought to seduce the children of light and tear them from their God Source, as the story of the Garden of Eden reveals. Since then, the fallen angels have positioned themselves everywhere among God's people in order to control them and thereby live off their light.

With the power and allure of their former attainment, these fallen angels have often seemed to the innocent ones of earth to be true interpreters of God's law, his universe, his hierarchical order and his divine plan. And so mankind have been led astray and become entangled with the fallen ones for the countless centuries since the Fall. Karmically bound to each other, the children of light and the fallen angels have continued to reembody side by side to the present hour.

Although Archangel Michael won the war in heaven, the war is now being fought on earth. And ever since, earth has been the scene of the epic battle that we are seeing played out to this very day.

Not only did earth become the new home of these fallen ones, but when the planet was further compromised by the Fall of man, it became host to other lifewaves from other systems of worlds.

COMING OF THE LAGGARDS

The interruption of God's plan for the root races that resulted from the fall of the fourth root race on Lemuria is well-known by students of the hidden mysteries. As man consented to the serpentine lies projected into his thought and feeling processes by the fallen Luciferians, there was a tearing of the veils of innocence that had formerly insulated his world with sheaths of light.

The first to fall were the high priests on Lemuria, whose subtle sense of superiority over the people yielded to spiritual pride. Once the high priests began to be influenced by the prideful rebellion of the Luciferians, wedges of darkness were driven into the consciousness of the people, separating them from their Source. Agitation and inharmony broke down the protection that is always sustained when people express true brotherhood to one another. Fear and doubt widened the gap between man and man, and man and God.

Once mankind had shown themselves vulnerable to the illusions of duality, the entire planet lost the protective sheath that had sealed the virgin consciousness from intruding evil and man lost his protection. As like attracts like, so the level to which man's consciousness had descended became a magnet for any interplanetary consciousness vibrating at the same level.

And therefore the laggards came, those who had been influenced by fallen ones on other planetary bodies and had failed to fulfill their divine plan on schedule on their home star. They are called laggards because they have lagged behind in their spiritual progress wherever they have embodied.

In the case of the planet Maldek (a former planet in our solar system), the fall of these individuals was so great, and their rebellion was so complete, that war ensued. The devastating use of atomic energy resulted in total destruction—the blowing up of the planet.

The asteroid belt between Mars and Jupiter, the remains of Maldek, is a stark reminder of what can happen when a people forsake their God. We have a clear physical record, then, right within our own solar system, of the consequence of the misuse of free will.

As a penalty for waging war and bringing about total nuclear annihilation of their planetary home, two-thirds of the evolutions of Maldek—those who had totally denied God—went through what is referred to in Revelation as the second death,[4] the death of the soul.

The remaining third, a remnant of souls considered salvageable because they had taken a stand against the evil ways of their brethren, were allowed by heavenly councils to embody on earth. Heaven's hope was that these individuals would work out their karma and once more walk in the ways of righteousness and truth. For in the far-distant past they too had known the Edenic state; they too had come from God; they too had departed from innocence. Among them were humanitarians, philanthropists, scientists and talented artists and artisans who had resisted war and inharmony but whose peaceful and constructive efforts had been drowned out by the din of their more warlike and destructive brethren.

THE CAIN CIVILIZATION

The laggard remnant that incarnated on earth had been given the opportunity to choose good and shun evil. But instead of being drawn into perfection by the members of the fourth root race embodied on Lemuria, very few—even among the most spiritually evolved laggards—were ultimately inclined to choose the path of light, despite their past attainment from prior golden ages.

The majority of these laggards, although highly advanced materially and scientifically, had willfully rebelled against God. They refused to use their talents and their free will to glorify God and to execute his plan on Maldek. On earth, they continued in the ways that had caused the destruction of their planetary home. Those who persisted in their rebelliousness thus contributed to the tearing down of the virtue of the fourth root race.

The ascended masters tell us that Cain, the first-born son of Adam and Eve, was one of the laggards from Maldek who incarnated on earth. Cain, though born of the seed of Adam, was conceived through the uniting of Eve's consciousness with that of the Serpent, the Liar who told her that she would not surely die if she ate from the tree in the Garden.

So Cain, whose name means "hollow root," contained within him the seeds of his rebellion, which he had outplayed in his prior incarnations on Maldek. In the Genesis account of Adam and Eve, Cain's brother, Abel, a shepherd, brought his offering to the LORD and it was accepted. When Cain, a tiller of the ground, brought his offering to the LORD and it was not found worthy, Cain rose up in anger and slew Abel.[5] The willful Cain wanted to please God in his own way, in the way of the ego, the way of the pride and ambition of the Serpent, who had sired his consciousness—not in God's way.

Cain and his descendant Tubal-cain, an "instructer

THE KILLING OF RIGHTEOUS ABEL

of every artificer in brass and iron,"[6] taught their arts to those among the fourth root race, as did laggard scientists. The laggards had learned the manipulation and mastery of material substance in previous embodiments on Maldek and on other planets, and they taught this knowledge to the less experienced evolutions of earth.

The techniques they taught included how to split the atom and harness nuclear power for peaceful as well as destructive purposes, how to create various forms of life in a test tube, and how to use ultrasonic waves, laser beams and astral rays as implements of healing and conquest. Their advancements in aeronautics, space travel and many other branches of science were far ahead of those of today's scientists.

Thus, the generations of Cain injected into earth's future civilizations the know-how to use these sciences, even the manipulation of DNA of both the highest and lowest evolutions, to further their evil designs. These rebels managed to perpetuate themselves and their lineage for thousands of years, and therefore they were there as civilizations rose and fell through the ages.

Because of their greater development and longer experience in the physical plane, when the laggards took embodiment on Atlantis they gained complete control of the materialistic society they built there. They held key positions in government, religion, science, the economy, the arts and the media, which they dominated with their recalcitrant consciousness. Then and now, they have sought after wealth and power as an end in itself rather than as the means to exalt the spiritual nature of man and life. Ultimately, they are materialists. They have no desire to love and serve God but rather to amass wealth and comfort.

By their efficiency in material things, the laggards reinforced the Luciferian lie that man does not need

God because he can do all things for himself. Thus, many children of the light who desired to return to their lost estate (including certain Maldekians who had retained their allegiance to God) soon fell under the almost total domination of the more advanced life-waves. Every effort of these more advanced laggards, no matter how socially progressive it might have appeared, was intended to preserve the status quo and to prevent the spiritual enlightenment of the race.

The most rebellious among them were determined to reverse the upward course of golden-age civilizations. They sought to deprive mankind of the higher spiritual teachings and the mysteries of the Christ, thereby attempting to ensure, as centuries passed and the dust covered the records of man's devotion to God, that no one would be able to ascend.

Why, you might ask, would God allow these laggards to incarnate through the fourth root race, knowing the risk that was involved? The masters have said there were two reasons: There were already seeds of the laggard consciousness here (meaning the people of earth had a karmic receptivity), and the people of earth had volunteered at inner levels to give bodies to these souls and to assist in training them to live a higher way of life.

Yet the laggards, having already evolved for millions of years before coming to earth, were older and more experienced souls than those who had more recently come forth from the heart of God in the fourth root race or who were to come later in the fifth and sixth root races. And therefore they have been able to outsmart the innocent ones.

DESCENDANTS OF SETH

After Cain killed Abel, Adam and Eve gave birth to a third son, Seth—the LORD's replacement for Abel. Seth's descendants began once again to "call upon the name of the LORD,"[7] to follow in God's ways. Through their obedience to God's laws, the generations of Adam through Seth brought forth great lights in the history of the earth.

However, as recorded in *The Forgotten Books of Eden,*[8] some of Seth's descendants, the children of Jared, were lured down the holy mountain of God (their dwelling place in a level of higher consciousness) by the children of Cain, who committed all manner of abominations and enticed them with sensual music from the valley below.

As noted in chapter 1, early Christian writer Julius Africanus did not believe that the "sons of God" who "saw the daughters of men" and "took them wives" (as recorded in Genesis) referred to angels but to the sons of Seth, even though the term "sons of God" is used elsewhere in the Old Testament to mean angels.[9]

With the understanding we now have from the Book of Enoch, which is older than Genesis, we know that those who lusted after the daughters of Cain were indeed angels who had descended into material form from the heavenly order of Watchers. It is possible that some of them incarnated through Seth and then took wives from among the daughters of Cain. The point is, they were angels—whether they came into embodiment through Seth and subsequently fell when tempted by the daughters of Cain or whether they fell directly from heaven and cohabited with them.

When these fallen angels had intercourse with the daughters of Cain, the genes of the sons of God were mingled with the genes of the fallen angels. This is why the Torah prohibited intermarriage among the Jews[10]— to prevent them from diluting their seed of light and from giving it to those who would use it to perpetuate their own existence in a more powerful and evil way.

Nevertheless, the culture of light was defiled, both through intermarriage and through imitation, and we now live in what I call the Cain civilization, a civilization corrupted with everything Cain represented— materialism, debauchery and the compromise of the seed of light.

A Mechanical Creation

The masters have given us a teaching that is the vital link, the key, to understanding what has transpired in the cosmic history of earth. It is the lost teaching about the fallen ones and their mechanization man in our midst—the teaching that Enoch gave to his sons and that Noah held in his heart for his sons— that we might understand in this day and age the true nature of the battle of Armageddon.

The Master R,[11] who is Saint Germain's sponsor, identified what he refers to as the Mechanization Concept. He spoke of the coming of the laggards and the darkness that ensued:

> Long ago, from a certain system of worlds there came bands who descended to earth, the hordes of shadow who were invited here by mankind (for mankind thought by the power of good example to elevate the consciousness of the laggard bands).
>
> Now, it is not so well known that these laggards were accompanied by some who were not invited. Some of these brought knowledge to mankind and to the earth, and some of this knowledge was degenerative and destructive. In addition, they also brought with them strange creatures of their own creation—seemingly intelligent beings not created by God, however, but by advanced scientists on other systems of worlds.
>
> The extent of the evil of these hordes and that of their mechanical creations has been very great, and the oppression they have wreaked upon mankind has been terrible to behold. The infiltration of the planet by these creatures is indeed a manifestation of human creation, not of the divine creation. God did not create evil; neither did he create destruction nor hatred nor egoism nor any form of vanity whatsoever.[12]

Speaking of the relevance of this knowledge to our lives today, the Master R said:

And so you may consider that these old histories of past civilizations where the powers of both good and evil entered in are relatively unimportant to you today, but this is hardly true…. For it is well that mankind understand the origin of evil, even as they understand the origin of good, in order that they may effectively eliminate the cause and core of "that which seemeth to be but is not."…

…You will recall that Jesus, in his parable of the wheat and tares, announced that an enemy had sown tares among the wheat.[13] These tares are the counterfeit man. Jesus said they were the children of the Wicked One, which exist apart from the original creation of God. And yet, inasmuch as nothing cannot create something, that which was created must have been created by someone who at some time somewhere drew forth the necessary information to so create.

In many cases in the New Testament it is recorded in the life of Jesus that he referred to certain individuals as a "generation of vipers" and as "hypocrites," addressing them in these words: "Ye are of your father the devil, and the lusts of your father ye will do. He was a murderer from the beginning, and abode not in the truth, because there is no truth in him. When he speaketh a lie, he speaketh of his own: for he is a liar, and the father of it."[14] This reference obviously does make a distinction between all men and some men.

Let me hasten to assure you, then, that there do exist upon the planet creatures who did not come forth from God—who are the counterfeit of the real manifestation. Many of these are consciously in league with the insipid and insidious purposes of the powers of darkness. They seek through conspiracy and plot to ravish the world of its good, to set brother against brother, to confuse, disturb and destroy harmonies wherever they exist.

These function on the physical plane, utilizing and directing their energies in a concerted effort against the light. They are, however, the pawns of "spiritual wickedness in high places."[15] And the league of the spiritually negative forces with these embodied wicked individuals has resulted in the slaughter of many noble souls down through the ages.

I am not so interested in identifying and describing these individuals as I am in calling to your attention that they do exist....

In the Bible these soulless beings are referred to throughout as "the wicked," for they have seen to it that all more specific descriptions of their race have been removed—lest mankind discover them and rise in righteous indignation against their overlords.

The Master R then gave us the perspective, the lens, through which to view and deal with this evil among us:

> I do not bring forth this information in order to frighten any, but to warn mankind that there are beings among them who are not the creation of God, who are not possessed with the same beautiful...[spiritual] body with which a manifestation of God is endowed.
>
> I propose no so-called witch-hunt. I propose that no one search out specifically these beings for identification. For your own...[God] Presence is the fullness of all that you desire, and I urge that the result of this release of knowledge shall be that you will turn more and more to God for your supply of every good thing, that you will determine more than ever to be alert to assist the mankind of earth in overthrowing absolutely all that is darkness and shadow and pain upon the earth planet. In order to do this and to break the monstrous plots that the sinister strategies have launched upon mankind, harmony and unity must remain the forte of all who love the light....
>
> The existence upon the earth planet of what we may term "simulated man" is a fact carefully hidden from the masses of mankind. Although it is the knowledge of the few, it may become and perhaps should become the knowledge of the many. Yet great care must be used in the dissemination

of this knowledge, for it is never the desire of the ascended masters to do anything except that which would result in the greatest blessing and the release of mankind from every binding condition.[16]

CHAPTER 3

STRATEGIES, TACTICS AND LIES
OF THE FALLEN ANGELS

Now that the earth is no longer a Garden of Eden but a compromised paradise in which many have been led away from the truth, some have been led to believe that the warfare between good and evil and the seduction of the sons and daughters of God by Lucifer and by those who are called devils are simply myths. The fact is, many of the scenarios outlined in the Book of Revelation have already occurred and are being outplayed in the great drama of tens of thousands of years of history that we have all experienced but do not remember.

As we take incarnation again and again, there is a veil that descends, a loss of memory. We do not recall the experiences we had in past lives—but our curiosity about them is not quenched. And so we watch science fiction movies and read science fiction books, searching for clues to those memories that are just below the surface of our present awareness.

We have all had encounters with the fallen angels. However, this may be the first time that this is being brought to your conscious attention. You can find in scripture several keys to this otherwise unrecorded and unrecalled history, such as in Revelation, Saint John's vision of the apocalypse, where these fallen angels—referred to collectively as the dragon—are cast out of heaven into the earth.

In reality, heaven and earth are simply frequencies of vibration. When these rebels against God could no longer occupy the higher frequencies and were cast down, they decelerated in vibration into earthly bodies to take their place among us. We have forgotten this scenario, but it looms in the subconscious and we cannot get away from it. That is why we were intrigued when we were children with Western movies, with the good guys and the bad guys, and now with the forces of good and evil translated into the skies in science fiction. We have an ongoing desire to watch the outcome of this interplay of forces of light and darkness.

FALLEN ANGELS PREEMPT THE OFFICE OF THE SON OF MAN

Our failure as sons and daughters of God to recognize the evil incarnate of these fallen angels in our midst is perhaps the greatest stumbling block on our spiritual path. It is the major test that we have failed again and again. And until we pass that test, not only will we be vulnerable to the forces of evil, but those who follow our lead in future generations will also be vulnerable. Therefore we must be "wise as serpents and harmless as doves"[1] and not whitewash the deeds of the fallen ones.

If we can understand the serpentine lies of the fallen angels, we can understand what they are after. We can learn how they go after it, step-by-step.

In a nutshell, the strategy of the Nephilim and the Watchers is to preempt the office of the Son of man in the earth.[2] These fallen ones have set themselves up as pretenders to the throne of grace. They have perverted the principles of divine abundance to create a materialistic and mechanistic civilization that has become, to a large extent, devoid of the spirit of living truth.

They have sponsored the laggards and other wayward evolutions in intellectual pursuits and secured for them the most prestigious professional positions and posts of leadership in international affairs. Having courted them and promoted them into prominence in circles of commerce, banking, government and industry, the fallen ones can maintain, through these individuals, control of the destinies of the majority of the people on earth.

The angels that fell with Lucifer abandoned their reason for being—serving God, and serving God in his children—and they have been angry ever since. Thus the warning is written in scripture: "Woe to the inhabiters of the earth and of the sea! for the devil is come down unto you, having great wrath, because he knoweth that he hath but a short time."[3]

When the Watchers fell, they too abandoned their reason for being. Thus, the "woe" that is upon the people of earth is that these fallen ones, with their superior science and technology and evolution, are in a position to outsmart the children of God. Therefore, great woe is come upon this planet, and we see it today in every form of manipulation of the people, nation by nation. It is not confined to communism or capitalism; it is, across the board, an international power elite bent on their ambition for power and the control of the earth and earth's people.

Ever since the Nephilim and the Watchers were cast down into the earth, they have promoted themselves as gods among us. They are not gods, but many people elevate them to that status by idolizing them and participating in their godless cult. The fallen angels have surrounded themselves with material trappings as a substitute for the spiritual kingdom they once knew. They have created a kind of "kingdom of heaven" on earth. They have used and abused both technology and earth's natural resources to fashion and sustain their kingdom—and they have used mankind, the children of God, and their own mechanical creation as their slaves.

These Nephilim have usurped the rightful place of

the sons of God nation by nation and even planet by planet. And they have been doing it for a long, long time. This is the hour for the turning around of this situation by the lightbearers, those who bear the light of God in their hearts. But if we are to meet this enemy as David met the giant Nephilim Goliath,[4] we must first have firmly within us an understanding of the strategies, tactics and lies of the fallen angels.

SUBVERSION OF THE DESTINY OF EMPIRES

In olden days, ascended masters walked and talked with unascended man. Under the inspiration of these great beings, man built great empires of light in various parts of the world—for example, the city of Ur of the Chaldees and early civilizations in ancient China, Egypt and the Americas. These ideal societies existed in the far-distant past. They fell gradually as a result of the evil influences of foreign invaders who cultivated in mankind an increasing familiarity with and acceptance of their godless ways.

From the beginning, the alliance between the Luciferians and the laggards had one objective: the overthrow of all God-oriented societies and the removal of the sons of God from the control of the governments of the nations and of the education of the youth.

In the biblical story of Nimrod's Tower of Babel,[5] we see the archetype of the fallen ones' desire for world control. A monolith of Luciferian pride and ego, the tower was constructed for spiritual as well as material power. But when the fire of God's judgment descended, it confounded the speech of the seed of the wicked who had built it, as well as the speech of the children of God who had been enticed by their unbridled desire for world power. The law of karma returned upon the

THE TOWER OF BABEL

fallen ones' heads their own evil intent. And "the LORD scattered them abroad from thence upon the face of all the earth"[6] to thwart their ability to communicate evil. Thus, when men forsake the Great Law, they lose contact not only with their Source but also with one another.

When the nations were scattered, the fallen ones capitalized upon people's differences and made their separation more important than their unity. They then used that discord and inharmony to their own advantage.

STRATEGIES AND TACTICS

When Archangel Lucifer and his angels were cast down into the earth to live as mortal men, they were given an allotment of time in which to outplay their existence. In Revelation and the Book of Daniel, this is recorded as a "time, and times, and half a time."[7] This refers to cycles, not years—a single cycle sometimes comprising tens of thousands of years. These are cycles of opportunity that come from God for the individual being who was once with him in heaven to repent and declare allegiance to "the light that lighteth every man [son of God] that cometh into the world"[8] and to bow before that light.

Yet these high and mighty ones have refused to bend the knee and acknowledge the light within God's creation. Were they to do this, the Nephilim and Watchers who control the higher levels of government, the economies of the nations, and the media would lose their stronghold.

For them to elevate and recognize God in the children of light upon earth would mean that they would acknowledge them as superior to themselves. They would have to relinquish their positions of power nation by nation and acknowledge that the true government should be upon the shoulders of the sons and daughters of God. In their desire to maintain the upper hand, though, the fallen angels have done, and are *still* doing, everything in their power to weaken and divide the children of light.

Divide and Conquer

Since men have the tendency to take sides, those who would manipulate nations and peoples find it to their advantage to divide humanity and to pit them against one another as a means of controlling the world. Using this strategy, the fallen ones have succeeded in polarizing the children of light into right- and left-wing factions in politics, economics and matters of faith and morals. God's children have been manipulated into positions where they can be milked of their energy— fighting for this cause, fighting for that cause—and while they're fighting, the manipulators are manipulating behind the scenes and doing exactly what they please.

Down through the centuries, the fallen ones have manipulated the wave of returning karma, taking advantage of it and using it toward their own ends. For example, once the sons of Belial convince the children of God that hatred and war are justified, they have no need to engage in the slaughter of the innocents themselves. For by first creating two opposing philosophies or systems, and rallying blocs of people around both, it then takes very little effort for them to convince people of the need to defend the sovereignty of the system or philosophy they have embraced. These ideologies soon become inseparable from their egos and the ego-centered civilizations in which they live. Goaded to war in defense of false ideals, the children of God effectively wipe each other out, leaving the dark ones in control of both sides—which they conveniently play against the middle whenever it suits their ends.

This type of manipulation of mankind's energies, thoughts and feelings at an individual and a mass level has been the principal tactic of these dark spirits, whose goal is the total domination of man and society.

Those who seek to rise politically in the world often capitalize on the weaknesses of humanity in order to achieve their ends. Their strategy is to set one segment of society against another by using both secular and religious issues to divide and conquer the minds of the people, whose hearts are, in reality, one. Using a stream of divergent ideas, they set people against each other as a means of unbalancing the population—pushing them either farther and farther apart or closer and closer together as it suits their purposes. This tactic is often the root and only cause of the underlying social problems that confront individuals and nations today.

The masters have given us deeper insight into this strategy:

> While political parties, various interest groups, and matters of foreign policy provide the means of dividing people on a national scale, miniature power blocs are sustained even within families and small business firms. Furthermore, the smokescreen that is created through the deliberate release of misinformation through the press and other news media makes it literally impossible for either the people or their elected representatives to properly assess the issues and to formulate sound policy.

> Strange as it may seem, from time to time both sides of a question have their own peculiar rightness. But as a means of preventing popular support in a given body for a certain issue, minor points are emphasized and major points are distorted in such a way that the pros and cons cannot be systematically and objectively evaluated. Then, too, once an individual has committed himself to a particular view or has taken a particular side (human nature being what it is), he is reluctant to consider the other side of the question. Thus, many are bound to their peculiar philosophy, politics or religion for a lifetime, never knowing the freedom to reevaluate their positions.

Occasionally people or parties make changes. Religious theology or dogma can become progressively more informed or retrogressively more bigoted. But in general the up, down and sideways movements of human attitudes and public opinion create uncertainties and vagaries that never allow the soul to clarify the real meaning of life.[9]

While we are all embroiled in fighting one another over silly little issues, the larger goal of our oneness in God is forgotten. Meanwhile, the ones who are pulling the strings are gaining more and more control through the bills that get passed through our legislatures and through all kinds of activities that are going on just below the surface of our awareness.

By dividing people on two or more sides of a given issue, political divisions have often turned into religious, social and even personal schisms. These schisms can breed fanaticism in individuals and groups. In my study of people, I have noticed that those who are polarized to the extreme right or the extreme left also polarize an extreme hatred of the other side, an extreme intolerance. They forget that we are brethren; they forget the unity.

Hatred is a deadly energy. It is blind, intolerant, prejudiced, proud, rebellious and seething, and it gives the wrong type of revolutionary enormous power. Those who bear that hatred are often unknowingly focusing a thrust of energy against the light. Thus, some souls of light who have embodied for the purpose of freeing this planet have gotten off track. Locked into splinter groups, they have lost the vision and lost the concept of the brotherhood of light.

Political, Economic and Religious Schism

Various systems of government and economics have been contrived by the fallen angels to get the children of light into opposing camps that will fight one another in support of seemingly righteous causes. But the cause is never realized; no side wins. And the blood of the lightbearers has been taken at the hand of those who profit by war—the Watchers and Luciferians, who control the manufacture of armaments and other accoutrements of war.

The plot of these fallen angels is a skein of maya that stretches across the planetary body like a spider's web. The worst thing about it is that they have successfully divided the lightbearers. They have divided them on the religious scene into camps of opposing and warring factions until those who identify with this or that religion or creed are against one another with great viciousness and fanaticism. This is an absolute tragedy.

We see the same thing in the political arena, where the fallen ones often control the elections. In the case of America, they would let the children of God think that the electoral process is fair and that opposing views are fairly represented in the two-party system. But who wins? The one who wins is often a plant of the fallen ones in whichever party they decide to back.

All of this is camouflaged by nice words and carefully crafted speeches quoting all of the right phrases. And the people think: "He's a good guy because he believes in freedom of speech and democracy. He's asked us to pray for him, so he must be a good guy."

Establishment of an Inner False Government

The perverted philosophy of the Luciferians is an individualism that excludes the inner Christ of each one, that excludes the merging of the Christ consciousness of all for the good of the many. Luciferians are individualists to the point that they will not cooperate with society. They milk society while claiming that their policies are for the good of the people.

Through perverted and corrupt political and economic systems, they have taken from the masses the light of their divine inheritance. They have taken the wealth of nations and they have put it into their pockets. They have organized an inner false government through which they intend to control the world.

One group through which these fallen ones operate is known as the Illuminati. The Illuminati was begun in Bavaria on May 1, 1776, by Johann Adam Weishaupt. Through this organization, the fallen ones have infiltrated the governments, economies and banking systems of the world. They always operate behind the scenes, attempting to draw into their camp the young and brilliant, the children of God as well as their own kind.

They flatter these recruits, appealing to their spiritual and intellectual pride by telling them that they are part of an elite group and will become the rulers of mankind. They tell them that the masses are not worthy to rule themselves and therefore must be ruled by the intellectual elite and the men of science. By perpetuating their power elite, the fallen ones deprive the children of light of their God-given opportunity to rule themselves according to the dictates of conscience.

Whether in the West or in the East, no matter what the form of government, no matter what the rationale, the movement is toward more and more power in the central government with less and less authority given to the individual. Through this tactic, power and wealth are concentrated and hoarded in the hands of the fallen ones in every nation.

Popularizing a Culture of Death

Having turned their back on God, the fallen angels cannot endow their offspring with a desire that they themselves do not have—a tremendous desire to be one with God. Rather, since they are committed to death, they endow their creation with the death wish, the desire for self-annihilation. And this is done for a purpose.

The plot of the fallen angels is to have enough laggards, enough rebellious or perverse individuals in embodiment to carry out that death wish, whether through the use of drugs, the consumption of unhealthy foods and beverages, or the misuse of energy through activities that squander light and the life force. All of this is popularized in the media as well as in the schoolyard to set an example, to show that those in the in-crowd are going the way of "sweet death."

The fallen angels promote their anti-God philosophy and behaviors so that the children of light who remain true to higher principles will be outnumbered and will feel that somehow, by popular opinion, their concepts are wrong. Those who go against the crowd find themselves unpopular and alone, sometimes painfully so

Going against public opinion can be hard on people who lack a strong will, great courage and great vision. It can be very hard for an individual, especially a child, to go against the group activities of his peers. And when an individual's resistance of peer pressure results in ostracism, this can and often does affect that individual's psychology.

In its various manifestations, then, the Luciferian drive to death promotes and relies on a certain herd instinct, a certain collectivism that has become a lifestyle upon earth.

Belittlement and Self-Condemnation

The fallen ones never cease in their condemnation of souls of light. Their goal is to make us feel as though we are worthless sinners, condemned forever. They do this because people who feel worthless are more likely to allow themselves to be absorbed into the mass consciousness. They are less likely to take a stand for truth, because they no longer understand that the truth is within them. Thus, lightbearers who have no sense of their worth or of their mission can be lured into alliances and sympathetic entanglements with the fallen angels.

To this end, the devils attempt to keep our attention on every bad deed we have ever done. They will never let us forget our sins. They will hang out our dirty laundry even in the moment that we are ascending into heaven. They attempt to make our "deep, dark past" (no matter how minor our infractions) seem like an enormous problem that we can never overcome. This is a lie!

This is the condemnation spoken of in the Book of Revelation as being delivered by the accuser of the brethren "which accused them before our God day and night."[10] The accuser of the brethren puts this burden of condemnation upon us so that no matter what we do, we never feel that it's good enough. This is what we tell ourselves when we listen to the lies of the fallen ones instead of to the voice of the good angels and of Christ speaking in our heart.

Many lightbearers have picked up this habit of criticism, condemnation and judgment from the fallen angels, and we tend to apply it to others and to ourselves. We look at the human part of ourselves and feel inadequate. But we aren't here to perfect our human self. We are here to liberate our own inner greatness and to manifest the full potential of our spiritual self.

We should never forget that we have the right to make mistakes. Why else would God have given us free will? Free will is the grand and noble experiment whereby, through our life on earth, we learn to focus our individual God consciousness.

Making mistakes is not what causes people to fail. What can be their undoing is making the same mistake over and over again and not getting to the root of why they are doing it. It takes diligence and self-mastery to avoid condemning ourselves or others as we engage in self-examination and strive to root out the obstacles to our spiritual growth.

LIES

On an esoteric level, the word *evil* is a shortened form of the term *energy veil*. The masters have told us that the English language comes down from the Atlantean tongue, and many of our words are abbreviations for concepts of cosmic law that we understood when we lived on Atlantis. Today we know the words, but we no longer remember their inner keys. Our memory of these laws has been clouded by the doctrine and dogma of the world's religions, into which has been sown the seeds of the one we call Liar.

Whoever this Liar is (it does not matter), the fact that the lie exists, the fact that we still contain it within our consciousness means that in time and space it has become a temporary reality and an enemy of the soul that seeks to reunite with the Spirit of the living God. We can trace these lies against the Spirit of God within us and, thread by thread, one by one, we can uproot them. They are totally illogical, but until we take a close look at them, the truth may not be obvious or easy to discern. That is because these lies have been sown and woven into our consciousness embodiment after embodiment by Church and State alike.

My quest for truth began when I was very young, about the age of three. Beginning at that time and into my teen years and twenties, I was searching everywhere for truth. I talked with priests, ministers and rabbis. I talked to everyone who might be a spiritual authority, including people who were students of metaphysics.

But none of them could give me the understanding that I sought. They would tell me about the mysteries, and as soon as I would ask a question that a child would naturally ask, they would say, "That's a mystery. We do not explain it. We simply accept it." And so I knew that they had no contact with the inner mystery of which they were the self-appointed guardians.

You and I have been intimidated by our teachers. How many of us have dared question the hierarchy of our respective religious movements? Jesus confounded the doctors in the temple, but it takes great courage and great inner conviction to do that. Most among the children of God do not have that courage, so they have gone on, year in and year out, accepting a blind belief taught by the blind followers of the blind.

The truth is that the Church was invaded centuries ago by fallen angels who were cast into physical embodiment in order that they might work out their karma on earth for their sin against the sons and daughters of God. These fallen ones, instead of embracing their earthly sojourn as penance for their rebellion and as a continuation of life's opportunity, penetrated the Church hierarchy to continue their blasphemy against the Son, the universal Christ, by betraying his little ones.

Thus the children of God's heart, who deserved true shepherds, trusted these wolves in sheep's clothing and have been led doctrinally astray by them. Many who are ministers today were also taught from childhood to believe the lies of Serpent as though they were truths out of the mouth of Christ himself.

Therefore, having lost the memory of our cosmic history, many of us have lost the knowledge of our divine identity. No one told us about our indwelling divinity, that we could become the Christ. And so the veil of maya became very thick. Without a teacher, we could not know the way. We believed the lie of the fallen ones that Jesus is the only Son of God, and we accepted their mass condemnation.

Through our acceptance of the fallen angels' lies and our intermingling with them, we have made karma. We have reacted to them and been seized by their anger, and we have responded in revenge. And therefore our karma has tied us to the fallen ones, sometimes in a very personal way in a family situation. This is one reason that in some families we see both people of light and people who don't love the light.

We find, therefore, that almost without exception— and it is important not to have that spiritual pride that makes us think we are the exception—the children of light on earth have absorbed the influences of the fallen ones. Without even realizing it, we have taken in at subconscious levels their philosophies, their way of life, their sense of morality, their emphasis on "the good life." "Eat, drink, and be merry, for tomorrow you die" is the byword of the Luciferians and the Watchers, because they know they will ultimately receive their final judgment. So they teach that doctrine to the lightbearers and draw them into a pleasure cult, a cult of sensual thralldom.

The fallen ones, knowing that their souls will be canceled out, have only one goal. They say, "If we're going, we're going to take the children of light with us." This is why they continue in their ways. They would destroy the planet—whether through wars, nuclear holocaust, environmental disasters or other means— in order to take with them as many souls of light as they can. To further their cause, they enlist those who unwittingly give allegiance to them.

Through the false governments the fallen ones have set up, they have drawn many into their camp. Nazism is a clear example of a government controlled by fallen ones taking millions of children of light into their camp by the sounding of the fierce voice, the beating of the drum, the military rhythm, and the exultation of the concept of a superrace.

Appealing to the pride that the Luciferians had already instilled in the children of light and drawing them in by it, they brought them into a mass hypnosis. This scenario has happened over and over and over again. Civilizations have risen and fallen as the result of the Luciferians, the Nephilim and the Watchers entering into the top echelons of government and only slightly perverting the true philosophy of the Christ and of Almighty God.

"There Is Only One Son of God"

The great lie of the ages that the fallen ones have perpetrated is that the only Son of God is Jesus Christ. This is the lie that has been the watering down of true Christianity. Through a similar lie, the fallen ones have taken from the children of the East the understanding that they have the potential to realize Buddhahood in the *here and now,* not in some astronomically distant future.

I believe that Christianity and Judaism in particular have been stripped of the very meat of the Word because Jesus, Moses and the great prophets of Israel have been made an exception to the rule rather than the rule of living for us all.

This is the diabolical lie that has caused confusion

in people of many faiths, because if they believe that they are miserable sinners and incapable of rising to great heights, they will not rise to their fiery destiny. Yet Jesus said, "He that believeth on me, the works that I do shall he do also, and greater works than these shall he do; because I go unto my Father."[11]

Jesus was calling for the belief upon the inner Christ. Therefore, if you believe in the Christ in Jesus, then you must believe that the Christ, the Son,[12] also lives within you, that this is your spiritual birthright. The apostle John affirmed this when he said that Christ is "the true light, which lighteth every man that cometh into the world."[13]

All sons and daughters of God have the potential to become the Christ, as Jesus did. Christhood is not something that is unique to Jesus. It is something he achieved through becoming one with the Logos, or divine Word. *Logos* is a Greek term for that aspect of God which mediates between Creator and creation. We, too, can become one with the Logos—in other words, become the Christ, become full-fledged Sons and Daughters of God.

When God created man, he gave us the power of his Spirit. The power of the Holy Spirit is always the consummation of the Father and the Son taking up their abode in our temple.[14] And wherever there is the power of the Holy Spirit, there is also an abundance of the gifts of the Spirit.[15] This power was with the early apostles—hence the testimony of the Holy Spirit, hence the testimony of miracles.

A true miracle is a transfer of energy from God to the soul for a permanent change in consciousness and the turning around of the energies of being. This is the type of miracle that we seek. This is the type of power that we seek. And this is the power that was our original birthright as sons and daughters of God.

Man's access to this power has been curtailed for two reasons: First, mankind misused the power. Because of his misuse of and disobedience to the laws of science governing the release of God's power, man was no longer qualified to receive it in full and thus was stripped of its use until he could prove himself worthy.

Second, certain individuals, recognizing the power that God had given to man, placed themselves between this power and the people through a priestcraft whereby they could reserve these powers and the secret mysteries for themselves and deprive the people of them.

We have seen this happen in both East and West and in most of the religious traditions upon the planetary body. The result has been that either through an individual's own disobedience to the laws of God or through the manipulations of the archdeceivers, mankind en masse have been deprived of the power of God. They have received some of the wisdom, but the knowledge of the use of this power as the science of the Christ, the science of the inner potential of the soul, has been lost.

Original Sin

The belief that there is only one Son of God and that no one else can be like him because we are all sinners goes back to the concept of original sin, which has been carried on and on for generation after generation. Saddled with this belief, people do not even try to master the basic principles of life that Jesus taught. This belief has permeated the faiths of people throughout the world, depriving them of the very essence of the life that Jesus and other avatars have lived.

The lie of original sin burdens all mankind with a weight of condemnation. Ever since the time of the Church Father Augustine, the churches have preached that we are conceived in sin and born in sin.[16] Yet even before Augustine, the psalmist lamented, "In sin did my mother conceive me."[17] He, too, was the victim of planetary condemnation.

This condemnation is subtle, and most of us are completely unaware of how it is directed against us. Yet often the root cause of our discontent stems from the belief sealed in the unconscious that our souls are stained. This is the doctrine of original sin—the belief that the soul has sinned and somehow that sin is linked to procreation. And therefore the most wondrous act of creation, the giving of life to souls on earth, has become compromised by the so-called stain of sin.

Our understanding, then, should not be of original

sin but of "original bliss." Our souls came forth from the Father-Mother God not with the sin of Adam and Eve but with the original blueprint of our Maker. This divine blueprint remains inviolate, and it endows us with the ability to become joint heirs with Christ[18] and all the avatars that have ever lived.

"One Must Experience Evil to Know Evil"

The Luciferian lie that one must experience evil in order to know evil, or any aspect of it, is the great lie that has been put upon mankind for thousands upon thousands of years. The fallen angels have told us again and again that the only way to make a decision and to ripen into maturity is to taste the fruits of the tree of knowledge of good and evil.

When we accepted this lie and decided to taste of the sensations of the energy veil, we left the Garden (higher consciousness) and entered into the shades of gray of relative good and evil, which became grayer and grayer until, in some, the light was eclipsed by the darkness of conceit, ambition and the ego consciousness.

While we were in Eden, we were innocent. We dwelled in the purity of our native soul consciousness. But our young souls were susceptible to the sophisticated wiles of the serpentine logic, and so we fell.

And over the long centuries of our souls' incarceration on planet earth since the Fall, we created an unreal self and then fed it, allowing it to mushroom until in some it has threatened to displace the hidden man of the heart, the inner Christ.

CHAPTER 4

THE TARES AMONG THE WHEAT

After the fallen angels incarnated on earth, many of the angels of light who had remained loyal to God volunteered to also take incarnation to offset the evil with good. Therefore, there are also abiding on earth many angels who serve the light, who help mankind, who carry the love of God in their hearts, who teach mankind the higher way.

Since our own incarnation upon the planet—whether we were originally sons and daughters of God, angels, or beings of light from other planets—most of us have forgotten the history of the Fall and our purpose for being here. We love the light, yet we find ourselves entangled within skeins of darkness and enmeshed in karma with souls of light and souls of darkness.

The ascended masters have revealed this ancient history from their archives[1] so that we would have the

understanding we need to reclaim our spiritual birthright, overcome the attempts of the fallen angels to
destroy our souls, and reunite with God.

Jesus spoke of two distinct evolutions on earth.
His teaching is specifically concealed in his conversa-
tion with Nicodemus: "Except a man be born again,
he cannot see the kingdom of God."[2] Or so the translation usually reads. However, the original Greek
reads: "Except a man be born from above, he cannot
see the kingdom of God." The Gospel of John cor-
roborates the Greek version: "And no man hath
ascended up to heaven, but he that came down from
heaven, even the Son of man which is in heaven."[3]

The phrase "born from above" mirrors Jesus'
statement to the Pharisees, "Ye are from beneath; I am
from above."[4] In chapter 8 of the Gospel of John,
Jesus is quoted as making an even stronger statement
to distinguish these two evolutions. Here he declares
that the Pharisees are the seed of the "devil."

EVIL AND THE DEVIL

Just who was Jesus talking about when he used
the term *devil*? The Greek word for devil, *diabolos,*
means "slanderer" or "accuser." Devils, in general,
invert the creation and slander the name of the Godhead. They are those who deify evil (d-evil), or the
energy veil, and worship materialism as opposed to the
living Spirit of God.

The fallen angels have already given up their place

in heaven. This we know from reading Revelation and the Book of Enoch, which records God's pronouncements to the Watchers: "Never shall you ascend into heaven," and "Never shall you obtain peace."[5] Thus, the fallen ones have nothing else to lose and everything to gain from taking the life-essence of the sons of God by stealing their money and murdering them on the battlefield.

They have no remorse for their misconduct, no pity for their victims and no ability to empathize, but rather legitimize their murderous intent by couching it in terms such as "wars of liberation." Jesus called them "whited sepulchres, which indeed appear beautiful outward, but are within full of dead men's bones, and of all uncleanness."[6]

Renowned psychologist Erich Fromm commented that "necrophiles" have "precisely the reverse of the values we connect with normal life: not life, but death excites and satisfies them"[7]—death in all of the sensational downward spirals of a selfish, purposeless existence.

Few have ever understood the "why" of this segment of the population, who seem to be the antithesis of the life-loving sons of God—the angry, the blasphemous, raging, restless, dying race whose core is rotten, rebellious and irresponsible toward the light and the honor of God. But then, few have explored the teaching of Enoch and the early Church Fathers on the incarnation of demons and fallen angels.

SEPARATING THE TARES FROM THE WHEAT

While we must be careful not to try to identify people as fallen ones, we can probably safely say that certain individuals, if not fallen ones themselves, are at least influenced or controlled by the Nephilim or the Watchers, as in the case of an Adolf Hitler and his chiefs of staff. Wherever murders in cold blood occur en masse, behind them are manipulation and the bloodthirsty designs of people who are somehow not quite like the rest of us.

But then there are those who pose as benign benefactors, taking our tax dollars and giving them away in order to earn a good reputation, and it becomes difficult for us to know whether they, or those behind them, are of the seed of light or of darkness. The children of light have not always recognized who their oppressors are. They do not realize that the destroyers of the people sometimes pose as their deliverers in order to keep a good name while they are destroying the very people they want to conquer.

Jesus carefully explained the difference between the tares and the wheat. He said the wheat are the children of light and the tares are the seed of the Wicked One that the enemy had come and sown. He said that they would not be separated until the last days, when the angels will come and bind the tares into bundles and burn them as chaff,[8] and the children of light will be free.

Somehow that message of Jesus Christ has not gotten through, and we are not taught that it is relevant today. But it is very relevant. And so the tares grow side by side with the wheat, and we can never know until the final judgment whether an individual is living on the borrowed light of the sons of God or whether he is a source of light and truly one with God. Therefore, Jesus warned us, "Judge not, that ye be not judged."⁹ But an absence of judging does not mean that we should not use discrimination and discernment to see what we will see and to choose our representatives well.

Most people today are simply not willing to face the facts and figures at hand. The Watchers, the Nephilim and their godless creation are alive and well on planet earth. They are the spiritually wicked in high places of Church and State, in economics, education, the arts and the media, and in the forefront of the scientific manipulation of the future.

Until now, these fallen ones have stood unchallenged. But as sons and daughters of God, we can claim the future for all of God's children. We do have that option. The apostle Paul said we can elect to be joint heirs of the universal Christ consciousness that Jesus embodied. This is the same higher consciousness that Gautama embodied, that the saints of East and West have embodied.

The fallen ones want to take from us that Christ

consciousness. And for the last two thousand years, they have succeeded to some extent in doing just that. Now, at the end of the age of Pisces, we have the opportunity to catch up on the God-mastery that Jesus showed us we could attain. Many have fallen behind because these fallen ones have convinced us that there is no such thing as fallen angels coming down to earth in flesh-and-blood bodies. This is the knowledge that the Church Fathers stripped from us, but which we must now have in order to be truly free.

It's time that people update their concept of devils running around with tails and pitchforks. It's time to realize that the devils are fallen angels who have mis-used God's light and science and elevated their energy veil—their entire soulless creation and their culture of death and materialism.

While the angels of light who never fell are seeking to exalt God's children to a higher way of life, a higher light, a higher acceleration in the spiritual universe, the fallen angels are working to entrap the children of God in a perpetuation of a quasi-life in the material universe. As long as the fallen ones can keep the light-bearers reincarnating in these dense earth bodies, they can daily milk them of their light, their supply, their money, their talents and their consciousness. This is how they have sustained the seemingly endless, unreal materialism on which they thrive.

IDENTIFYING CHARACTERISTICS
OF THE FALLEN ONES

When God created the angels, he gave them power to convey tremendous feeling through the emotional body. That power is inherent in all angelic hosts. Thus, the angels who descended into material form—both angels of light and angels of darkness—have retained some of that power.

This characteristic is one reason the fallen angels are such a dangerous group of individuals. They are very magnetic and can sway large crowds with their emotions. They can expand their tremendous emotional body to take in a whole audience at once, moving them to tears or laughter. When they are aligned against God, their fury is unbridled.

The angels of light who took embodiment to minister to the children of God also have an innate ability to convey emotions in a powerful way. Among these good angels are very powerful angels of the higher orders. These angels embody great light and can inspire millions.

Thus, we can never judge by appearances who is an angel of light and who is an angel of darkness. The student of higher truth must also be careful not to attempt to identify the laggards, the Luciferians and the Watchers according to religion, nationality or race; for these advocates of Antichrist have infiltrated every walk of life, and no church, government or nation can claim immunity from their presence.

They are the tares that the enemy has sown in the fields of human endeavor, growing side by side with the wheat. Since the Lord has said that the tares will not be separated out until the harvest, any attempt to label, classify or categorize these dark ones can only be met with failure, and to try to do so is to fall prey to their schemes of dividing and conquering the people. From the outer standpoint, there is no clear-cut line of demarcation between the sons of Belial and the sons of God.

It is also important to be aware that because evil imitates good, one's actions are not always a clear indicator of one's basic nature. In order for evil to win good souls to its cause, it must appear to be good. This is where we find that the children of light are most often fooled. Unless they have the discernment of the Spirit, they may think that because people are parroting good, they must be good. Evil is foreign to the nature of the children of God, and this is precisely the reason that they are such unwitting victims of the ploys of the evil forces. They do not understand the subtle nature of evil.

When those with evil intent go through the motions of doing good, being outwardly personable and appearing to be good human beings, those who do have the discernment of the Spirit can see at subtle levels that these parrots have evil motives. They are simply putting a patina of good over an evil core.

Evil has nothing original of its own. It's a copycat. So beware. Beware and "try the spirits"[10] and don't make hasty judgments or hasty alliances.

Also understand that people are not willfully evil unless they are tied to absolute evil. Many people of light have taken on, through many lifetimes, the ways of the fallen ones. They may have compromised truth, compromised their speech and compromised their actions; and therefore their actions alone are not an indication that they themselves are fallen ones.

Neither should we judge the laggards, as some among them yet retain a seed of light. The Master R explained that those who were given the opportunity to embody on earth had some spark of divinity left within them.

ABSOLUTE EVIL

There is a difference between relative good and evil and absolute good and absolute evil. Absolute good is God; absolute evil is its opposite.

When we metaphorically partook of the tree of knowledge of good and evil, our vision fell and we began to see good and evil as relative. Our habitation became a relative world, in which there was no longer the concept of absolute good. And so we began making relative choices. Relative good and evil includes the actions we take and the mistakes we make. It is when we seek to do good and choose the best that is available, what we believe is right. And if we err and regret it, we can ask for forgiveness, make amends and move on.

Absolute evil is the intent of those who have evil at their core, individuals who are the seed of evil and who have never forsaken their one reason for being: to destroy God's offspring, his sons and daughters. Absolute evil, embodied by the fallen angels, is the state of those who declared war against God in the Great Rebellion. It is the absolute dedication of the fallen angels against God and the Christ potential in his people.

That drive is part of the psychology and personality of every fallen angel. They no longer have the glory of the sons of God, nor do they have the approbation of the heavenly Father. So they must put down, in some way, the lightbearers so that in their own eyes and in the eyes of their cohorts they appear great. They constantly strive to reinforce the synthetic self (the antithesis of the Real Self[11]) and the ego.

Some express this drive through physical sadism and other horrific acts. It is also expressed through people who are much more sophisticated and who impose their hatred upon society at large through legitimate business—for instance, the slow torture and death of our population by chemical wastes, by pollutants, by dangerous drugs, pharmaceuticals, and all kinds of experimentation on the human body. It's the same vibration, but it's conducted with clean hands in a polished way, in a socially acceptable mode. That's the only difference.

This is hatred of the Mother (the feminine principle of God, which is the body of God), and it comes in many forms. One expression of this hatred is in the tobacco industry, which manufactures a product that causes people to die of cancer by the thousands. That is slow death; it is torture; it is sadism. And behind it is the murderous intent of the devils.

It may horrify some to hear this stated so bluntly. That is because many have been neutralized to the socially accepted forms of murder that exist, such as in the alcohol industry, the pharmaceutical industry and the food industry, which poisons our food with chemicals, refined sugar and other harmful substances. We also see this evil intent in the popularization of recreational drugs and the drive to make them socially acceptable.

More obvious to us is the presence of fallen angels —or those whom they have corrupted—in gangs, drug cartels or Mafia families, where they become the nucleus of the group. In these cases, there is almost always one who has in past ages been the captain of that particular unit of fallen angels. And the others fall right in line behind their leader every time.

They often reincarnate as karmic groups. Having committed their crimes together in the past, they have to reincarnate together to undo their group karma. For example, if a group of eight individuals murders some-one, they have to reincarnate and help give life to that person.

These individuals embody again and again, and

they have a powerful momentum. What the police forces, the ministers and the good people of America do not realize is that they are dealing with a momentum of absolute evil that is centuries, if not millennia, old. The fallen angels know that they will face the final judgment. Anyone who does not care whether he lives or dies will live dangerously, live at the expense of others, play with life and death, and take gambles on a daily basis. This attitude is something you have to have in your blood if you're going to be a member of such a gang.

Because these karmic groups of international gangsters have been reincarnating with one another, they even know at a soul level that when they die they'll keep coming back (until the final judgment). This gives them a sense of their immortality even while they embody death itself.

"How Long Shall the Wicked Triumph?"

Those who once had great light may be given an even longer opportunity to balance their karma and return to the throne of grace than those who had less. This is a corollary to the law of karma, as it is written: "For he that hath, to him shall be given [opportunity]; and he that hath not, from him shall be taken even that which he hath."[12]

And so, we know that the opportunity given to some of the fallen ones has been very, very, very long, until even the psalmist thousands of years ago cried out, "How long, O LORD, how long shall the wicked triumph?"[13] For the power of their darkness seems endless as they move against the children of God, who seem much less powerful and often helpless.

Indeed, the fallen angels who swore their eternal enmity against God in heaven move freely on earth, embodying darkness with bravado, sophistication, wealth and worldly wisdom. And they will do so until they are confronted by those in embodiment who have the courage to be the spokesmen for the Elect One—those who bear the light of the Christ consciousness and who elect to do God's will and to judge the fallen ones, as Enoch prophesied. For by definition, that Elect One who comes in the name of God has the attainment necessary to challenge the fallen ones.

This is why John the Baptist and Jesus Christ, as well as the prophets and the avatars of all ages, have come to the earth: "For judgment I am come into this world."[14] They come because they want to give a reprieve to the blessed children of God who are tormented by these fallen ones and who do not yet have the ability—the externalized Christ consciousness—to move against them.

PART 2

The Profile of Evil

Amassing Power and Control

Thus far we have looked at the psychology of the fallen angels and of absolute evil. In summary, evil has nothing to lose and everything to gain. This means that it is irresponsible, trigger-happy and power-minded. The fallen angels are not interested in money; they already control the money of the world. They are interested in power and control over the planet itself. They may put forward many seemingly humanitarian schemes and plans, but behind them all is their one-pointed goal of amassing greater world control. This is the profile of those who face the judgment.

When we know the profile of the fallen angels incarnate we can understand why, by their inner alignment with darkness, they are determined to snuff out the candle of freedom in the heart of every freedom fighter on earth, nation by nation, people by people.

I would also reiterate here that this profile and destiny of the evil ones is in contrast to that of the masses of mankind on earth, who are committed to good, who are facing their returning karma (which can be balanced), and whose ultimate destiny is union with God.

The Book of Enoch gave us the initial understanding that a group of fallen angels known as the Watchers had embodied on earth and that the LORD God had pronounced their judgment. But I am perhaps one of only a few spiritual teachers in the world who will tell you that the Watchers are still in embodiment today.

The Watchers are the most wicked and most powerful of the embodied fallen angels. They are not a class of any certain race or nationality or religion— they come through any and all. They are the powerful ones who pull the strings. They are beyond the super-rich; in fact, they control the superrich. They have the power and the control of the world's wealth. We do not necessarily see or know them, but we all know or feel their influence.

Given that the Watchers had such great light when they fell from their high estate and even now have greater residual light (i.e., power) than we have, we may well wonder: How can we ever hope to deal with them? How can we ever hope to escape their control? There is only one way: God in the person of his mighty archangels and legions of light will come to our defense.

In answer to our call, the legions of light will deal with the fallen angels in our midst. Our role as sons and daughters of God is to use our free will to invoke heaven's assistance in bringing about the prophesied judgment of these fallen ones. The ascended masters have taught us how to do this through the Science of the Spoken Word.

The Science of the Spoken Word is a step-up of the prayer forms of East and West. It combines prayers, mantras, affirmations and meditations with dynamic decrees—powerful spoken petitions to God—to bring forth a dynamism of energy that we pass through our chakras,[1] our spiritual energy centers, out into the entire world.

When we turn over any situation to the masters and the mighty archangels by daily invoking their intercession, we are giving to them our authority as sons and daughters of God in embodiment to intercede so that the wicked ones can no longer oppress humanity. (An explanation of how to invoke their aid will be given in Part 5.)

Anyone who knows even a fragment of earth's history over the last two thousand to five thousand years understands that war and oppression have been wreaked perpetually upon humanity. There is a cause and a core to these conditions, and I tell you that everyone who is alive upon planet earth today has the record of this infamy of the betrayal of the fallen angels in his subconscious.

Each one of us has our own threshold of awareness. There are certain things we are willing to face and certain things we are not willing to face. Some people do not want to face the fact that absolute evil exists. They find it hard to fathom that beings who once dwelled so near to God could rebel and take that absolute power of good and invert it to absolute evil and then use it against the children of light.

For many of us, our threshold of awareness does not allow us to admit that there is a conspiracy of fallen angels against the light. It is too frightening to maintain this awareness in our conscious mind on a daily basis. Yet we see the manipulation of our commodities, our money, every aspect of our society and culture, and even our educational systems and the minds of our youth. We see it here and we see it there, and within our minds and hearts we hear the whisperings of the good angels, who tell us: "Put two and two together. Who would want to create this contrived situation to the destruction of the souls and bodies of the people?"

One of the top priorities of Saint Germain and the brotherhood of light has been to help us put two and two together and unmask the profile of evil as seen in the activities of the fallen angels among us.

CHAPTER 5

GLOBAL ECONOMIC MANIPULATION

Today, people in America are divided on virtually every issue. Never has the country been quite so fragmented. Perhaps the only thing that everyone really agrees on is the economy—and everyone agrees that it's in bad shape. But why it's in bad shape and how to fix it are again divisive issues.

The situation in America in many ways mirrors the problems faced by other nations. A nation's economy is more than a mechanism for the production and distribution of goods and services. When we talk about the economy, we're talking about a way of life.

Abundance is the natural law of life, as Jesus showed us. He and his disciples were never wanting and yet they did not live in excess. Jesus brought to us the understanding of the abundant life, of manifesting every good and perfect gift from God. And he also spoke of the manipulation of the abundant life by the powers that be.

Today, the understanding of how to realize the abundant life has been taken from us by the manipulation of the spoilers in our midst. By our naiveté, many of us have given them our attention through idolatry. According to cosmic law, we become energetically tied to that which we place our attention on or give our devotion to, because attention is energy flow. In this way, we have become karmically entangled with the fallen ones and have given them our power, our light.

Acting out their drama before an unwitting audience, the fallen angels have chosen politics, the media and the entertainment industry as their center stage. Although there are people of light with great integrity in all of these fields, these areas are often dominated by those who, knowingly or unknowingly, are promoting the fallen angels' dark agenda. By attracting our attention to their performances—whether outrageous, hilarious, spectacular or deeply moving and evocative —they take in our money *and our light*. This is how the fallen ones walking the earth today, though spiritually bankrupt, can gather more and more power unto themselves. The light of the people is thus turned to darkness in schemes that subjugate and destroy the very ones from whom that light was taken.

Many of these schemes center on money, because money is power. Money in any form, even if it's a paper note, represents energy—the energy of God, the abundance of God. When money is amassed by those who have chosen to embody evil instead of the Christ, that money gives them power—and both money and power are necessary coordinates of control. These serpents use this power to turn world conditions and world events toward their own ends.

The problem of the economy is a spiritual problem. If you do not have bread and butter, if you do not have a roof over your head, if you are fighting a daily battle of survival, then it will be harder to pursue the path of your soul's integration with God.

Economic survival is becoming the plight of more and more people around the world as the economy falters and appears increasingly vulnerable to collapse. We are now in the midst of the most challenging economy since the Great Depression of the 1930s. The manipulation of the world's economy by central banks, both leading up to and since that time, has resulted in an almost constant inflationary trend, although there are now some portents of deflation in the United States and around the world. Whether the manipulation of the economy results in inflation or deflation, some will benefit from it. Historically speaking, however, inflation has been the biggest economic challenge, and many argue that it will be a great challenge again.

ECONOMIC CANNIBALISM

Inflation is economic cannibalism. It devours savings and makes it impossible to plan for the long term. It's a covert way of robbing from future generations by causing people to spend tomorrow's capital today. While inflation affects everyone, it causes the poor to suffer most.

Vladimir Ilyich Lenin correctly noted that the quickest way to destroy the capitalist society was to debauch its currency. This is accomplished, in large part, by inflation. Inflation has never started without an increase in money. And inflation has never ended without corrupting society in proportion to the degree of the inflation itself. In recent history, it has destroyed more lawfully constituted governments than any other force except war itself.[1]

Sometimes people in high places, both inside and outside of the government, treat inflation as if it were a mystery. Yet some of these same individuals are the very ones who manipulate the money supply behind the scenes.

Adolf Hitler rose out of the ashes of the German economy that was destroyed after World War I, not by the war, but by inflation. Between 1916 and 1923, the Reichsbank—Germany's central bank—hyperinflated the German currency. Prices rose so fast that the price of a meal in a restaurant went up while the customer was eating it. The Germans decimated entire forests trying to print currency fast enough to keep up with the inflation.

Max Warburg was the head of the Reichsbank at the time, and Paul Warburg, his brother, came to the United States and joined the banking firm of Kuhn and

Loeb. Warburg traveled all over the United States pushing for a central bank like the Reichsbank.

The new central bank, ultimately called the Federal Reserve System (the Fed), was the product of a conspiracy of bankers. The Fed is little more than a complicated mechanism for the manipulation of the economy and the creation of fictitious money. It can be used to create inflation, deflation, recession, depression or a collapse at any time. It is totally out of the hands of the people themselves. And that, above all things, is what is so dangerous.

This is not only an American problem. Every nation's central bank is structured similarly and serves the same function as the Federal Reserve.

Between 1923 and 1929, the Fed created a terrific inflation and then suddenly stopped it. The inevitable happened: In October 1929, the Wall Street market crashed, swiftly plunging both the U.S. economy and the worldwide economy into the Great Depression. The economic crisis lasted for a decade and affected virtually every nation, wealthy or poor.

The U.S. Congress today does not control the Federal Reserve System; the power elite does—and the power elite controls Congress. Only an act of Congress can uncreate the Federal Reserve. In 2010 the U.S. Congress did attempt to audit the Federal Reserve but that effort failed.

The same scenario exists in political systems everywhere. Governments throughout the world actually like inflation because it gives them a covert means of taxing the people. Many countries would welcome the return of inflation as a way of paying their sovereign debts with devalued money. And, as Saint Germain tells us, those in control have another, ulterior motive:

> A part of the problem as we see it is that those who are in the position to pull the purse strings are often those with a vested self-interest who lack the spherical vision of a very complex problem....
>
> The system of political parties and frequent elections, though designed to preserve democracy in a republican, representative form of government, makes severe demands upon those seeking office. In order to be elected, they must secure the popular vote.
>
> Inasmuch as the control of inflation and the cutting back of government spending must affect vast segments of the people adversely, it is never a popular cause for politicians to preach the real cure for inflation, which is the sacrifice of immediate gain, inordinate profits, and even the life of leisure for the long-term gain of prosperity and the sound management of the nation's government and business based upon the realities of the money supply and the resources at hand. Thus, those seeking election are unwilling to place before an uneducated populace the gravity of the issue or the consequences upon all of the people of the real solutions.
>
> This generation and their prosperity is built

upon the credit system. The increase of the money supply has created an unreal concept of the abundant life.[2]

If Congress does not uncreate the Federal Reserve System, there is little chance that the U.S. government—which was established to be responsive to the people—will be able to control long-term inflation. Although we are currently not experiencing inflation, it has been the general trend since the Great Depression and could again pose a significant problem in the future. Historically inflation has served the purposes of the central bankers who created the system, and they have had a vested interest in maintaining the status quo. As long as the central banks are autonomous and not under the control of an objective outer body of people, namely Congress or the legislatures of the respective nations, it will be in their interest to continue an inflationary trend.

This manipulation of the economy is a direct manipulation of people's lives. By the labor of their hands and minds, the people have earned the right to accumulate abundance, to save it, to draw interest upon it. Yet because of inflation, the fruits of their labor are stolen—and that which is earned in one day is no longer adequate to feed one's family the next.

Saint Germain appeals to the stalwart among us "to consider the critical condition of inflation side by side with the manipulation of the free market." He says that "many who express their opinions in economics today are not fully qualified to run the economy," nor do they have the necessary understanding of the spiritual component of economics. Thus, despite their educational and worldly credentials, they are, from the higher perspective of the ascended masters,

> mere amateurs, [who] approach the subject of the nations' money systems, a balanced budget, taxation, and the financial burdens of a federal bureaucracy as though they were experts in the science of supply.
>
> ...The real laws of economics and the God-solutions to the international economy are not to be found in the most elite schools of the day nor in the minds of the experts (if they were, we should have no problems of such immense proportions)....
>
> Let the governments and the people learn to live within their means, and let the real value of goods and services be based upon the theory and the altogether practical application of the law of the sacred labor[3] performed to the glory of God, who is resident within his humanity.

Saint Germain explained that the manipulation of the free market and the free governments of nations through monopoly capitalism or corporate socialism will not work because manipulation destroys individual creativity and snuffs out the individual's desire to be self-sustaining in God. While he did not tell us what will work, he said that the solution begins with this fundamental principle: Whatsoever a man soweth, that shall he also reap;[4] and its corollary: Whatsoever a man soweth not, that shall he not reap. Saint Germain admonished:

> There are too many people in every walk of life who still want something for nothing and they are willing to espouse any economic philosophy that will deliver to them immediate pleasures and material prosperity. These are not noble hearts but they whose names go down in history as the ignoble and as the destroyers of the abundant life of the soul....
>
> Let the value of life rest upon a gold standard that comes from the golden rule, which is the principle of the divine economy: Do unto others as you would have them do unto you. This golden rule is applied to the gold of the heart, the golden wisdom that serves the needs of the community through love—applied love that becomes compassion, charity, and the sharing of the joys of the abundant life with those who entertain the impoverished sense.
>
> If you ask me why the economy is in such a disastrous state, I will tell you that it is because not enough people care for God or for one another. They see solutions only in terms of more money and more government control and the regulation of life. But without heart or attunement with the [Divine], the light of God does not flow to meet the needs of the people.

ABOLISHMENT OF THE GOLD STANDARD

The replacement of gold by silver and more common metals, and finally the substitution of paper as the medium of exchange, is a plot of the manipulators to magnetize people's consciousness to the lower vibrations of these metals and to deprive them of the benign, healthful and stimulating qualities of gold.

The masters have spoken about the problem of creating paper currency that is not backed by gold:

> Inasmuch as [the seed of the wicked] have implanted themselves in the structure of civilization itself, it is inevitable that in some quarters and in some levels major change take place. You have seen therefore the signs in the heavens and the signs on Wall Street of conditions in the economy that do not augur well for America or the world. You have seen the frantic and frenetic movement of those who control international banking and the money systems and the currencies of the nations, moving almost in a stepped-up film in fast motion here and there and everywhere to create more money to stop the inevitable descent of karma. Think how ludicrous this is: Can paper money forestall the karma of the seed of the wicked?[5]

The masters have explained that gold is necessary for the stability of the economies of the nations as well as for the stability of the individual consciousness.

Gold is intended to be the standard of exchange throughout the earth. With a meaningful gold standard, there would be no way to spend so much money so recklessly, because new money could only be created by governments as the stock of gold to back it was increased. In other words, money could no longer be created out of thin air but only as a result of real economic growth.

The reestablishment of the gold standard is critical to the nations. People must understand the great fraud that has been perpetrated upon them by the printing of money without backing and that the continued rolling out of paper money by the printing presses will cause the eventual collapse of the economies of the nations.

From a spiritual perspective, gold is precipitated sunlight and a focus of the Christ light. As such, the gold standard was ordained by God as the means to keep the balanced radiation of the sun flowing through the hands of the people for the health of their four lower bodies and for the perpetuation of brotherhood. In every civilization where gold was in circulation as the medium of exchange and was worn by all the people, there was a corresponding attainment of great illumination, abundance, health and self-mastery. The custom of using gold as an adornment in primitive tribes comes down to them from the ancient civilizations of which they are the last remnant.

WAR AND THE LUST FOR MONEY

Money and greed are all too often the motivation behind war, and it is the greed to increase money that causes the Western nations to supply armaments and all types of defensive and offensive weapons to other nations around the world.

It is the money beast, as the masters call it, that drives the feeding of technology, of commodities, and so on, throughout the planetary body. And that greed has its origin in the Nephilim and the Watchers themselves, who long ago began to lust after the light of the people of God. It is this lusting after the light that is behind the lusting after the abundance, the energy, the very life force of the lightbearers.

The lusting after money, regardless of the cost to human life, has spanned the centuries. Jakob Fugger (1459–1525) is the original archetype of the modern financier, investment banker and venture capitalist. Fugger, often called "the Rich," was born into a family of wealthy merchants. His motto was "I want to gain while I can."[6] Through numerous lucrative business ventures, including even the financing of armies to wage war against each other, Fugger expanded his already sizable investments and amassed a fortune. Using his vast wealth to buy influence, Fugger literally purchased the position of Holy Roman Emperor for Charles V and, in exchange, leaned upon his political connections to further expand his own business empire.

He is considered to be one of the wealthiest persons of all time.

This archetype appears in every generation as those who finance wars, monopolize national resources, promote munitions factories, and create and destroy industries, nations, lives and fortunes. These individuals, whether acting alone or in groups, can be ruthless in their pursuits. They support conflicting systems financially, militarily and in other ways, pitting them against one another in war, economic strife or ideological clashes, driving brother against brother. And they're confident of gaining greater power and control over the nations by manipulating both the conflict and the outcome.

GREED AND ADVERTISING

The use of black magic is prevalent upon the planet. We aren't ordinarily aware of it on a conscious level because it is often disguised, sugarcoated and legitimized by the most ingenious minds and methods.

Black magic is the scientific, or systematic, practice of evil. It is a necessary function of evil, for without it evil could not exist. Black magic involves the misuse of God's energies for any purpose that is inconsistent with the will of God. It is employed by the forces of evil to gain control over the manifestations of God and to secure for themselves, by fraudulent manipulation of cosmic law, the things of this world—money, fame, and the power to manipulate men and nations.

The advantages gained are then used to place obstacles in the pathway of those who aspire to do the will of God and to serve the light.

Aligned with the forces of evil are momentums of human greed that have become focused through various institutions. These institutions have become a necessary and integral part of our civilized world. Some were sponsored by the brotherhood of light upon the principle of the golden rule taught by the avatars, but over time even these have largely become instruments of darkness.

In the advertising world, a legitimized form of black magic is practiced in various forms, sometimes without the knowledge of the top executives. Through the perversion of pure art forms and the skillful use of symbols, advertisers can control both minds and the markets, thereby controlling the energy of the people. Thus, advertising agencies can become agents of control if they employ artists and creative people who have been trained to be masters in mind manipulation.

Almost all advertising contains elements of hypnosis. Engaging the attention and training the eye of the viewer on key images causes the viewer's energy to flow to the object of attention. This sets up automatic reflexes in the brain, nudging the viewer toward a predetermined outcome—in this case, the purchase of the advertised product without the correct use of his free will.[7]

In the past few generations, the glamorously advertised use of liquor and tobacco (both of which impede the flow of light to the brain, not to mention that they can cause lung cancer, heart disease and other serious side effects) has wreaked havoc on the physical and subtle bodies of mankind. On another front, the display of evocative and partially or wholly nude figures in motion pictures has compounded the frightful toll upon the energies of the people, especially the youth. All of the contact media—radio, television, the Internet, national magazines, newspapers, books and motion pictures—have played a significant part in promoting a lifestyle centered in materialism and sensuality.

When people's attention is focused on materialistic pursuits, they are essentially feeding the creation of the fallen angels with both their money and their energy. This is the only way the fallen angels can sustain themselves. As noted earlier, when they rebelled against God, they were cut off from their Source and they no longer received the continual flow of light that had previously given them life. That is the price of rebellion. Since their fall, they have walked the earth as if they were gods, but most of them are, in effect, the living dead.

These living dead, unless they turn around, will not regain the throne of grace. In the end they will be judged, and they know it. Thus they are unscrupulous because they have nothing to live for except to eat, drink and put off that tomorrow wherein they shall surely die. Their motive, besides putting off the day of their judgment and establishing a synthetic kingdom in the interim, is to strike out at God in vengeance. And since the fallen ones can't reach God, they try to destroy the souls of God's children by enticing them with the good life and telling them that they "shall not surely die"[8] if they sin against God's laws.

Getting the populace caught up in a materialistic existence devoid of the presence of God has been their goal. Saint Germain spoke of the toll this has taken on the lightbearers:

> The surfeiting of the people in consumer products bought with unsound money unbacked by a gold standard has produced a profound insecurity in the people, a subconscious resistance to take the responsibilities of living and working together... to produce the abundant life, which is the only true foundation for a golden-age civilization....
>
> Materialism is a disease which is as debilitating to the human spirit as is that of Communism. Both of these products of the minds of the manipulators have affected millions of lightbearers, and their acceptance of the philosophy of the Serpent has left them in a euphoric nightmare. Their [false] peace, the product of their psychological separation from God, has left them [feeling] nonthreatened in an era when all around them... are the most threatening conditions to the human spirit which have ever existed in modern history.

CHAPTER 6

INTERNATIONAL TERRORISM AND ANARCHY

The root of world terrorism is suicide, so let us begin with an understanding of the origin of suicide. The original suicide was the rebellion of the fallen angels against Almighty God and their letting go of the hand of God. Through this act, the fallen angels committed spiritual suicide. Ever since, they have set the example of spiritual suicide by the many indulgences, abuses and perversions they have taught us and our children throughout the ages, including the taking of life through physical suicide.

Terrorist suicide missions combine suicide with murder. The promise behind these acts is that those who kill in the name of God will have an eternal reward. For example, those who die in the process of killing the so-called enemies of Allah believe that they will go straight to heaven, see Allah, and reap abundant rewards.

Today's suicide bombers seek immortality through death instead of through the elevation of the soul. The fallen ones have provided this false path—all the way to an individual's last breath—as a shortcut to union with God.

At inner levels, the false hierarchy of fallen angels has always enlisted the support of their mechanization man and underlings as well as those children of light who are ill-informed and have become convinced that they are serving the real hierarchy of light and the cause of worldwide truth and freedom. And with that misguided belief and false understanding, even the children of God have functioned as instruments of absolute evil to carry out actions against the light.

The varying degrees and types of terrorism we see depend on the type of evolution involved, what the motive is, and where the hatred comes from. Some terrorist acts are motivated by the absolute evil of the fallen ones who have sworn eternal hostility against the living Christ. They have an absolute determination to the death to destroy all that represents the light and freedom of the planet. Others are acts of relative evil, motivated by those who have been manipulated into believing that terrorist acts will bring about good.

Many times this false path has been taken up by lightbearers who have been misled and duped. We must remember that relative evil consists of those acts that can be forgiven because they were committed by children of God who would do better if they knew better. Nonetheless, a good end never justifies wrong means. We should never say, "Let us do evil that good may come."[1]

Terrorists might declare that they want a better life for the people and that they are working for good, but in fact their acts foster anarchy. They seek to break down society, to destroy the lawful means and the democratic process by which representatives chosen by the people are brought to the seats of government and to positions of responsibility, authority and power.

Terrorism is a rent in the garment of God-government, society and institutions, and the beginning of anarchy. The original anarchist was Lucifer himself, who rebelled against the authority of God and therefore has, from the beginning, advocated the violent overthrow of the established order of the universe.

The fallen ones have infiltrated the governments of the nations and introduced many irresponsible elements. Once in power, they have deemed the very corruption that their own kind have sown to be justifiable grounds for overthrowing the entire system. Thus, the terrorists of this planet, as we have seen, are the worst gang of hellions walking the earth. If their activities were to gain sufficient momentum, the life of every man, woman and child would be in jeopardy twenty-four hours a day.

Terrorist acts have as their underlying purpose the instilling of a state of terror in people. There's no greater degree of fear than terror. The gradations of fear include anxiety, nervousness, tension, doubt and fear. Terror is the ultimate fear. When something strikes terror in the heart, it's like facing a living death or a living hell. And that is the very point, the very goal of terrorism.

The devils and fallen angels take a great deal of satisfaction in being able to extract the reaction of ultimate fear from the children of light, because when there is terror in an individual, there is an opening of the chakras. The state of terror evokes a spilling of light in the same manner that a terrorist act causes the spilling of blood. An individual in a state of terror does not have the God-control to retain the light, and so the light that is spilled flows to the fallen ones in the same manner that light, or energy, flows to the object of one's attention.

Terrorists always prefer to incite extreme fear before committing murder. When someone is in a state of fear, their chemistry changes radically. And therefore, inciting mass terror and fear in a population before killing them extracts the greatest amount of light from them.

So we see that besides the destruction of democratic institutions, the fallen ones' purpose in committing acts of terrorism is to extract light from the people in large quantities and then use it to further their own ends.

CHAPTER 7

GENETIC MANIPULATION

When the fallen angels lost their place in heaven, they lost their opportunity to be co-creators with God. But they took with them what they knew of the science of creation, and they have never stopped trying to create a superior being to man. They do not do so for any benevolent reason. They do this only to get even. The creation of what the ascended masters call mechanization man is the ultimate revenge of the fallen angels against the sons of God.

We see, then, in this relative plane of maya, that Antichrist and the fallen ones have had their day. They have had their day of preeminence in which the serpentine mind has held sway in mankind, especially in those darkest periods when mankind did not know the one true God. The fallen ones' consciousness contributed to the wickedness that was accomplished in the days of Atlantis, which led finally to the edict that went forth from the heavenly councils that resulted in the Flood, the sinking of Atlantis.

From the akashic records[1]—the impressions upon the ethers of all that has ever transpired in the physical universe—we read the history of mankind's self-ruination through their cooperation with the genetic engineering experiments of the Nephilim. There was no end to the vile things they created for their pleasure, including animated robot slaves that did their bidding, which ultimately got out of hand. The genetic engineering of the human race and lower creatures became their modus operandi of controlling man, and the relationship between God and man.

Because their creations were not inspired by the Spirit of God but by their ego and desire for control, the creations of the Atlantean scientists were hideous, even mixing the seed of animal and human life. The creatures we read about in our mythologies bear witness to the product of their experimentation. These fallen ones stole the genetic material of the lightbearers to imprison God's creation in monstrous creatures that were not only distortions of God's purposes and intent but also a defilement of the divine image itself: the head and torso of male or female humans on the bodies of horses and all kinds of abominations, such as the mythological satyr (goat-man), and other strange types too grotesque to even speak or think about.

According to the readings of Edgar Cayce, the most renowned seer of the twentieth century, these mutants were the result not only of genetic tampering but also of the union of humans with what he called "THINGS." Cayce left us the following record on the Atlantean era:

> There was not a laboring for the sustenance of life (as in the present), but rather individuals who were children of the Law of One—and some who were the children of Belial (in the early experience) —were served by automatons, or THINGS, that were retained by individuals or groups to do the labors of a household, or to cultivate the fields or the like, or to perform the activities of artisans.[2]

Interpreting his father's readings on Atlantis, Edgar Evans Cayce says the term "THINGS" refers to

> the life form creations of the spiritual beings [the Nephilim] who had projected themselves into materiality.... The earth was proceeding along an evolutionary pattern...which was interrupted by the projection into materiality of these thought forms. It sounds as if they, in many cases, mixed with animals, the results being sometimes quite bizarre.[3]

Based on his Cayce research, Brad Steiger in his book *Atlantis Rising* concludes that some of these creations carried

> physical deformities such as feathered appendages, webbed feet, and other animal-like features.... As

an extra, insidious feature of Atlantean culture, the sons of Belial soon discovered cybernetic control of the human brain. They cracked the DNA code, enabling them to shape heredity. Such control resting in unethical hands could only result in the creation of more "THINGS."[4]

This is why God had to destroy the products of Nephilim experimentation. And thus, Atlantis was destroyed by earthquake and tidal wave.

So nature shrugged off the imbalances imposed upon her by a wayward generation, and the miscreations of the Nephilim and the laggards were destroyed. And thus the edict went forth: Henceforth every seed shall bear "after his kind."[5] The possibility of crossing animal and human life was thus forbidden by divine decree.

CONSEQUENCES OF GENETIC ENGINEERING

By tampering with the RNA and DNA chains, the sons of Belial (to use the Cayce term) interfered with and severely curtailed man's relationship to God. Through the control of the brain waves and the neurological system—with its delicate balance in the interchange of the life force from Spiritual Man to the organs and cells of generic man—they altered humanity's genetic capacity for psychic (soul, or 'solar') awareness.

They interfered with the web of light that interconnects the etheric, mental, emotional and physical bodies through which the intimations of the Godhead are received in the spiritually evolved lifestream. By this genetic 'brainwashing' and then the control of the four lower bodies through the mass media and the programming of the young from their earliest years, the sons of Belial reinforced the blunting of the thought receptors in generic man and short-circuited his receptivity to the higher frequencies of spiritual man attuned to the universal Mind. In other words, the sons of Belial purposed to stunt the soul faculties of the light-bearers by tampering with the physical instrument.

The ascended masters teach that the Atlantean records of genetic horror and cataclysm, which remain in the subconscious of everyone alive today on planet earth as an indelible race memory, are an underlying cause of modern-day anxiety, insomnia, hysteria, psychosomatic diseases, mental disorders, and so many karmic ailments of the flesh.

Likewise, mankind's vulnerability to religious and political fanaticism (seeking a savior or a demagogue for deliverance from impending genetic manipulation, the nuclear nightmare and ensuing cataclysm) derives from their prior subjugation by the "giants in the earth"[6] and the records of the sinking of both Lemuria and Atlantis.

This is why people are so affected by stories such as the one about the frightful golem (the sixteenth-century robot that rebels against its maker and terrorizes the townspeople),[7] the story of Frankenstein, and endless science fiction on the subject. This fascination shows their need for a periodic discharge of the "THINGS" lurking in the collective unconscious. Because people are unable to deal with these soul memories, they have a desperate need to experience films on horror and disaster, murder and the macabre in order to neutralize what is underneath. They watch the movies all together in packed theaters as a group catharsis. They scream, cry, eat popcorn, and then it's over: "It was only a film." "Fascinating food for thought." "A release of physical/emotional tension." "Such things can't be real." Or so they tell each other.

CHAPTER 8

DESECRATION OF THE CULTURE OF THE MOTHER

Our bodies and the earth itself are the gifts of God, the vehicles we have been given for our sojourn on earth. Without them we could not fulfill our mission in life or balance our karma. Our physical form is sacred, as Paul told us: "Know ye not that ye are the temple of God, and that the Spirit of God dwelleth in you?"[1] Thus, when we do not honor and respect our body or the bodies of others, when we harm or abuse the body, when we pollute the environment or mistreat animals, we are creating physical karma.

The mystic Kabir said, "The formless Absolute is my Father, and God with form is my Mother."[2] It is the Mother aspect of God that corresponds to Matter and the Matter universe. The Latin word *mater*, meaning "mother, origin, source," is considered by some etymologists to be the origin of the word *matter*.

Matter is the body of the Mother. There is nothing in the Matter universe that is not the province of the Divine Mother. She sustains the civilizations of the world and all the details of life that pertain to it. She is everywhere—in science, technology, government, the economy, health, education, the arts, the environment. She is fire, air, water and earth. She is nature.

We live in a time when our need for the Divine Mother could not be greater: Our bodies and the very earth that sustains us are being polluted and ravaged by agricultural, environmental and pharmaceutical chemicals, toxins and toxic wastes. Our children are not receiving a proper education. They are surrounded by violence in the news and entertainment media, in the streets, at school and at home. And most outrageous, more and more are being imprisoned in sex-slave trades and child sex tourism, and forced into prostitution, pornography and all manner of evils. Women are having abortions at an alarming rate. Rape and sexual harassment are frequent occurrences. Governments and economies are falling apart because our leaders are spineless.

These and other ravages of darkness are working together to tear apart the family and the family ideal in our society. Symptoms of the besieged family include high divorce rates, widespread unemployment, bulging welfare rolls, rising crime and drug abuse, domestic violence and child abuse, teen pregnancy, and so on. Saint Germain has said that the loss of the Father energy within families and society is also a contrived desecration of the Divine Mother. The crux of family life is at stake.

Understanding our relationship to the Divine Mother means coming to grips with our relationship to the feminine principle wherever it is found in life. Both men and women have a feminine side. It is the sensitive, intuitive side. It is the inner child, the soul. If we are to respect the Divine Mother, we must examine how we treat the feminine—how we care for our own soul and the souls of others.

CRUCIFIXION OF THE MOTHER

Woman has been mistreated because she represents the power of God that descends into the plane of Matter for the judgment of the Evil One. It is the Divine Mother that goes forth to defend all of the children of God against the forces of evil. As Revelation 12 records, ever since Lucifer was cast out of heaven, he has gone forth with a vengeance to persecute woman and her seed:

> And there appeared another wonder in heaven; and behold a great red dragon, having seven heads and ten horns, and seven crowns upon his heads.
>
> And his tail drew the third part of the stars of heaven, and did cast them to the earth: and the dragon stood before the woman which was ready to be delivered, for to devour her child as soon as it was born.

And she brought forth a man child, who was to rule all nations with a rod of iron: and her child was caught up unto God, and to his throne.

And the woman fled into the wilderness, where she hath a place prepared of God, that they should feed her there a thousand two hundred and threescore days....

And when the dragon saw that he was cast unto the earth, he persecuted the woman which brought forth the man child....

And the serpent cast out of his mouth water as a flood after the woman, that he might cause her to be carried away of the flood.

And the earth helped the woman, and the earth opened her mouth, and swallowed up the flood which the dragon cast out of his mouth.

And the dragon was wroth with the woman, and went to make war with the remnant of her seed.[3]

As we have seen through the ages, that which represents the Divine Mother upon earth has been persecuted, murdered, denied, desecrated by the fallen angels and their tools. Through the desecration of her body, of her offspring and of life itself through the pollution and problems in the ecology, and so forth, the Mother is crucified.

In the Piscean age, Jesus the Christ was on the cross. In this age, the Aquarian age, it is the feminine principle that is on the cross—not women alone, but the feminine polarity in man and in woman, that energy which fell in the final days of Lemuria and which is destined to rise again. The allegorical account of that fall symbolized the decadence of the age, and the subsequent destruction and sinking of the continent resulted from the desecration of the Mother light in that civilization.

In the ancient Motherland of Lemuria, located along what is now known as the Ring of Fire that surrounds the Pacific, stood twelve temples dedicated to the Divine Mother. They surrounded a central altar. Before the desecration of Lemuria, priests and priestesses tended the altar and kept the flame of the Mother. This Mother energy is more than, but also includes, the fire at the base of the spine, the Kundalini upon which yogis meditate. This is the sacred fire of the Mother. The worship of the Mother light is an ancient, enduring tradition of India, which was carried over from Lemuria, as was the ancient Sanskrit tongue.

In the decline of the Lemurian civilization, priests and priestesses who tended and worshiped at the altar compromised the sacred energies of the Mother through perverted practices. This perversion culminated, just prior to the sinking of the continent, in the assassination of the highest representative of the Divine Mother on Lemuria. And so, in the ages that have passed since that time, we have had to discover what it is like to live in a culture that has ceased to honor the Mother light in ourselves, in science and technology, in the media, in government, in our religious institutions and in nearly every aspect of life.

REEMERGENCE OF THE MOTHER

Now, at the dawning of the Aquarian age, we are feeling the powerful vibration of the Mother energy rising once again. Men and women are coming into their own—their own identity—and feeling the renewal of the flame of the Divine Feminine.

We know from the archives of the Brotherhood that those ages in which the Mother flame has taken dominion within the individual have been marked by great advances in science, art and culture. Earth's more recent civilizations have not reached the heights of science as it was practiced on Lemuria.

The Mother, as the Matter aspect, is the feminine polarity of the masculine Spirit, and yet she is inherent in Spirit. The Mother is the great womb out of which we are born, not only into physical bodies, but also to eternal life. The Mother has the most tender love for us, and at the same time she knows that we are spoiled, that we are given to self-indulgence and to playing with the trinkets and baubles of this world. And so she hides herself and says, "Come and find me." The Mother wants to draw us out of our illusions. She wants to help us untangle the skeins of our karma. She wants us to have the sense of duty that will drive us to fulfill the inner blueprint that has been placed within us by the Father.

The Mother has come to us after twelve thousand years behind the veil. When the culture of the Mother disappeared with the sinking of Lemuria, the feminine aspect of being became latent, and mankind, dominated by the masculine aspect, went forth to conquer in time and space.

Since the Fall on Lemuria, the fullness of the Mother's reality has been outside our reach. This is part of the race karma of mankind that we share. Since our expulsion from Eden, we have suffered a collective unconscious guilt for our self-imposed separation from God.

Ever since that moment, which our souls remember well, it has been like going through a long, dark tunnel, a dark night of the soul. We have been the dissatisfied ones, sons and daughters of God—a people identified as the elect of God, the chosen ones—who are not satisfied with the status quo or with materialism or with going the way of a strictly human existence. We have sensed that there is more to life than the material, more than we have been told.

When the culture of the Divine Mother began to reemerge during the decade of the 1960s, it was eclipsed by the fallen ones. The result, as the Master R commented, was that "the very ones who caused the destruction of Atlantis have come again…into embodiment. Joining forces with darkness, they have created a culture in direct antagonism to the culture of the Divine Mother."[4]

THE SIXTIES

The revolution of the sixties was perhaps among the strangest revolutions in history. And at the same time, we also saw history repeating itself, from the decadence of Lemuria to the decadence of Atlantis to the decadence of even several thousand years B.C. The generation of the sixties lived through one of the most paradoxical, perplexing, yet truly amazing revolutions in recorded history.

People felt the approach of a relentless wave of light. This was not a revolution of guns and political movements, although they played a role. Nor was it solely a revolution of music, sex and drugs, of youth casting off and taking on fads, although these too were a part of the scene. So were mysticism, Zen, vegetarianism, wine drinking, coffeehouses, folk music, and rock and roll.

The sixties also saw a rebellion against an old order that was rapidly fading, a rebellion against tradition, against mothers and fathers throughout the land. Singer-songwriter Bob Dylan captured the spirit of the times in his 1964 song that became the anthem for a generation: "The Times, They Are a-Changin'."

The sixties brought an alchemical change. It was a flushing out. It was an intensification of the flame of freedom bringing out the highest aspirations in people —people desiring to penetrate to the depths of their souls and the heights of new planes of consciousness.

Simultaneously, people were falling prey to leaders who had no right to be leaders, many of whom were agents of the archdeceivers who were about to stage their great counter-revolution against the light. This is how it played out:

The hypocrisy of the old order was obvious to the souls riding the wave of Aquarius. The new spirit abroad in the land was the oncoming tide of freedom. Everyone felt this tremendous wave. If you couldn't understand it or you couldn't explain it, you could still feel it. It shook people free from their moorings. Instinctively it made you want to get up and do something, anything. It was a revolution of individualism, a celebration of the self, of creating, of glorying in being who and what you really were—if only you knew what that was.

It didn't matter if the revolution struck everyone differently and made them do diverse things. That was its nature. But it was also a new awareness of the unity of life: Each individual was a part of the movement and somehow tied into the great cosmic mind. There was an increased feeling of brotherhood, a willingness to be together and to share, a sense of mobility and of no longer being boxed in by the old order.

Yet there were many on hand who took advantage of that energy of freedom. Some became footloose and fancy free, irresponsible, working out the repressions of centuries, bringing forth the very rebellions that had caused the sinking of Atlantis.

The leaders who came to the fore in the sixties spoke of the revolution. They were able to articulate for the rank and file many of those things they felt but couldn't express. They saw through some of the flaws of society, the blunders of Big Brother. In the minds of the youth, the failures of the war in Vietnam became the positive proof that the leaders of the revolution had caught and maintained the vision.

Many of these leaders had incarnated under a dispensation from the Lords of Karma[5] that decreed that those individuals who had been kept out of embodiment since their part in the sinking of Atlantis had to reincarnate to be given a final opportunity to bend the knee, call on the law of forgiveness and go through repentance, remission of sin, and regeneration in the service of God. It was required by the Great Law that these individuals reincarnate one final time so that by their actions, by their words and works, they could be judged.

The Lords of Karma had faith that the sons and daughters of God held in their hands, if they would invoke them, the laws of the land and the laws of God with which to rebuke and refute the Liar and the lies of these reembodied fallen ones.

God used these fallen ones to test the leadership of the generation. The majority of that leadership, however, failed to challenge these false leaders of the people and instead allowed their subculture—the counter-revolution that they worked on Atlantis to that civilization's destruction—to become a part of the mainstream of life in nearly every nation upon earth.

CHEMICAL MANIPULATION

The prevalence of drugs in our culture has spiraled out of control among certain segments of the population, whether with recreational drugs, pharmaceuticals, or nicotine and alcohol. More and more people are relying on chemical substances to treat every imaginable health condition, including a host of so-called problems in children at younger and younger ages. And then there are those who just want to get high—many of these also at alarmingly young ages. Although taking intoxicants is not new to modern times, we saw a surge in the use of recreational drugs during the decade of the sixties.

The Drug Conspiracy

A big part of the sixties culture revolved around the use of marijuana, which Saint Germain calls the death drug. There were two sharply conflicting views about marijuana. Some defended it as a harmless intoxicant or a mind-expanding sacrament, and others claimed it was a killer weed that could produce violence, insanity and licentious behavior. Although the focus has shifted over the decades, the controversy over marijuana is ongoing. Today the battle is over the legalization of medical marijuana.

Saint Germain reveals that the modern trend to

use drugs is part of a conspiracy that began beyond the dawn of recorded history:

> The story of these drugs—of marijuana, cocaine, heroin and all the synthetic, fabricated drugs—is an ancient one. I pinpoint, therefore, the conspiracy of fallen angels known as the Nephilim... and as the Watchers... to control the populations of the worlds....
>
> ...Nefarious powers moving against the evolution of life everywhere have seen fit to use mechanization man, computerized man... as trendsetters, jet-setters climbing after the gods and the fallen angels to tempt, to taunt and to hypnotize... the seed of Christ in embodiment.
>
> Their end is manifold, but it centers on the desire to steal the light..., to draw the lightbearers down into the valleys,[6]... where they would engage in the practices of darkness. And therefore,... fallen angels in embodiment demonstrate the "way that seemeth right"[7]—[they] provide the drugs, direct the processing and draw mechanization man into the entire conspiracy... as storefront manikins to be copied by the children of light.
>
> Thus, those who are the glamorous and those who comprise the multitudes of the mass consciousness exert a momentum that is planetary in scope to magnetize the lightbearers into their practices of drugs and perverted rock and nefarious deeds— and therefore karmically ally and align these light-

bearers with the darkest forces of the pits of hell....

...Understand that the original conspiracy against the lightbearers and the various evolutions and creations that began long, long ago with the fall of the fallen angels did... have its origin with a chemical manipulation and a genetic manipulation, and did come about not only through this vein of addiction and the supplying of the people with all manner of stimulants, but with other modes of conspiracy, thereby to limit the extent of the people to rise, to take dominion over their destiny, to make contact with the octaves of light, or to in any way challenge the fallen angels.

Since their fall, it has been the goal of the fallen angels to keep in subjugation all evolutions and the planetary bodies they have invaded and to prevent them from rising to any form of equality— to contact the power of God or to learn the secrets of the Great White Brotherhood, which they themselves [the fallen angels] have perverted from the beginning in their arts of black magic, war and witchcraft, necromancy and sorcery....

...These false hierarchies of fallen ones are positioned everywhere because they must control the people in order to take from them their light.[8]

Studies have shown that the use of marijuana results in the persistent poisoning of the deep centers of the brain necessary for the awareness of pleasure. Thus, it poisons the part of the brain that allows us the full awareness of being alive. As a result of this, many marijuana users have a kind of sensory deprivation, a symptom of marijuana that is the slowest to recede and the one least likely to go away. The inability to experience pleasure to the fullest makes one constantly pursue pleasure because one isn't quite realizing the full satisfaction of life. And therefore the taking of marijuana involves one in an ever-receding goal of more pleasure, which can no longer be experienced.

Relying on their own personal experiences, marijuana users believe that it is harmless because they perceive no difficulties. They do not perceive the difficulties because their faculties of perception are being destroyed while they use it. And so they have a diminishing ability to discern within themselves levels of their own God-awareness. Day by day they perceive no harm because marijuana is destroying not only the physical senses but the senses of the soul. This is one of the most subtle dangers of marijuana and most psychostimulant and psychedelic drugs. The user is rendered incapable of detecting the changes in himself.

This is the subtlety of the cult of death. With each joint, the smoker is deprived of a certain essence of life within the cells and the ability to perceive that he has indeed lost just a little bit of the essence of life. Therefore, he can never see himself as he was or as he is, because inherent in the drug is the gradual destruction of the ability to perceive life and to perceive that that life is waning. And having lost the tie to life, the way is opened to experimenting with heroin and other hard drugs.

To this day, some people justify that God has made everything, and therefore whatever he has made is for the blessing of his offspring. But God did not make marijuana, opium or any of the drugs that are in use today or the plants from which they are taken. What is not common knowledge is that marijuana and these other drugs were created by the great advancement of Luciferian science on Atlantis and Lemuria.

Saint Germain says that the reason the people want marijuana is because they want the Holy Spirit. The descent of the Spirit imparts light, bliss and an infilling Presence. The fallen Atlanteans and Lemurians knew they had been cut off from the Holy Spirit; therefore they attempted to simulate bliss chemically. Even though they understood the harm it would cause them, they nevertheless did this, knowing already that they were self-destroyed by their rebellion against God. In the meantime, they would enjoy the "synthetic Spirit," and furthermore, they would not enjoy it alone—they determined to take the children of God with them in their "sweet death."

We hear from many individuals that through the taking of drugs they attained a perspective of life that they would not otherwise have had, and that this new perspective led them to spiritual seeking and spiritual paths, which in turn led them to a higher spirituality and enlightenment. My thesis is that these individuals attained spirituality and enlightenment because they were ready, not because they smoked marijuana, not because they partook of certain mind-transforming drugs.

I do not accept the premise that the spiritual senses are opened by such drugs. The individuals who took drugs, and ultimately gained enlightenment, gained that enlightenment because the Christ within them strove and worked with them in spite of those drugs, in spite of the conditions associated with those drugs, and not because of them.

If you just look at the vast thousands of people who take drugs and who never attain enlightenment, never attain higher consciousness, you can see that the theory does not hold true. Inherent in it is a very subtle serpentine logic, and it is precisely that type of subtle logic that has become a justification for all sorts of practices that are not in keeping with the laws of God, including a very relaxed morality in our society.

As the 1960s saw an explosion of marijuana use in America, so the succeeding decades saw the rise in use of cocaine and a host of other drugs, too numerous to name.

The drug issue cannot be cast aside. It is eating away at the very vitals of our nations and our own souls, because every one of our souls is touched every time someone falls prey to drugs. Needless to say, our youth are under the most vicious attack through this drug epidemic, and that attack is on all levels of con-

Please tell us how you liked this book!

Book title: *Fallen Angels Among Us*

What did you like the most? _____

Other comments? _____

May we include your comments in our advertising? ☐ Yes ☐ No

☐ **YES! Send me a FREE catalog.** ☐ **YES! I'm a seeker—send me more info and new title announcements.**

Name _____

Address _____

City _____ State _____ Zip Code _____

E-mail _____ Phone no. _____

Your tax-deductible contributions make these publications available to the world.

Thank You!

Summit University Press, 63 Summit Way, Gardiner, MT 59030-9314 USA
1-800-245-5445 • Outside the U.S.A., 406-848-9500
www.SummitUniversityPress.com • E-mail: info@SummitUniversityPress.com

SUMMIT
UNIVERSITY
PRESS

*Nonprofit Publisher
since 1975*

491-#7235 FAAU 10/10

BUSINESS REPLY MAIL

FIRST-CLASS MAIL   PERMIT NO. 20   GARDINER MT

POSTAGE WILL BE PAID BY ADDRESSEE

SUMMIT UNIVERSITY PRESS®

63 Summit Way

Gardiner, MT 59030-9902

sciousness within their being. On one level, the aim of the fallen ones is to destroy the body temple so that it cannot house the consciousness of God.

Pharmaceutical Drugs

Another point of grave concern is the rampant use and misuse of pharmaceutical drugs. Prescription drugs are not difficult to obtain, and they have become an increasingly popular alternative to illegal drugs for adults and teens. Their use is widespread among younger children as well.

One of the overarching strategies of the fallen angels is to destroy the ability of future generations of lightbearers to contain light. U.S. pharmacists distribute five times more Ritalin than the rest of the world combined. This translates to as many as two million elementary school children in the U.S. alone being treated at any given time for attention deficit disorders. Of these, 60 percent to 90 percent (between 1.2 million and 1.8 million children) are being treated with Ritalin. Others receive another type of medication or treatment.[9] If a child is a little bit active in the classroom, the way children normally are at their age because they're excited about exploring the world around them, he is given drugs to calm him down.

Often these children are lightbearers who have come forth with great creative energy, and they are feeling the creative energy of God. Instead of being allowed to express that energy, they are given drugs to suppress it. This drugging of our children is inspired and promoted by those who are determined that these souls of light will not rise to manhood and womanhood with the fullness of the light that God has placed within them.

A report by the Florida Medical Examiners Commission showed that the number of deaths caused by prescription drugs surpassed those caused by illegal drugs. An analysis of 168,900 autopsies conducted in Florida in 2007 found that the number of deaths from legal drugs was three times the number from cocaine, heroin and all methamphetamines put together. A sergeant in the pharmaceutical drug diversion unit of the Broward County Sheriff's Office said, "The abuse has reached epidemic proportions; it's just explosive."

In Florida in 2007, illegal drugs were responsible for 989 deaths. In contrast, 2,328 people were killed by opioid painkillers, including Vicodin and Oxycontin, and 743 were killed by drugs containing benzodiazepine, including the central nervous system depressants Valium and Xanax.[10]

A July 2010 *St. Petersburg Times'* article, "Prescription Drug Epidemic Spreads to Babies," reported:

> The prescription drug epidemic, well documented among teens and adults, now is claiming victims before they are even born. Tampa Bay area doctors and addiction specialists are reporting a dramatic increase in the number of pregnant addicts

and infants needing treatment for withdrawal from prescription drugs.

The trend is reminiscent of the "crack baby" epidemic of the 1980s, when mothers used crack cocaine during their pregnancies....

And doctors say that treating a baby with drugs like oxycodone, methadone or Xanax in the system takes longer, and involves more medication, than treatment for heroin or cocaine.

"Babies are suffering more," said Dr. Terri Ashmeade, medical director of Tampa General Hospital's neonatal intensive care unit. "Withdrawal patterns seem to be worse (with prescription drugs) than what we were seeing with heroin."[11]

Nicotine

Although God gave the fallen angels "time, and times, and half a time" to repent of their sin, many have not repented but continue their diabolical activities as purveyors of drugs, alcohol, nicotine and other substances that go against the true law of our being. The burden of drugs on the people does not end with illegal or pharmaceutical drugs. Cigarette smoking is currently the primary avoidable cause of death in America.[12] Worldwide, at least five million deaths each year are caused by smoking at the present time.

Nicotine attacks the user at the lower level of the mental body. It is a narcotic that strongly affects the nervous system. It accelerates the heartbeat, raises the blood pressure and in large doses produces tremors, convulsions and vomiting. It causes the paralysis of the skeletal muscles, which eventually brings about impaired respiration.

Nicotine is one of the most toxic substances known. It is a poison used in insecticides, ranking with cyanide in rapidity of action. Nicotine has no medical use. In addition to nicotine, there are some four thousand chemicals in cigarette smoke. Several of these are known carcinogens. Smoking increases the incidence of heart disease as well as cancer in the lungs, larynx, esophagus, bladder, pancreas and kidneys.

Nicotine is one of the most perniciously addicting drugs in common use. It is so hard to stop smoking that it is a common occurrence for those with advanced cases of emphysema to continue to smoke cigarettes right up until death. Heroin addicts who have stopped smoking and kicked heroin have found that it is easier to quit heroin than cigarettes. Most smokers continue smoking only because they cannot stop; about 70 percent of them want to quit smoking.

The masters teach that nicotine creates a density on the surface of the brain that blocks the flow of divine intelligence into our beings. Thus, it is a hindrance to our spiritual development.

THE MISUSE OF SOUND AND RHYTHM

The priests and priestesses who tended the flame of the Mother on the altars of Lemuria knew the sacred science of sound and rhythm. But they perverted these during the era of their rebellion. That perversion of sound and rhythm was also in vogue in the last days of Atlantis and was one of the factors that contributed to the cataclysm that caused the sinking of that continent.

The rhythm of the Mother is the 4/4 time and corresponds to the base-of-the-spine chakra, which has four "petals." The rhythm of 4/4 time, which we hear in marches, is a disciplined energy that causes the chakra to gently spin and the Mother light to gently rise up the spine through the other chakras.

Rock music, on the other hand, has a syncopated 4/4 beat, which is a perversion of the rhythm of the Mother, and therefore channels energy through the chakras in a counterclockwise spin. As a result of this perversion, the life force descends instead of ascending up the spine.

When a person listens to rock music and enters into that beat, the light of the chakras descends with violence. Because it is not a gentle descent, it tears the delicate membranes on the inner bodies—the astral, mental and etheric bodies. These tears occur at the places where the chakras tie into the central nervous system. As a result, the light is released, giving a sensation that is often called a rush. Furthermore, this beat also goes counter to the heartbeat.

This means of assault upon the youth was reintroduced through rock music during the era of the sixties.

Unwittingly and ignorantly, many people on earth have come to like this music and have developed a habit of listening to it to the point that it has become an addiction.

The fallen angels seek the bliss of reunion of the light of the Mother with the light of the Father, but they can't have it without submission to the living Christ. So they invert the beat, and the vibration of the energy descending becomes the synthetic experience, or the inverted experience, of the raising of the Kundalini fire. The raising of the sacred fire of the Kundalini on the spinal altar is one of the great experiences of the soul in her reunion with God—when this experience occurs lawfully, when you are strong in your ability to contain God's light.

As the Kundalini ascends, the upward movement of the light through the chakras results in the wholeness of the light of Father and Mother. The descent of the Kundalini, which occurs with the syncopated beat, is also a movement, a vibration, a sensation of light, albeit in a counterproductive direction. If one has never tasted the pure nectar of God, how can one know that the synthetic nectar is inferior? Thus the rock beat causes the descent of the Kundalini and has its own perverted bliss, which is the substitute experience for reunion with God. This is the reason people are addicted to rock music—because it does create a movement of energy.

The light of the sacred fire is very powerful, and

when it is released, there is a high. Individuals who get used to that release want to listen to more rock music in order to experience it again. When they're not listening to it, they feel an uncomfortability. They feel temporarily better when that energy is released through listening to the music again. So this becomes a habit that they can't get out of easily.

When that energy is released, it is lost; it isn't retained. Thus, there is a slow bleeding of the life force, and this causes early aging, early mental degeneration, chaos in the chakras, and a short concentration span. This lack of ability to focus happens because of the loss of energy in the third-eye chakra and in the crown. What has also come to pass is that the energy descending into the lower chakras and not rising again puts all of the weight of the life force in those chakras. That energy must go somewhere. So with the advent of rock music in the sixties, the logical result was a sexual revolution, free sex and greater promiscuity.

ABORTING THE DIVINE PLAN OF SOULS

The sexual revolution of the free-love generation of the sixties led to the abandonment by many of the traditional concepts of marriage and family. Living together became fashionable. Premarital and teenage sex became widespread. Birth control became a necessity. And once the new morality was established, it was a relatively small step from birth control to population control and the social acceptability of abortion.

Consequently, many souls who should be a part of Aquarius—souls of light who are prepared to take their place and help bring in the New Age—are not in embodiment. They have been denied entrance into the portals of birth because one or both of their parents considered the pregnancy "untimely." Abortion has become a means of birth control.

Many people today have an inner sense of what karma is. Beyond karma is dharma—the fiery destiny of the soul, the desire to fulfill one's reason for being. Every soul who is prepared for rebirth is charged with that sense of completing unfinished business. The soul wants to give the world something of herself. It might be a creative gift or a gift of love, sweetness and kindness. It might be a small act of charity or a monumental achievement. The gift each of us will give will vary according to our divine plan.

We find confirmation of some of these spiritual truths in the fascinating work of Dr. Helen Wambach, a clinical psychologist and regression therapy expert who pioneered past-life and prenatal research beginning in the mid-1960s. Her studies give a glimpse into the spiritual life of the unborn child and the continuity of the soul. She once said of her work: "Ninety percent of the people who come to me definitely flash on images from a past life."[13]

In one study, she asked 750 people under hypnosis questions about their life before birth. She analyzed their answers in her book *Life before Life*.[14] Although hypnosis can be dangerous under certain circumstances and is not recommended for those on a spiritual path,[15] Dr. Wambach's findings are worthy of study. They reveal the soul's sense of the timetable of its mission.

Many of Dr. Wambach's subjects knew they were born in the twentieth century for a specific reason, and the majority of these said they chose this time period "because of its great potential for spiritual growth." Thirty percent of them knew they had to live during this time in order to be with certain people. Some stated that their purpose in this lifetime "was to be with one or several other people they had known in past lives in order to work out their relationships." Others said they had come to fulfill a certain mission.

Dr. Wambach observed that "the largest group of the sample said that the purpose of this lifetime was to grow spiritually and to teach others." One of her subjects said, "Before my birth there was a conference, and I had a feeling of deep love from one of my advisers. He talked of my yearning to reach my life plan. When you asked about purpose, all I felt was a strong feeling of a plan."

The solution to the karmic dilemma of abortion is not threatening or killing abortion providers or making threats against abortion clinics. The solution is compassionately providing a safe haven for the parents and their children.

Individually and as communities, we can support

single mothers and mothers-to-be. We can also pray for mothers to carry their babies to term and, if they do not wish to raise them, to put them up for adoption. There are thousands of couples eagerly awaiting the opportunity to adopt a child.

One of the most interesting conclusions of Dr. Wambach's research is that some of her subjects who were adopted children said, while under hypnosis, that they knew before they were born that they were destined to be adopted. It was part of their life plan.

"Some of them knew before they were born of the relationship they would have with the adoptive parents," says Dr. Wambach, "and felt that they would not be able to come to them as their own genetic child but chose the method of adoption as a way to reach their parents." Her research led her to conclude that "chance and accident apparently played no part in the adoption."[16]

This puts a new light on the attitude among some today that if a woman is pregnant and doesn't want to keep her child, she might as well abort it. In fact, it may be someone's karma and destiny to give birth to a certain child and then put him up for adoption so that the child can find his rightful parents, who are unable to have children.

Those who have supported abortion and want to balance that karma should realize that God is merciful and has given us ways to become sponsors of life. We can rectify our karma not only through prayer work but also by giving birth to children, adopting children or sponsoring them financially. We can participate in community programs, become a mentor or support organizations that care for underprivileged, orphaned or needy children, for example.

THE BATTLE VICTORIOUS

The intertwining of the karma of the lightbearers and the fallen ones is being outplayed today on a world scale. In order for us to understand our personal karma, we need to see it juxtaposed against the background of world karma (the combined karma of the fallen angels and all mankind). It is essential that we have the perspective of our entanglements with the Nephilim and the Watchers and understand where we have lost ground in this and past lives by giving in to or forming alliances with them.

This chapter has highlighted some of the ways in which the children of light have been entrapped by the fallen ones' schemes. Over the millennia, many have become enslaved to the lifestyle promoted by these rebellious ones. Through the dulling of our minds, brains and sensitivities, the fallen ones have managed to prevent us from coming into our full God-power and recognizing our spiritual destiny.

In this age, we have an opportunity to use the Science of the Spoken Word to effectively deal with the energies of the fallen angels, as well as our own karma. It was Saint Germain who first introduced the science of decrees in the twentieth century. This method of prayer has become widely used by those desiring to undo their past mistakes.

Above all, everyone who goes forth to do battle with the Goliath of the fallen angels must remember that God is the only reality, the only life and the only power in the universe. God and man are inseparable as the Divine One. All that has determined to manifest imperfection has placed itself outside of this oneness, far afield from God's saving grace—until it elects to return to the state of divine union.

Those imperfect models of creation that have set up an existence apart from God must one day relinquish the energies they have pirated from the Deity, for their existence outside of him is a myth. Those who are always conscious of God within as real, always aware that, in reality, nothing has the power to oppose the divine will, will emerge from the battle victoriously.

The dire prophecies that we face today are a reflection of the karma that has been created by the Nephilim and the Watchers and mankind's interactions with them over aeons.

One with God is a majority. With this knowledge in hand, we can, by the grace of God, do our part to turn the tide of the darkness that is upon us, our nations and our planet, and mitigate the handwriting on the wall of prevailing prophecies.

PART 3

PROPHECY

A FORECAST OF RETURNING KARMA

God has never willed destruction or death or famine; the prophecy is of mankind's own returning karma and specifically of the returning karma of the lightbearers and of the fallen angels....

Seek ye first to live, to endure, to survive the age. And know that it is possible to live through the worst of prophecy.

I may speak it, but I am not the origin of prophecy! Every living soul upon this earth and fallen angels and godless ones—all are harbingers of that which must descend. For the law of karma is inexorable, irrevocable, saving where the violet flame, the sacred fire, does consume mankind's karma.

—Saint Germain

Recalling Enoch's Prophecy

The end of the Piscean age is the end of the opportunity of the fallen ones to work their evil. They must either come into alignment with God or face the consequences of the judgment prophesied in the Book of Enoch and in Revelation 20.

These are key prophecies for our time because they apply to the fallen angels who hold positions of power and influence in the governments, the military establishments, the banking houses and the economic institutions of the nations. Many of these fallen ones have sworn their enmity against God and his people, and they have no intention of recanting or relenting.

As you will recall, the Epistle of Jude speaks of the destiny of the fallen angels, quoting Enoch directly:

> And Enoch also, the seventh from Adam, prophesied of these [the Watchers], saying, Behold,

the Lord cometh with ten thousands of his saints,

To execute judgment upon all, and to convince all that are ungodly among them of all their ungodly deeds which they have ungodly committed, and of all their hard speeches which ungodly sinners have spoken against him.[1]

The Book of Enoch makes it clear that the judgment of the Watchers is the key to the liberation of the souls of light and is necessary in order to purge the planet prior to the Lord's kingdom come. Enoch's premise is that this judgment will occur "in a generation which is to succeed at a distant period *on account of the elect.*" (En. 1:2, emphasis added)

We have defined the elect as those who elect to be instruments of God's will, having received the calling from God to bear the light of the Elect One. Enoch 1:2 indicates that the judgment will be a direct and inevitable consequence of the coming of the Elect One, the incarnate Word, and his chosen in this and succeeding centuries. This means that the judgment prophesied by Enoch will come through the Christ light ignited in the hearts of his own, the lightbearers.

I invite you to consider whether you are being called today to bear that light—the light that will ultimately judge the fallen angels and defeat the prophecies of karma returning as recompense for the deeds of both fallen angels and men at the end of the Piscean age.

Let us now look at the role prophecy plays in helping us to balance both personal and planetary karma and thereby foil the agendas of the fallen angels among us.

CHAPTER 9

Understanding Prophecy

As we enter Aquarius and both personal and planetary karma are coming due, the handwriting on the wall is becoming clear for all to see. The turmoil and upheaval around us and on the evening news are the signs of the times that Jesus foresaw over two thousand years ago:

> And ye shall hear of wars and rumours of wars: see that ye be not troubled: for all these things must come to pass, but the end is not yet.
> For nation shall rise against nation, and kingdom against kingdom: and there shall be famines, and pestilences, and earthquakes, in divers places.
> All these are the beginning of sorrows.[1]

The beginning of sorrows is the beginning of the return of world karma. World karma is upon us. We can scarcely understand each day and each year the acceleration of darkness through war, new types of diseases, genocide and all manner of problems on the earth. People seem to have become more disturbed, and there is no longer an overall sense of native innocence and purity that had existed prior to the 1960s.

CYCLES OF RETURNING KARMA

The ascended masters have revealed to me that the cumulative karma created by those who have lived on earth during the past twelve astrological ages (a 25,800-year cycle) actually fell due at the dawn of the Piscean age. That karma would have descended in full at the beginning of that age if Jesus had not stepped in to mitigate it, just as other avatars before him had borne mankind's karma. Because Jesus chose to take embodiment and to fulfill his mission by assuming that role, this karma was allowed to descend in a series of cycles that would last throughout the Piscean age.

I thus came to understand the full meaning of Jesus "bearing the sins of the world": Jesus perceived the plight of earth's people and agreed to take embodiment at that crucial hour in history to mitigate the full impact of the karma that was scheduled to descend.

Before Jesus Christ's coming, it was evident to all of the host of heaven that the failure of many sons and daughters of God to deal with their karma and with the karma of the laggards and fallen angels was due in great measure to their being deprived, by the forces of darkness, of the truths of Christ's teaching. Jesus imparted these truths to his innermost circle of disciples, and God has given them to us today through the ascended masters. This divine doctrine is not confined to any particular religious tradition; it belongs to all.

The fact that Jesus took upon himself the full weight of that karma does not mean that we who made it (both souls of light and those committed to darkness) are not responsible for it. It does not mean, as some Christians have misunderstood, that Jesus "wiped away" our sins (karma) or that he will "save" our souls without us having to lift a finger. It simply means that Jesus bought us time. He bore world karma for a time to give us the opportunity to gain self-mastery so that we could better deal with that karma as and when it descended.

Jesus' purpose in coming was to demonstrate the path of personal Christhood so that the children of light could follow in his footsteps throughout the Piscean age and beyond. But infiltrators into Church and State withheld the knowledge of this path from them.

These wolves in sheep's clothing—the embodied fallen angels who have usurped positions of power and authority in Church and State—have taken away the true teachings of the Christ. For they knew—and feared—that the lightbearers would exercise the power, wisdom and love of Christ to lawfully overcome them and to cast them out of the temples of God and man.

Thus, having had no teachers to teach them the sacred mysteries that Jesus imparted to his disciples, many souls of light have missed the point that their soul's calling from God is to walk the path that Jesus taught. And so they are ill-equipped for their mission in this new age because they do not have the fullness of self-knowledge of the indwelling Christ as we enter the two-thousand-year dispensation of Aquarius.

Today, as we are reaping the personal and world karma of many astrological cycles, the accumulation of these past sowings is boomeranging upon the nations and upon every one of us.

Karma is never a punishment, although those on the receiving end of it may experience it as such. Karma is the effect of whatever thoughts, feelings, words and deeds a person has set in motion through the freewill qualification of God's energy.

Most of us have set in motion good causes that have produced a harvest of good effects. But we have also been putting out negative vibrations and then recycling those same negatives as they have come full circle. And we've been doing this for a long time. Often we have sown error unwittingly, in ignorance of cosmic law; but most of us will admit that at times we have knowingly directed harm toward some part of life. The Great Law requires us to pay the price for these wrongdoings. We must pay our karmic debts.

THE ROLE OF THE PROPHETS

Divine intercession has always been God's solution to man's nonresolution. Examples abound in the

Old Testament of prophets warning the people about the consequences of not changing their evil ways. The word *prophet* means, literally, "one who has been called" or "one who speaks for another."

Prophecy is exhortation—God exhorting us to right action through his messengers. Prophecy is delivered through them by the ascended masters and higher heavenly beings who guide earth and her evolutions. These beings read our collective karma as the handwriting in the skies and then tell us through their prophets what will come upon us and our generation if we do not obey the laws of God.

God has always given people an opportunity to change a prophesied outcome, yet they have seldom taken it. The book of the prophet Jonah illustrates that God will even intercede on behalf of those whose actions have shown great wickedness when they heed his prophet's warning and repent.

When Jonah prophesied to the people of Nineveh that God would destroy their city in forty days because of their wicked ways, they believed God, renounced their evil behavior and prayed to God to spare them. They proclaimed a fast and put on sackcloth. The king of Nineveh then arose from his throne, covered himself with sackcloth, and sat in ashes. He proclaimed:

> "Let neither man nor beast, herd nor flock, taste any thing. Let them not feed, nor drink water. But let man and beast be covered with sackcloth

and cry mightily unto God. Yea, let them turn every one from his evil way, and from the violence that is in their hands. Who can tell if God will turn and repent and turn away from his fierce anger, that we perish not?"

The Book of Jonah records that "God saw their works, that they had turned from their evil way."[2] He relented and did not inflict the disaster that he had threatened. From this example, it is clear that God is always seeking to give us opportunity.

In 1981 in Medjugorje, Yugoslavia (now Bosnia and Herzegovina), the Virgin Mary began appearing to six teenagers, warning of coming calamities. She said that some of these could be mitigated through prayer and fasting. She also revealed that because of the response to her messages, one of the calamities had been averted. This is a confirmation of what the masters have been teaching us for more than fifty years. Knowing that we can mitigate returning karma gives us great hope even as it goads our souls to more earnest prayer.

None of us knows what we will face tomorrow, next week or next year. The future is unknown, but not entirely. When we stop and think about it, the sudden destruction that comes upon a people has often been predictable. Had they studied the times and trends and been students of their own history and of the laws of Mother Nature, they could have foretold their probable future. The givens and the knowns were there. That's why you often hear the expression "I might have known this would happen." And indeed people do.

Their souls know beforehand what will come to pass if they (or a sufficient number of them) do not change their ways. But the reasoning mind, locked in its own labyrinthine logic, cannot see the straight line of causal relationships leading more and more inevitably to a predictable conclusion.

Saint Germain read the handwriting on the wall on November 27, 1986, when he forewarned of economic crisis. Several months later, on October 19, 1987, which is now known as Black Monday, stock markets around the world crashed. In the U.S., the Dow Jones Industrial Average tumbled 508 points, a 22.6 percent drop. This remains the largest single-day *percentage* decline in stock market history. In light of current world events, Saint Germain's warning bears heeding as much as ever:

> Economic debacle is foreseen. Prepare. Setbacks will be sudden. Be not lulled by the heyday. Many Band-Aids upon the economy, the money system, the banking houses. These will not prevent the collapse of nations and banking houses built on sands of human greed, ambition and manipulation of the lifeblood of the people of God.[3]

There is a handwriting on the wall today of the course of human events. And yet, as we learn from the events in Nineveh, we can at any moment decide to change the events and to change the graph of life.

THE FREEWILL FACTOR

One of Saint Germain's great rallying cries is *Prophecy is never set in stone*. He says that if we respond to the prophets' warnings and apply the spiritual solutions they place before us, calamity can be averted.

When Jonah went to Nineveh to warn the people that calamity would ensue unless they repented, much to his disappointment they did repent. They heeded the voice of God through him and their city was spared. Concerned that the people would consider him a false prophet, Jonah complained to God.

We understand from this story that prophecy is not final and that karma can be transmuted, which in essence means that it can be transformed from a state of negativity, or a misuse of God's energy, to a higher state or form. In the matter of prophecy, the unpredictability of human will (that it can at any moment change its course) must be taken into account. If the fulfillment of divine predictions were inevitable, this would circumscribe man's free will.

Instead, the science of prophecy always takes into account mankind's ever-present opportunity to change. If men change, prophecies may also change. Since the plotting of trends on the graph of human consciousness is done at divine levels, the masters can and do foretell with great accuracy the outcome of returning personal and world karma. And since the harvest of current events is so delicately intertwined with mass and individual sowings, the latter often determine the former. Current events can therefore be predicted with a large degree of certainty by the masters, who have access to the karmic records of the earth and her evolutions.

THE MAYAN CALENDAR AND 2012

In the mid-1980s, the Mayan calendar and the date 2012 began to be mentioned as having great significance for the future of our planet. It started with a series of books on the Mayan calendar, which, according to some, predicts "the end of time" in 2012. Other prophecies for 2012 followed with increasingly rapid succession. These cover a broad spectrum of doomsday scenarios as well as scenarios that describe a time of great transformation that some believe the earth will pass through.

Many 2012 articles start off with a generic sentence like this: "The ancient Mayan calendar predicts the end of the world in 2012." Given such emphatic claims, it's important that we understand more about the Mayan calendar.

As explorers, archaeologists and anthropologists penetrated deeper into the Mayan civilization in Central America, they found that the Maya had some twenty or more different calendars. These calendars were based on very accurate observations of the seasons and the heavens.

The most intriguing of the calendars, with roots going back to earlier Mesoamerican cultures like the Olmec, is the one known as the Long Count. In this calendar, a "Great Cycle," or "Sun," consists of 1,872,000 days—a fraction more than 5,125 years. These cycles of 5,125 years are also referred to as "World Ages." Mayan mythology says that before the current Great Cycle, there were four earlier World Ages. Each of these ages ended in destruction, followed by the emergence of a new kind of human being.

According to that system, the current World Age is very close to completion. When properly correlated with the Gregorian calendar, it will end sometime in or around 2012. The exact end date remains disputed.

Different people who have studied the Mayan Long Count calendar have calculated different end dates. The date used most often is December 21, 2012, with its built-in numerical symmetry of 12-21-12.

An interesting aspect of the Long Count calendar is that beyond the end of the current Great Cycle, there are no further specific future dates found in the Mayan records. This has led researchers and speculators to claim that the Mayan calendar literally says that when this current cycle ends, there will be no more time, no other World Ages. This "end of cycles" or "end of time" concept lies at the core of the 2012 prophecies.

Predictably, this "end of the Mayan calendar" concept has been approached with very different mindsets. Some people claim that it signifies the end of civilization as we know it by means of tremendous cataclysms. Others claim that it means that the earth will go through a major transition in consciousness, a transformation that will result in the birth of an entirely new kind of human being.

The ascended master El Morya, Chief of the Darjeeling Council of the Great White Brotherhood, commented on the Mayan calendar and the date of 2012:

> We address the topic brought to the fore concerning an ancient calendar and a date.... Understand, then, that their calendar is the calendar of the Nephilim and of their cycles. Thus, one can learn from a false... teaching the cycles that they are plotting on the graph even according to the heavens [the stars]....
>
> These fallen ones have placed their races upon this planet for this hour when they might be the negative electrode in embodiment for the anchoring of their energy, their control and their final manipulation.... Understand the complexity of a half a million years, ten million years of programming. Understand the nature of false hierarchies and of the anti-Mind itself. It is a giant network and it has moved throughout the Matter spheres long for only one goal—to take millions of its own kind in order to devour the light of one son of God who has descended into Matter. They will stage a conspiracy for thousands of years to accomplish the undoing and the fall of a single son of God....

Understand that the Sons of God in earth are not in great number. Yet the salvation of these is the reason [for the presence of the Great White Brotherhood in your midst]. There is a chaff that is burned and there are the tares that are bound in bundles and burned. Realize, then, that that which is saved unto everlasting life is the good wheat of the genetic seed of Christ.

When you have this seed and you know that you have this seed, for the fire burns in your heart, you have two goals in life—first, to preserve your personal integrity and to disentangle yourself from the enmeshments of karma with these fallen ones. And second, to bring the knowledge of the Great White Brotherhood and the religion of the Divine Mother to all others who have this divine spark. Two goals alone: disentanglement with the dark web woven by the [fallen ones] and the ascent of the heart and mind to the octaves of safety.[4]

PROPHECY OF THE SEVENTH ROOT RACE

During the first three golden ages and in the early days of Lemuria and Atlantis, the ascended masters and the angels walked and talked with those whose consciousness had never departed from the unity of good. Under the tutelage of the masters, these civilizations reached tremendous heights of scientific and cultural achievement.

As noted earlier, the first three root races lived in harmony with each other and with the laws of the universe. They expressed the highest potential of their souls, fulfilled their reason for being, and reunited with God.

When the souls of the fourth root race were derailed from their spiritual path, they lost the vision of their quest for divine wholeness and created karma. Some have been reincarnating on earth to this day. Thus, the souls of the fifth and sixth root races embodied into an imperfect world and they, too, became misguided, made karma, forgot their divine origins, and lost sight of their purpose in life. Many members of the fifth and sixth root races are also still in embodiment.

As a result of the unpredictable conditions on earth today, the souls of the next root race, the seventh, have not yet been allowed to embody, for it would jeopardize their spiritual development. The seventh root race is being held back because the Lords of Karma have determined that they will not send another root race of pure souls into the earth and run the risk that they will be influenced by the fallen angels and impressed with the imperfections of the planet. Therefore their incarnation has been put on hold, so to speak, to give the lightbearers time to invoke the light, clean up the pollution of this planet at all levels, and make it a fit habitation for these new souls.

Saint Germain spoke of this concern, which he shares with other members of the Great White Brotherhood:

The entire planet shall have the opportunity to bring in a golden age of Aquarius, but it is South America that God has chosen as the place that must be prepared for the incarnation of these holy innocents....

Yet, as I have said and as other ascended masters have said, this is a time when we must hold back even though we would move forward, for we cannot recommend... that the souls of the seventh root race be born to mothers and fathers on this continent [South America] until the leadership of the nations with the support of their constituents will right the wrongs of society.[5]

PREPARING FOR THE SEVENTH ROOT RACE

Saint Germain has explained how we can prepare for the precious souls of the seventh root race, who can do so much to help us once again enter a golden-age culture:

Top on our agenda is the defense of the child. We must have guarantees that the street children will receive equal protection of the law and that night stalkers who hunt them down and kill them will be arrested, tried and serve time in prison. The children must not be fair game for night stalkers![6]...

Let the people of South America rise up en masse and call upon the Lord Jesus Christ and his hosts... to bind the forces of organized crime, drug trafficking, police corruption, child pornography, child abuse...and the desecration and degradation of women. Let them call for the judgment of those who openly display women's bodies on billboards and in stores, advertising everything from cars to cigarettes, thus debasing the image of woman and corrupting children.

Let the people of South America call for the judgment of dishonest politicians and businessmen and their manipulation of the economy and the resources of the land, which rightfully belong to the people. Let them call for the judgment of spiritual wickedness in high places and for the judgment of the heads of state and their cabinets who fatten their wallets at the expense of the people.

Let them call for the judgment of those who misappropriate funds that ought to be going for food, clothing, medical care and housing—housing to replace the cardboard dwellings of the poor that fall apart every time it rains.

This continent must be delivered of the corrupt ones who go about corrupting the souls and the bodies of the people! Again I say, call upon the Lord Jesus Christ and the... archangels to purge the earth of those who do not have the best interests of the people at heart, who siphon off their very lifeblood and use it to gain power over the nations.[7]

CHAPTER 10

NATURE'S ROLE IN PROPHECY

In past ages when mankind's discord and negativity have reached proportions greater than what the nature spirits could bear, nature herself has convulsed in cataclysm, as with Lemuria and Atlantis.

Profit seeking at the expense of the environment, the insensitive treatment of any part of life, and discordant thoughts, feelings, speech or actions all create an accumulation of negatively charged energy that becomes a weight on the earth body, the oceans and the very air that we breathe. We see the effects in all manner of disturbance in the elements: for example, storms, floods, droughts, wildfires, earthquakes, tornadoes and hurricanes.

The masters have warned that if civilization continues on its present course, it will literally tear itself apart, and nature will prepare to begin a new cycle. Such an occurrence, they say, would cause a quaking in all those who witness it. And yet, this need not come to pass. If men and women begin to give the same attention and devotion to the power of light that they have given to darkness, they may be spared this fate.

What the world needs is a wave of light to counteract the potential oncoming darkness and destruction. Diligent application of the violet flame can forestall cataclysm. This high-frequency spiritual light can literally change the electronic vibration of matter. With the violet flame, negative energy can be requalified as positive energy through its action of transmutation and its attributes of mercy, justice and freedom. (This subject will be addressed in Part 5.)

If mankind knew they had the ability to transmute the karmic causes of cataclysm that are brewing just beneath the surface of everyday life, they would invoke the violet flame before that karma breaks out with violence in the physical plane. Of course, any invocations to the violet flame must go hand in hand with a judicious care of the ecosystem and a profound respect and reverence for the laws governing nature's cycles of self-renewal.

When there has been an absence of reverence for life and God, an absence of divine justice—brother to brother, nation to nation—and the desecration of women and children in society, major earth cataclysms have been unleashed at the end of cosmic cycles. And they will be unleashed again unless people abandon their selfish and shortsighted violation of our planet's resources. For when these transgressions against life and nature are not transmuted, karmic law decrees that nature's form of transmutation must act.

ECOLOGY AND THE THREAT OF CATACLYSM

After the Fall of man, when mankind and fallen angels began to create negative karma with one another, the forces of nature became the instruments of karmic judgment. Famine and pestilence, drought and flood returned to all on earth the thrust of their collective rebellion against natural law, their extravagant waste of natural resources, and their defiance of life's oneness.

Thus mankind was beset with the problems of ecology, which in effect are the problems of karma. This is the price mankind has had to pay for his failure to live in harmony with God and nature.

In recent generations, citizens of every nation have taken concerted action to find solutions to the problems of the ecology. Though their intentions are in many cases honorable, they often do not have all the facts. When individuals have lacked the awareness that Spirit is the great coordinator of the cosmic flow in nature, they have often mistakenly focused their efforts on shortsighted goals or been misled by those with ulterior motives. Therefore, those who promote a falsely based ecology must come under closer scrutiny before their premises and conclusions are universally adopted.

While the concern for earth's ecology mounts,

people are often oblivious to the cause and effect relationship between the soul and its environment. In fact, all that man beholds around him is the effect of causes he has set up within his own consciousness. These are but a reflection of his misqualified emotional and mental energies.

Those who are unaware of the interchange of energies between Spirit and Matter do not see the relationship between the pollution of the elements and personal and planetary karma. These same individuals would also have a hard time comprehending that the destruction of Maldek, the sinking of the continents of Lemuria and Atlantis, and the burying of other ancient civilizations were karmic penalties exacted by God through nature. They regard cataclysm as the result of an interplay of natural forces.

When people's spiritual senses have not been quickened, they do not recognize the presence of God in nature. We come to understand, then, that there is an unerring spiritual law. It is tempered by a God who reserves the authority to either restrain or unleash the momentum of mankind's karma, sometimes mercifully restraining it for centuries as he gives mankind the opportunity to balance their debts to life.

HEALING OUR INNER ECOLOGY, HEALING THE EARTH

Man is not at the mercy of an overpowering force outside himself. If humanity could bring themselves to admit that their wars and their hatreds, their economic opportunism and their inhumane treatment of all forms of life have a direct bearing upon the balance of forces in their environment, they would be taking the first step in solving the problems of ecology. The second step is no less important—mobilizing their resources and know-how in a concerted effort to eliminate violations of natural law. These actions would go a long way toward bringing about the desired rapprochement with the forces of nature: oneness with life.

Instead, mankind occupy themselves with building fences around what they have come to regard as their own little patch of earth. If they can secure their families from the pollutions of the masses, they are satisfied; but their No Trespassing signs cannot keep out the gathering clouds of personal or planetary karma. And those who fail to observe on a world scale the ancient maxim "I am my brother's keeper" have failed to understand that the only one who can avert total cataclysm in the natural order is man himself.

Unless people come into harmony with God's laws and his creation and cease blatantly disregarding and abusing them, they will set in motion the only alternate method by which nature can correct those abuses. Natural law will respond through disaster as the earth convulsively shrugs off the perverted creations of man in order that a nobler image may once again be brought forth. Yet nature ever prefers the gentler way.

THE WAY OF MERCY

Prophecies and predictions of natural disaster come, then, as an act of mercy so that the people might change their ways before it is too late, so that they might know that their fate is pending in the halls of cosmic justice, and that the outcome will depend entirely upon their attitude and their actions.

The way of mercy is still open. Man *can* approach the altar of God seeking forgiveness. He *can* avert calamities by right action and by invoking the light of Spirit to descend into the planes of Matter. By making an about-face he *can* depart from a self-centered existence and glorify God in man and in all his works.

PART 4

The Path of Light

In the Twinkling of an Eye

The revelations of Enoch and the masters concerning the fallen angels' conspiracy against truth within both Church and State need not bring a message of despair. If we take heart and courageously lay the ax to the root of the trees of these devils and their doctrinal error to make way for the tall tree of Truth noted for its good fruit,[1] then there is hope.

There is much we can learn about ourselves from this exposure of the seed of the wicked: Is our faith in man or in God? Have we made gods of the saints, East or West, believing them to be incapable of human error during their lifetimes? Do we stand for truth or do we still grovel in the idolatry of mortals and embodied fallen angels? And, most importantly, where do we go from here now that we have this knowledge?

The purpose of the ascended masters' intercession in this time is to reconnect you with your divine memory and your soul blueprint. They have come to return you to your Real Self rather than tying you to yet another organization, yet another spiritual teacher, yet another individual in time and space who, because he is in time and space, is still subject to error.

By the overdevelopment of the physical senses, the carnal mind and the intellect, the souls of mankind over tens of thousands of years have become divorced from their inner identity and from communion with life in all nature. For many, their soul senses have grown dull; they have atrophied. Even so, in the first glimmerings of the light of Aquarius, we sense a growing soul awareness.

As explained in chapter 9, our opportunity in the last two thousand years of embodying upon the planet has been to follow in the footsteps of Jesus the Christ and to realize the Christ consciousness. But for want of a teaching and a teacher, for want of the preservation of his words and works as they were given, many have lacked the understanding of what it means to become the Christ.

People have believed the lie that the position of Christ belongs only to one Son of God and that therefore they cannot become Christs. That lie is a mockery of the love of the Creator for his creation. It has been foisted upon Christians, who are taught that they are saved simply by accepting in faith that Jesus' exclusive Sonship and death on the cross constituted full payment for the sin that mankind incurred as a result of the Fall of man.

If it were true that Jesus' crucifixion saved all

of us for all time, then from the moment of Jesus' last breath on the cross, the sin of Adam and Eve (known as original sin) would have been wiped out and men would have been forever granted the gift of eternal life that was enjoyed in paradise prior to the Fall of man.

The truth is that by the demonstrated attainment of the teacher, the disciples can learn from that one's example and gain their own attainment. The teacher's attainment can never replace the individual's responsibility to realize his own self-mastery. Therefore, those who have believed the lie of the fallen angels have conceived of themselves as hopeless sinners and have not taken personal accountability for their own salvation. They have instead been condemned by that lie to a limited awareness, a limited expression of their own inner being. And so we find that our civilization and the consciousness of the children of light have not evolved according to schedule.

We come, then, to the threshold of Aquarius and we do not have the tools in our hands, the acceleration of consciousness necessary to carry the torch of the new dispensation. And so the masters, seeing the plight of mankind, have come forth to give their teachings. We can apply their teaching right now, starting this very moment; and step by step we may find that "in the twinkling of an eye,"[2] as Paul prophesied, the transformation that has been neglected for two thousand years will take place.

CHAPTER 11

ACCEPT YOUR DIVINE IDENTITY

The true inheritance of the children of God is the indwelling Son of God. But the Watchers as well as the Nephilim who were cast out of heaven by Archangel Michael have denied the living God and the living Christ within every child of God on earth. That denial of the present potential to realize the universal Christ light within us is the crux of the problem of Christianity—and it is *not* Jesus' teaching.

As was mentioned earlier, the word *Christ* comes from the Greek, *Christos,* meaning "anointed one." Jesus was referred to as 'Christ' because he was fully anointed with the light of Almighty God. You, too, can receive that anointing by the way you lead your life and the choices you make. For, as it is recorded in Acts 10:34, "God is no respecter of persons."

Lacking awareness of Jesus' true teachings, we have too many times believed the spoilers and false pastors when they have told us: "You don't have a chance. Only *the* Son of God has a chance. And you'll never be a Son of God, a Christed one, because there's only one Son of God!"

Falser words were never spoken. God has told us that he created us in his own image,[1] and there is no higher image than the image of God. The image of God is Christ, the Son, the light-emanation of the Logos, the Word. Although this light-emanation is referred to by different names in the world's spiritual traditions, it is still the same light.

I have revealed the nature of those who would enslave us to a culture of death. But what is the nature of those who yet retain the Spirit of God? When we can answer that question and more fully understand our inner identity in God, we will then have the confidence and the sense of self-worth—and above all the sense of the power of God—to go forth and meet the challenges that beset us in our nations.

"COME APART AND BE A SEPARATE PEOPLE"

Moses freed the children of Israel from their captivity in Egypt to bring them to a place where they could fulfill their divine destiny. But along the journey, they forgot their purpose; they forgot who they were. Instead of living according to God's commandments, they patterned their lives after the idolatrous cult of the fallen angels and their mechanization man. They hankered after the society of the Nephilim and the

Watchers. And so they needed another reminder that they were gods—gods in the sense that the spark of life was within them and that to realize its fullest potential would make them one with God himself.

And so the psalmist, who knew about the fallen angels, reminded them once again of their divine origin and destiny. With the fierceness of the Holy Spirit, he delivered an intense rebuke to the children of Israel: "I have said, Ye are gods; and all of you are children of the most High. But ye shall die like men, and fall like one of the princes."[2] He was saying: "If you are going to behave like the fallen angels, you are going to die like them; you will fall like the princes of the Nephilim."

Our destiny as lightbearers is to be Christed ones, Sons of God—those in whom the Spirit of the living God dwells. All of the avatars and Christed ones of East and West have come to remind us of this. Century after century they have come to expose the fallen ones. They have rebuked the Liar and the father of lies, the murderer from the beginning.

Yet the children of light have abandoned the Christed ones in the hour of their persecution and crucifixion; they have sided with the popular way, the cult of materialism and spiritual death of the fallen angels. And so, within just one generation after the crucifixion of Jesus, the apostle Paul again had to remind the children of God of their divine origin: "Know ye not that ye are the temple of God, and that the Spirit of God dwelleth in you?"

This enchantment with the cult of materialism, spiritual decline and the death of the soul is the disease that besets the nations today. Those who have come to help liberate us, the ascended masters, tell us that if we would speak to God in his holy mountain, we must come apart and be a separate people.[3] They call us to separate ourselves out from the false hierarchy with its false gods, idolaters and mechanization man; from the false civilization, a mechanized lifestyle and materialism. These conditions were prevalent in the olden days and they still prevail today, and so the masters have come once again to remind us who we are.

YOUR POTENTIAL TO BE SONS OF GOD

When I was a child, I was taught that Jesus was the only Son of God begotten of the Father. I used to wonder how it could be that God created only Jesus, since I was also made in God's image and likeness. I prayed to Jesus to explain this mystery to me, and he revealed the truth that each soul who comes from God has the presence of Christ within his heart.

The role of this inner Christ, or Higher Self, is to communicate with the Father, the I AM THAT I AM, and to serve as a mediator so that the soul evolving in the material world can learn how to correct its human faults. Jesus explained that our Christ Self is our Teacher, who inspires us through the intelligence of God's mind and shows us how our soul down here can ascend back to our God Source up there, just as he did.

When God revealed his name as I AM THAT I AM to Moses on Mount Sinai, he commanded Moses to tell the children of Israel: "This is my name for ever, and this is my memorial unto all generations."[4]

The masters refer to the I AM THAT I AM as the I AM Presence, and they tell us that this Spirit of the living God is individualized for each soul. It is each one's divine reality. The Christ that is individualized in each of us is the Son of God who has come to show us the way back to the heart of God the Father, the I AM Presence. Jesus was an example of the law, not the exception to it.

The diabolical lie of the fallen ones that the only Son of God was Jesus has led people to believe that they are incapable of attaining the status of one such as Christ. Yet Jesus himself taught, "He that believeth on me, the works that I do shall he do also; and greater works than these shall he do, because I go unto my Father." He was telling us that the Christ consciousness is within all and that we *all* have the potential to be Sons of God. Whether we are Christian, Muslim, Hindu, Jew, or follow another spiritual path, it matters not. The universal path of higher consciousness, or of personal Christhood, is open to all. Christianity as it has evolved since the life of Jesus has become an inoculation against the real thing.

If we do not accept the calling to become Sons of God, Jesus' mission will have been in vain, and we may miss the potential of our mission. The mystery of the one Christ individualized and indwelling as seed potential in every child of God is the key to self-knowledge that has been taken away from us. It is the stone that the builders of orthodox systems have rejected. Where orthodoxy misses the boat is in its claim of an exclusive divinity and an exclusive Sonship for Jesus.

The Church has overlooked, misunderstood or misrepresented the clear message in the First Epistle of John, which speaks of our intended coequality with Christ: "Behold, what manner of love the Father hath bestowed upon us, that we should be called the sons of God.... Now are we the sons of God, and it doth not yet appear what we shall be: but we know that, when he shall appear, we shall be like him; for we shall see him as he is."[5]

The fourteenth-century Christian theologian and mystic Meister Eckhart taught that the birth of the Son of God within the individual is even more important than the incarnation of the historical Jesus: "It is more worthy of God that He should be born spiritually... of every good soul than that He should have been born physically of Mary."[6]

Attaining to Christhood is the goal of life and our reason for being on earth today. Each of our successive incarnations has been for the purpose of increasing the Christ light in our body temple.

This path of personal Christhood did not begin with the coming of Jesus Christ. For aeons, it has been the path of evolutions of souls on this planet, in this solar system and galaxy, and in universes without end. Ever since there has been a Matter universe and the descent of souls into form, the internalization of that Christ light has been the goal.

THE TRUE TEACHINGS OF JESUS

Though we can find some remaining keys to our inner divinity scattered throughout the Bible and in other scriptures of the world's religions, these teachings have either been misunderstood or deliberately misinterpreted by many religious teachers, leaving most of mankind in the dark about their true nature.

In 1977, a collection of ancient manuscripts published in English set off a storm of controversy among scholars and clergy. These texts, discovered at Nag Hammadi, Egypt, in 1945, say that they preserve Jesus' secret teachings. The texts date from the second century or earlier, and they corroborate entirely what the ascended masters have been teaching since 1958: The indwelling Christ, the indwelling God, and the kingdom (consciousness) of God are within you.

Jesus unveiled the great teaching of the universal Christ during his Palestinian ministry, but within just a few centuries after his crucifixion, Church councils (having neither the Spirit nor the fervor of his revelation) codified into doctrine and dogma certain things that Jesus never taught.

The Council of Nicaea, convened by the emperor

Constantine in A.D. 325, was a watershed in Christian theology. It was attended by only three hundred of the Church's eighteen hundred bishops, among them only six from the Latin-speaking West, and the proceedings were moderated by Constantine himself. The council produced a confession of faith called the Nicene Creed, which says that humans are separated from God by a vast gulf.

Nicaea set an important precedent. For the first time, a secular ruler was in a position to influence Christian doctrine. And the bishops in attendance had good reason to want to please their imperial patron—some of them still bore marks of torture from the persecution under the Roman emperor Diocletian.[7]

The decisions and doctrines of the Council of

THE COUNCIL OF NICAEA

Nicaea and later Church councils have altered Jesus' essential message, leaving a missing link. Thus, we have yet to fulfill our Christ-potential, which is a must if we are going to meet the challenges we face today. And we can only overcome them through the indwelling Christ.

GNOSTICS: GUARDIANS OF THE MYSTERY TEACHINGS

The Nag Hammadi texts teach that Jesus did not want to be seen as exclusive but as an example of what we could all become.

The word *Gnosticism* is derived from the Greek word *gnosis,* which means "knowledge" or "understanding." To the Gnostics, self-knowledge was the key to salvation, and ignorance was one's greatest enemy. Gnosis meant knowledge of self against the backdrop of understanding God, the universe, and good and evil.

Gnosticism was a movement within early Christianity that flourished during the second century at a time when the doctrines and organizational structure of the Church as we know it today were not yet solidified. Gnostic writings have provided insight, therefore, into some of the controversies that existed in the formative years of Christianity—controversies that centered around the crucial questions of what Jesus did and did not teach, what he did and did not intend.

The Gnostic movement was composed of a diverse group of sects with varied beliefs and lifestyles, ranging from a strict asceticism to a libertine outlook on life. As prominent Gnostic scholar Hans Jonas pointed out, "the movement itself transcended ethnic and denominational boundaries."[8]

What they did have in common, to a greater or lesser degree, was that they did not accept the Church's newly developed creeds, doctrines and hierarchical structure. The Gnostics did not agree with the early Church Fathers and ecclesiastics who had vested the sole authority for teaching and preaching in the hands of the clerics. And they did not accept the Church's strict criteria for deciding what was and was not to be labeled scripture.

The Gnostics themselves claimed to be the guardians of the mystery teaching handed down through certain of Jesus' disciples. These teachings, they said, had been given by Jesus to an inner circle of initiates during his ministry, during the period between his resurrection and ascension, or after his ascension as new revelation.

The Gnostics did not believe that at Jesus' ascension the door of access to the Word of the Lord was shut forever. They did not believe that on the occasion of his ascent, the scripture was finalized. They believed that they could experience for themselves an intimate communion with Jesus, that he could impart to them new insights and teachings very personally, spoken deep within the heart through that very same Christ Presence that he was.

The writings of the Gnostics that embodied these revelations are not among the accepted scriptures of Christianity that have come down to us today. Most of their works have not survived because the early Church Fathers, threatened by the popularity of a teaching that challenged the orthodox position, condemned the Gnostics and banned their works.

Church hierarchy denied the freedom of the soul's intimate, personal and individual relationship with Jesus Christ and with the angels and saints in heaven. Thus, orthodoxy has become the denial of individual spiritual freedom, both in the first centuries following Jesus and today.

PAGES FROM THE NAG HAMMADI LIBRARY

As a result of this banning of the works of the Gnostics, almost all of their writings were destroyed. Until the last century, all we really knew about the Gnostics came from their greatest enemies, the Church Fathers, who wrote scathing and lengthy denunciations of their ideological foes.

It wasn't until the translation of two original Gnostic documents in the late nineteenth century, Codex Askewianus (Pistis Sophia) and Codex Brucianus, and then the astounding discovery of fifty-two ancient Gnostic texts at Nag Hammadi that some of the lost teachings of the Gnostics came to light and the Gnostics could finally speak for themselves.

THE PATH OF PERSONAL CHRISTHOOD

The goal of the Gnostics was nothing short of personal Christhood, the realization within each one of all that was in Christ Jesus. As noted at the beginning of this chapter and elsewhere, the term *Christ* comes from the Greek *Christos,* meaning the "anointed one." The Gnostics sought the same anointing that was received by Jesus the Son of man—the anointing of the light of the Son of God.

Although Christian Gnostic groups differed in many ways, they shared the common belief that our soul's origin is divine and her goal is to return to God. They believed that God had given them a seed of light, a divine spark, that represented their divine potential. They saw Jesus as their Redeemer—but a very different sort of redeemer than the one the orthodox Christians claimed to know. To the Gnostics, Jesus had come to breathe life into that spark and awaken them to their own divinity. For them, Jesus was a way-shower who had attained gnosis, experienced union with the Father and then came to show them how they could do the same.

The Gnostic Gospel of Philip, named for that apostle and probably written in the second half of the third century in Syria, calls the one who has achieved gnosis "no longer a Christian but a Christ"—one anointed of the light of the I AM Presence. "You saw the Spirit, you became spirit. You saw Christ, you became Christ.... What you see you shall [become]."[9]

When we understand the mystery of the Old Testament teaching that no man can see God and live,[10] we will see that this teaching of Philip is the same. The true meaning of that statement is that no man can see God and live any longer as man; he must live thereafter as God. Therefore, the "seeing" is the taking unto oneself of eternal life.

THE CHART OF YOUR DIVINE SELF

The masters have given us a tool for understanding our divine nature. The Chart of Your Divine Self (see next page) illustrates what Jesus taught and the apostles knew—the son of man's unique relationship to God through Christ, the Great Mediator. The Chart shows the relationship of the Personhood of God the

THE CHART OF YOUR DIVINE SELF

Father, individualized in your mighty I AM Presence (the upper figure); and God the Son, individualized in your Holy Christ Self (the middle figure); with your evolving soul consciousness—the son of man (the lower figure). In other words, it illustrates your spiritual anatomy—your divine nature and direct relationship with God.

This Chart depicts three distinct levels of consciousness:

Your Personal Presence of God— the I AM Presence

The highest level of consciousness is represented by the upper figure—the Presence of God with you, the Father-Mother God—the all-loving, all-knowing, all-pure, all-powerful God.

For every soul that God sends forth from the very center of Being, he creates an individualized fragment of himself called the I AM Presence. It is the One God, and yet it is individualized. It is apart from God, and yet never apart from God. Your individualized I AM Presence *is* God. It is the I AM THAT I AM that appeared to Moses as the flame that burned in the bush that was not consumed.[11]

This Presence is our origin, our true Being, whereby we too can attain what is called cosmic consciousness. The energy of our own God Source is not remote. It is ever present within and above us, hovering as a cloud of infinite spiritual energy.

Surrounding the I AM Presence are seven concentric spheres of spiritual energy. These spheres of pulsating energy, called the causal body, contain the record of all the good works you have ever performed, stored as your treasures in heaven, your cosmic bank account.

Each sphere of the causal body is a different color, denoting one of the seven rays. Rays are frequencies of light, and each ray is associated with a different attribute, or aspect, of God's consciousness. The color and chief attributes of each of the seven rays are as follows: (1) blue—protection and perfection, (2) yellow—wisdom, (3) pink—love, (4) white—purity, (5) green—healing and truth, (6) purple and gold—ministration and service, and (7) violet—freedom, mercy, forgiveness and transmutation.

The particular gifts, graces and principles of self-awareness inherent within each ray can be developed by a disciple through his life's calling. Therefore no two causal bodies are exactly alike, because their shimmering spheres reflect the unique spiritual attainment of the individual soul. This explains the inner meaning of the Bible verse "One star differeth from another star in glory."[12]

Your Higher Self—the Holy Christ Self

The middle figure in the Chart represents the Holy Christ Self, who is also called the Higher Self. Just as the I AM Presence is the Presence of God that is individualized for each of us, so the Holy Christ Self is the

Presence of the universal Christ that is individualized for each of us.

The middle figure represents your inner teacher, your voice of conscience and dearest friend. Jesus discovered the Higher Self to be "the Christ" and Gautama discovered it to be "the Buddha." Thus, the Higher Self is sometimes called the Inner Christ or the Inner Buddha. Christian mystics sometimes refer to it as the inner man of the heart or the Inner Light. And the Upanishads mysteriously describe it as a being the "size of a thumb" who "dwells deep within the heart." By whatever name the world's spiritual traditions refer to the Higher Self, each of us is meant to become one with our divine identity. This Higher Self will give you unerring direction if you will tune in to this still, small voice within you.

The Holy Christ Self corresponds to the Second Person of the Trinity—the Son of the Father-Mother God. The Bible refers to Jesus Christ as the Son of God because Jesus had become one with his Holy Christ Self. In fact, both the Father (the I AM Presence) and the Son (the Holy Christ Self) dwelt fully in Jesus, as Paul testified when he said, "In him [Jesus] dwelleth all the fulness of the Godhead bodily."13

Most of us cannot yet say that we are the Son (or Daughter) of God, with a capital *S* and *D*. But we can say that we are sons and daughters of God, with a lowercase *s* and *d*, who are in the process of fully developing our divine potential.14

In the Chart of Your Divine Self, the descending dove of the Holy Spirit is depicted just above the middle figure. When a son of man puts on and becomes the Christ consciousness, as Jesus did, he merges with the Holy Christ Self. When Jesus was baptized by John the Baptist, the Holy Spirit descended like a dove upon him and the words of the Father, the beloved I AM Presence, rang out as a voice from heaven, "This is my beloved Son, in whom I AM well pleased."[15]

Your Divine Spark—the Threefold Flame

The shaft of white light descending from the I AM Presence through the Holy Christ Self to the lower figure in the Chart is the crystal cord. It is the "umbilical cord," the lifeline, that ties you to your I AM Presence. Ecclesiastes referred to it as the silver cord.[16] Through this cord God's light, life and consciousness flow to you perpetually.

Your crystal cord nourishes the threefold flame in the secret chamber of your heart. The threefold flame is the divine spark sent from the I AM Presence—it is literally a spark of sacred fire from God's own heart kindled within you. Through the love, wisdom and power of the Godhead that is anchored within it, the soul may fulfill her reason for being in the physical plane. Because the threefold flame is the link to the heart of the I AM Presence, it is a major key to our spiritual progress.

The mystics of the world's religions have contacted the divine spark, describing it as the seed of divinity within. Buddhists, for instance, speak of the "germ of Buddhahood"[17] that exists in every living being. In the Hindu tradition, the Katha Upanishad speaks of the "light of the Spirit" that is concealed in the "secret high place of the heart" of all beings. It describes this Spirit as "smaller than the smallest atom, greater than the vast spaces."[18]

The Katha Upanishad also tells us that this eternal, unchangeable Spirit, this pure immortal light, is a "little flame in the heart."[19] It teaches that only he who sees this indwelling Spirit revealed in his own heart will attain eternal peace.

Likewise, Meister Eckhart teaches of the divine spark when he says, "God's seed is within us."[20] There is a part of us, says Eckhart, "that is untouched by time or mortality: it proceeds out of the Spirit and remains eternally in the Spirit and is divine.... Here God glows and flames without ceasing, in all His abundance and sweetness and rapture."[21]

Jesus was referring to the secret chamber of the heart when he spoke of going into the closet to pray. The mystic Teresa of Avila called this closet her "interior castle." Truly, entering this closet is going into another dimension of consciousness.

Your Soul—the Living Potential of God

The lower figure in the Chart of Your Divine Self represents you on the spiritual path, surrounded by the violet flame and the protective white light of God. The soul is the living potential of God—the part of you that is mortal but that can become immortal.

The purpose of your soul's evolution on earth is to grow in self-mastery, balance your karma and fulfill your mission on earth so that you can return to the spiritual dimensions that are your real home. When your soul at last takes flight and ascends back to God and the heaven-world, you will become an ascended master, free from the rounds of rebirth.

Ascension—the Goal of Life

The Christ of Jesus was fully one with him while he was yet in embodiment, and at the conclusion of his lifetime, he ascended into the plane of the I AM THAT I AM and became the ascended master Jesus Christ. He achieved the integration of the three levels of consciousness shown in the Chart of Your Divine Self.

All sons and daughters of God have a divine spark, which is our potential to realize, or become one with, the Higher Self. This concept is at the heart of the world's major religions.

The culmination of the path of personal Christhood is the ascension, a spiritual acceleration of consciousness that takes place at the natural conclusion of one's final lifetime on earth. Through the ascension, the soul merges with the Christ Self and returns to the Father-Mother God, the I AM Presence.

An ascended master is one who has has used his free will to become one with God and to demonstrate

God-mastery in time and space. Through mastery of the flow of energy in his own being as well as his environment, he reaches a certain level of attainment, bringing his soul into congruency with his own God-awareness. This mastery propels him into the reunion with God in the ascension in the light, the ritual of the return that was demonstrated by Jesus.

We ascend by increments as we pass our tests and win our individual victories. Our thoughts, our feelings, our daily deeds are all weighed in the balance. The entire record of all our past lives and momentums of both good and evil must be counted; and then, when we have brought at least 51 percent of all the energy that has ever been allotted to us into balance with the purity and harmony of the Great God Self, we may be offered the gift of the ascension, which is indeed by the grace of God. The remaining karma (49 percent or less) must be transmuted, or purified, by the ascended soul through service given to earth and her evolutions from the heaven-world.

The masters come to initiate us in the ancient mysteries of Christ and Buddha and the teachings for the new age of Aquarius. They come to exhort and to help us to rise to the great God-potential within ourselves and thereby defeat the momentums of returning karma. They present a path and a teaching whereby every child of light on earth can find his way back to God.

CHAPTER 12

CONQUER THE ENEMY WITHIN

The sages of East and West conclude that ignorance is not bliss but the root of all obstacles to spiritual progress. Ignorance is not just ignoring the precepts of the Law or ignoring the inner voice of God, the conscience. These conditions are symptomatic of an even greater malady. Ignorance, first and foremost, is blindness to the true nature of one's Real Self and blindness to the true nature of the unreal self.

In spiritual terms, the ignorant are those who deny the singular principle realized by the mystics of all ages and all faiths—that we are one with God here and now. Ignorance of our true nature leads to suffering and is the reason we keep reincarnating.

Grounding ourselves in the knowledge of our Real Self entails also knowing our unreal self. When we know both, we can stand poised between the two, daily affirm our Reality and thereby dissolve the vestiges of the unreal self. This is the mark of wisdom.

The maxim "Know thine enemy" applies to both the enemy within as well as the enemy without. For both are anti our Real Self and would take from us the great truth of our divinity. This knowledge is the power of God within us that the fallen ones would deny, but which is our certain liberation.

THE NOT-SELF

When we study the writings of the Gnostics, we find that the emphasis on gnosis was a two-edged sword: They believed that gnosis is not only knowledge of the Real Self—the Christ Self that we are in the process of becoming—but it is also the knowledge of the lower self, the karmic self, which includes the not-self.

The Gospel of Thomas is explicit on this point: "If you bring forth what is within you, what you bring forth will save you." He is speaking of the great light of the Christ. "If you do not bring forth what is within you, what you do not bring forth will destroy you."[1] Here he is speaking of the not-self, the accumulated energy of all impure motives and actions from this and past lifetimes that remain untransmuted.

In the Gospel of Thomas, Jesus is quoted as saying to Salome:

> "I am He who exists from the Undivided. I was given some of the things of my father."
>
> Salome said, "I am your disciple."
>
> Jesus said to her, "Therefore I say, if he is undi-

vided, he will be filled with light, but if he is divided, he will be filled with darkness."[2]

The same teaching is given to us in the Bible—that we cannot serve both God and mammon. The house divided against itself cannot stand.[3]

The Gospel of Philip explains that rooting out the destructive element within us, which would, if it could, remain unseen and undealt with, is necessary on our path toward union. So long as the root of the not-self is hidden, it is strong. But when it is exposed and recognized, it will dissolve and perish. Because it can only be removed if we recognize it,[4] we must see it for what it is in order to render it powerless.

THE COUNTERFEITING SPIRIT

Other Gnostic texts examine in great detail this "root of wickedness," its origin and its defeat. They speak of a "counterfeit" or "counterfeiting spirit" (also translated as "antagonistic" or "despicable spirit") that seeks to lead mankind astray "so that he will not know his perfection."[5] The most intricate teaching on this subject comes from the third-century Gnostic text Pistis Sophia. This text includes a series of dialogues attributed to Jesus and his disciples in which Jesus reveals to them the higher mysteries.

In one section, Jesus explains that there are two elements given to the soul who is to reincarnate: the power and the counterfeiting spirit. The counterfeiting spirit is created by "the rulers of the great Fate."

We can see these rulers as being the fallen angels who move men and nations by their karma—*karma* being an equivalent word to *fate*. Our fate is our karma and our karma is our fate. And therefore, we have seen that the false hierarchies of Antichrist do seek to ensnare us through our own karma. Pistis Sophia records this teaching:

> The rulers of the great Fate... give the old soul a cup of forgetfulness out of the seed of wickedness, filled with all the different desires and all forgetfulness. And straightway, when that soul shall drink out of the cup, it forgetteth all the regions to which it hath gone, and all the chastisements in which it hath travelled. And that cup of the water of forgetfulness becometh body outside the soul, and it resembleth the soul in all its figures and maketh itself like it, which is what is called the counterfeiting spirit.[6]

This forgetfulness comes upon us early on in each of our embodiments. Just prior to taking on a newly formed body, our soul is fully aware of the heaven-world, our spiritual guides, the masters and other beings of light. And for a short time after we enter that tiny body, we remember. But very quickly, for whatever reason, the veil of forgetfulness comes upon us.

In our waking state, we no longer recall our inner experiences in the spiritual octaves of light. We forget that we have an I AM Presence and a Holy Christ Self.

And then, because we have forgotten our God-reality, when we see the darkness of the world we cry out in fear and despair. If we truly remembered who we are, we would be in the full glory of the Christ consciousness and the I AM Presence moment by moment. Until we are fully "awake" (as Gautama, Jesus and other living masters are awake), forgetfulness is part and parcel of being in a physical form.

THE DWELLER-ON-THE-THRESHOLD

On the road to self-mastery, we need the courage to explore how much of our identity is invested in our true, divine nature and how much is invested in the lower nature, the not-self. Kabbalists called this darker side the evil urge. Saint Paul referred to it as the carnal mind. In esoteric tradition it is known as the dweller-on-the-threshold. It is what the early Christian Gnostics called the counterfeiting spirit.

Everyone has a dweller-on-the-threshold. It is the antithesis of the Real Self, the conglomerate conceived through the inordinate use of free will, consisting of the carnal mind and a constellation of misqualified energies of which we are not aware.

This term has been adopted by the Brotherhood because it conveys the meaning that the dweller sits at the threshold of self-awareness, where the elements of the subconscious or from the unconscious cross the line into the conscious world of the individual. Once the individual becomes aware of some aspect of the not-self, the dweller has entered the realm of the conscious will. There, through the decision-making faculties of mind and heart, the individual may choose either to ensoul (to give energy to) or to slay the components of this antithesis of the Real Self.

We find an instructive portrayal of the dweller-on-the-threshold at its worst in Robert Louis Stevenson's famous novel written in 1886, *The Strange Case of Dr. Jekyll and Mr. Hyde*. You will recall that Dr. Jekyll is a respectable citizen who leads a double life, hiding from public view the sordid side of himself that secretly indulges in certain pleasures. We hear about this all the time. We hear about respectable citizens, people of high social rank, prominent members of our towns and cities whose hidden lives come to light.

In the story, Dr. Jekyll is able to concoct a potion that transforms him into Mr. Hyde, a separate personality through whom he gives vent to evil impulses. Of course, he has created this potion because he has a desire to live through his evil self some of the time. He has that desire as long as he can be in control of the evil self.

To one degree or another, this happens to all of us. We know we have a bad habit, but we believe that we have it under control. "I don't really have the coffee habit"; "I'm not really addicted to sugar"; "I can take or leave pot any time," and so forth. So we play this little balancing game. But it's a two-edged sword.

At first Dr. Jekyll is able to safely transform himself from Dr. Jekyll to Mr. Hyde and back again. But as he indulges Mr. Hyde to a greater and greater degree, Mr. Hyde gets the upper hand. So, too, as we indulge the dweller-on-the-threshold, we give it more power and then a little more power and a little more power. And yet that power remains hidden. We never really know how powerful that dweller is, so we allow ourselves to believe that we are always in control.

When Dr. Jekyll eventually commits murder, he recognizes that his creation has overpowered his own instincts for good. The power of his soul was reduced because he gave that power to the counterfeiting image.

INNER ARMAGEDDON

From time immemorial, men have predicted the end of the world and the coming of the great battle of Armageddon. The Hebrew word *Har-Magedon* means "hill of Megiddo." The Canaanite fortress of Megiddo guarded the pass to the Valley of Jezreel, through which ran the major commercial route from Egypt to Mesopotamia. Whoever controlled the pass governed the economy of Israel. Therefore, the stronghold has been the scene of many battles, ancient and modern. Thus the term *Armageddon,* both as a name and as a place, came to symbolize the final battle of the forces of light and darkness.

In the last two thousand years, this battle has been associated with certain eschatological concepts— the Second Coming of Christ, the resurrection of the dead, the Last Judgment, the Rapture of the saints, the punishment of sinners and the coming of the New Jerusalem.

Many Christians who are troubled by current trends expect the prophecy of the reappearance of Christ to be fulfilled at any time. Some feel that the signs of the times are preliminary to the battle of Armageddon. Others have believed at one time or another that we were engaged in the war that would end all wars. These find in the doctrine of "final ends" a hope of the appearing of a new order of the ages that will terminate the injustices of the old and establish a golden age of peace and harmony in every country upon earth.

While the prophecies of scripture have led many people throughout the world to believe that Megiddo in the land of Israel is the biblical, prophetic site of man's final days upon this earth, Armageddon has also come to mean the personal battlefield of every individual in a spiritual sense; it pertains to the battle between good and evil in each one's own inner world. Armageddon is, in reality, a battle between the light of the Real Self and the darkness of the synthetic self. It is a spiritual warfare waged so that the world might be stripped of illusion and prepared for the coming of the radiantly victorious Christ into manifestation in every heart.

Everyone who puts his foot on the path of the ascension is opposed by forces from within and from without, both personal and impersonal. Forces from within consist of the negative momentums carried over from past embodiments as well as those from one's present life. Forces from without loom within the mass consciousness, projecting energies of hatred, malice, jealousy, and so on, and drawing into lower vibrations the consciousness of susceptible individuals.

Whatever the form, whatever the source, none of these forces has any power, presence or permanence—for there is only one Reality, and that is God. Man derives his very life from Reality, from God. However, insofar as man places his attention upon imperfect conditions (unreality), he is freely giving God's energies to that which is unreal and is thereby prolonging the illusory appearance of those conditions.

The message of Armageddon contains archetypal patterns that will occur in the life of the soul who becomes the saint, who becomes the ascended master. Everyone who has ever ascended has gone through an Armageddon in the personal, microcosmic sense. For the initiate, the way is one of overcoming.

Because the God Presence in man is the highest reality in the earth, this battle is actually more central to the individual than it is to the world. How we deal with our personal Armageddon will ultimately determine the outcome of the Armageddon we find taking place outside of ourselves.

Therefore, there is an action of Armageddon that occurs simultaneously in the world of the advanced disciple and in the world at large. This is an example of the law of correspondence between the Macrocosm and the microcosm. This does not mean that we need to live our lives in anticipation of this Armageddon becoming concrete and physical around us (though all signs may point to that fact). In the days following the ascension of Jesus Christ, the early Christians expected the Second Advent of Christ and the destruction of world power. They did not realize that it was taking place in the very hearts of those souls who had reached that point on the path of initiation.

THE DIVIDING OF THE WAY

In the Dead Sea Scroll *The War of the Sons of Light Against the Sons of Darkness,* Archangel Michael is called the Prince of Light through whom God promises to "send perpetual help to the sons of light." Archangel Michael has spoken of the dividing of the way that occurs when the forces of light meet the forces of darkness:

Armageddon must be fought. And it will be fought in the psyche of the individual. It will be in the heart of the individual. It will be in the dweller-on-the-threshold. That is where Armageddon shall be, and it shall be multiplied in every individual upon earth.

And some will be on the side of the forces of light and our legions and will go after the Lord Christ as he does come. And others will go after the fallen ones. There will be the dividing of the way, but it may not come at all in the way in which

Christians interpret it.

Armageddon is the place where you determine whether you shall be a God-free being or go the way of the fallen ones....

Armageddon is taking place inside of you at this very moment. Most people have a warring in their members, but the dweller-on-the-threshold manages to cover it up. And so that war is never fought and won by the soul, but it is only left there. And that war and that warring is a festering condition within the physical body itself. Many of your problems in the physical body or the emotional body or the mind do come from the nonresolution that you have midst the forces of Light and Darkness.

...Because you have not forthrightly dealt with the issues of the unconscious, you are yet vulnerable. You do not have that certainty of wholeness, and therefore that certainty of your victory and of your ascension.

...That wholeness is your goal. Then you will be invincible. Then there will not be a part of you that is an open door to burdens of sickness, of darkness, of mourning, of suddenly wanting to go here and there, for you cannot find peace. If you cannot find peace, it is a serious condition in your psychology.

Peace must be with you.... The peace that passeth understanding[7]—when you have its full cup, you will reduce your misery and subconscious levels of misery. And then you will realize that God is where you are. You need not go here, go there; for the kingdom of God is fully ensconced within you, and no devil, great or small, can in any way tamper with your state of mind, your project, your goal.[8]

The battle of Armageddon must be waged and won by us while we are on earth. It is here in the arena of life and of consciousness that we must overcome the hordes of evil and put down all oppressions that we have created against any part of life until we are vessels for the pure energies of God. We are living in a time when people are making final choices. Because it is man and man alone, following the urging of the fallen angels, who originated imperfection through ambition and pride of the intellect, it is man and man alone who must undo this false creation by withdrawing those energies of God that he has unwisely invested.

For those who choose to do this, the reward will be great. Those whose Armageddon culminates in mystical union with the Higher Self will become integrated into the Godhead and experience once and for all the epic manifestation of peace—the true Om, the true Shalom. It is through the doorway of higher consciousness that each one comes to know himself—his Real Self—and in truly knowing himself, knows God.

THE POWER OF SELF-AWARENESS

Self-awareness is essential if we are to recognize and overcome the dweller-on-the-threshold and the manipulation of the fallen angels. Self-awareness is our only true self-defense, whereas unawareness leaves an opening for the fallen ones to step in and trap us.

Not one of us can deny that sometime, somewhere in our lifetime we have been overtaken by a situation or a compromise that was alien to our True Self, our true identity. And yet, because our powers of intuition were not heightened, our soul was not guarded at that moment and we either ignored or were unaware of our compromise. We've all experienced those times when we've said to ourselves: "Why did I let myself get into that situation all over again? I should have known better." When we have an unguarded moment and fall into that trap, our soul must again learn the lesson that it learned long ago and then forgot.

Identification with the unreal self makes us easy prey, so it's easy to see why the fallen angels continually strive to make us identify with the not-self. For when we do, we can be controlled. There is no possible way to control a person who identifies with his Higher Self, with his divine consciousness. When we wake up to this and take a good look at our world, we will begin to understand that the embodied fallen angels, the betrayers of the people in every nation, comprise a power elite—and that they would take from us our light if we let them.

The fallen ones can only live off our light if we give it to them. What they fear most is that we the people of God will withdraw our light from them when we become aware that they are not keeping their word and that they are not protecting this blessed earth for a path of peace and freedom, but are using it for their own purposes.

When enough of us withdraw our light from them and from the not-self, the dweller-on-the-threshold, then we as a united body of lightbearers will reclaim the earth as the platform for our soul evolution.

CHAPTER 13

RE-CREATE YOURSELF

Only you can re-create yourself after the original intent of your Real Self. The true alchemist is the mystic who goes within, discovers who "I AM," and understands that the I AM Presence and the Holy Christ Self are the Real Self. He also understands that there is an unreal self. The unreal self is the miscreation of the mind that is not tethered to the Christ mind but has lost the way of gnosis, of self-knowledge. That soul, therefore, has not created in consonance with the laws of God and so it has created karma.

You have created exactly what you are today. You can look in the mirror of self and if you don't like what you see, you can re-create yourself. You can assess your life, see what you have created, what you have accomplished, what you have not. You can see the good you have done and what has been the fruit of your effort.

And if you have little to show for your life or your effort that is of enduring worth, you can determine that from this day on you will do everything you can so that your future creations lead to the resurrection and the life of your soul. The reason you can engage in the mighty work of building the kingdom of God within you is because it is already there. You cannot create something that endures unless it already exists in the mind of God. And if it exists in the mind of God, you have a right to bring it into manifestation.

And so we understand that it takes attunement with the mind of God to formulate a plan for practical action that will succeed in creating that which is of enduring worth. This is strategic planning at its best. There's only one place that a son of God can learn this kind of strategy and that is within the threefold flame in his heart, the Presence of God within. And so we come full circle to the need for Christ consciousness. We cannot formulate a winning strategy for the light without the Christ consciousness.

The fallen angels, who are anti-Christ, pervert the Christ consciousness in their strategy, which comes from the inverse, or opposite, of the logic of the Christ mind. If you study the writings and tactics of the power elite through the ages, you will know what I am speaking about. The strategies of darkness that caused the downfall of the golden ages of Lemuria and

Atlantis have continued to work so well for the hordes of darkness that they have not needed to develop new ones.

Thus, in order for the light to win the day and vanquish darkness, not only do we need to understand the tactics of the fallen angels (discussed in Parts 1 and 2) but we also need to be ready with a strategic plan that will counteract and overcome them. Let us examine some of the winning strategies of light.

ALLOW GOD TO ACT THROUGH YOU

The ancient Chinese sage Lao Tzu taught, "Act without doing. Work without effort." To the Western mind, this sounds like a Zen koan. How can you act without *doing,* or work without *effort?* Lao Tzu was revealing the secret that all spiritual adepts have discovered. He was telling us that when our lesser self (our ego) gets out of the way, then our Greater Self can act through us effortlessly.

Jesus taught this truth when he said, "I can of mine own self do nothing.... The Father that dwelleth in me, he doeth the works."[1] Jesus, "being in the form of God, thought it not robbery to be equal with God."[2] Just as Jesus recognized that he was the issue of God and that God was the source of his authority, so we too must understand that it is not the individual but God in the individual that is the doer. We do not claim divinity for the outer human, the limited self. We claim our divinity as the I AM Presence and the divine spark in our hearts, and we acknowledge that God made us to be his instruments, his vessels.

We are intended to be the vessels of God, ever humble, ever conscious of our inadequacies but aware of God's Presence in us. Our God Presence is the all-power that can resolve the conditions in the world today, among them global terrorism, the potential for war and plague, and other conditions that defy human solution. These are giant conditions unless we have a giant God, the Almighty, with us to solve them. As lightbearers, we do have God with us.

We need not be fearful. We need but remember the promise of God through Moses: "As thy days, so shall thy strength be."[3] In other words, whatever you are called upon to do, whatever is the need of the hour, you will have the strength to overcome if you have entered into a covenant with God. If you allow God and his emissaries to work through you, they will supply you with all the strength you need. Just ask for God's help and see what happens.

It can be glorious to feel our own helplessness, our total absence of strength, or the barrenness of our mind for an idea or a thought or an understanding to do something. This is because when we cast ourselves upon the rock of Christ, allowing the human matrix to be broken, we find ourselves flooded with the creative power sufficient to meet all of our needs. This is a glorious moment in which we rejoice in the glory of God.

Thus, it is the commitment of the son of God to allow God to act through him that is the very first strategy of light. This commitment requires expanding the threefold flame of the heart, because this flame focuses the Christ consciousness. It is the fire of love, wisdom and power (the attributes of the threefold flame) that gives us the ability to move, to think, to act, and to overcome the subconscious records and momentums of our individual self and the planet as well as to meet and overcome the enemy in anyone who assails our Christhood.

Any interaction with the Nephilim, the Watchers or the laggard evolutions must be through the Christ Self, the mediator of each one. That Christ light thus forms a canopy of light around us that effectively prevents the impure stream of darkness from these individuals from entering our beings.

Those who remain at the level of the outer self without calling upon the Christ Self to act as the mediator and interpreter of their relationships inevitably enter into an energy exchange of random momentums of relative good and evil. Until we have purified ourselves entirely, this exchange goes both ways. Thus, for the best and highest interaction with other souls of light, we can invite our Christ Self to act as the mediator in all our relationships. Jesus Christ has promised us: "Where two or three are gathered together in my name, there am I in the midst of them."[4]

OVERCOME THE DWELLER

The novel *Frankenstein,* written in 1817 by Mary Shelley, provides another illustration of the momentous encounter with the dweller-on-the-threshold. In this case, the mad Dr. Frankenstein creates a living creature that is reminiscent of the golem of Jewish folklore. The golem was a robotlike servant created out of clay and brought to life by pronouncing the sacred name of God over its form.

The dweller is like the Frankenstein monster and like the robot creation of the fallen angels and the laggards. Once the monster-dweller is given life and fed, it begins to gain power over its creator and eventually turns on him in revenge. The dweller is angry because it is not the issue of God and is therefore not a living soul, and yet it does contain a portion of the power of God by virtue of having been created with God's energy, albeit a misuse of it.

To overcome the dweller-on-the-threshold that we have given life to, we call upon Archangel Michael, the great defender of the people of God. We need his assistance to subdue the individual dweller and the planetary dweller (the combined energy of all of the unredeemed negative karma, or misqualified energies, of all people living upon earth).

The planetary dweller also manifests through the false hierarchy of fallen angels. Rather than risk being overcome by Archangel Michael and the hosts of the

LORD, they have vowed first to destroy God's creation in one way or another. And to this end they would make nuclear war. They would destroy the economy. They would wreak havoc in the environment, destroy the ecology, poison the food and water supply, and create epidemics and pandemics by spreading premeditated and manufactured viruses in our communities. They would do anything to prevent the sons of God from regaining control of planet earth.

And so the lightbearers must strategize and defeat them through the power of God and the intercession of the hosts of the LORD. If we sit idly by, we run the risk of allowing both the personal and planetary dweller to overcome the souls of the lightbearers before they can be rescued, before they can manifest the light of the Christ consciousness.

It is up to us to determine whether, by the power of the Son of God within us, we will gain the victory over the personal dweller on behalf of all lightbearers. This we can do by calling daily to Archangel Michael to bind that dweller within us. (This subject will be addressed in Part 5.)

So long as there is any karma remaining in an individual, a vestige of the consciousness of the dweller also remains. For this reason, it is wise to invoke Archangel Michael's assistance daily to keep the dweller bound. After we have done so, we can join Archangel Michael and his legions to meet the adversary against our nations and our freedom.

DON'T WORRY

Mark Prophet used to advise us not to take our human selves so seriously, not even in light of the serious challenges we face from the fallen ones. Following is Mark's teaching:

> People never forget the wrongs you do or have done. Don't worry about it. Be glad that God forgets them. That's all that counts. And *you* forget it so *you* don't get hung up on it!
>
> Don't get hung up on your ideas of yourself—of how small you are, how impractical you are, or how some person has more talent than you, et cetera.... The biggest problem that people create is the problem of creating worries.
>
> Stop all the human nonsense of worrying over what's going to happen—concern about your family, concern about your economic future, concern about the problems of your country. Rest assured that you *can* do something about it.
>
> "Take therefore no thought for the morrow: for the morrow shall take thought for the things of itself" are the words of the great master, who then said, "Sufficient unto the day is the evil thereof."[5] What this means is that evil, being the energy veil, or net, of the fallen ones, lies in wait to trap you. But it's already there, so don't worry about it. Rather be concerned about maintaining a strong tie to your I AM Presence, who will guard you against the snares of the Wicked.[6]

The evil is also your own energy veil, the cocoon of illusion that you've surrounded yourself with: It is your karma. And that's already there too, and it comes up daily for your transmutation by the Holy Spirit's sacred fire, the violet flame. So don't worry about that either, because it will be there, as sure as the dawn, until you've cleaned it all up. Instead, have a lawful concern that your mind and heart stay steadfast upon God.

So the message is this: Don't worry. If you've got God, you've got everything. With God, you can beat anything that tries to tear you from him, especially your own karma and your vulnerabilities to the traps of the negative forces.

Don't become a worrywart about your past karma coming down upon you like a house of cards, because you can do something about it, and you can start right now.[7]

FORGIVE YOURSELF

Every one of us has made mistakes. Yet no matter what mistakes we've made, we were doing the best we could at the time. Now it's time to forgive ourselves, to get on with our life, and to keep our eye focused on the vast spiritual potential we have inside of us. We all have that potential, but we haven't always accepted it.

One of the reasons self-forgiveness and self-acceptance can be so hard is that many of us were belittled or ridiculed when we were growing up. In the face of this, we erroneously came to believe that we just aren't lovable. When those barbs of criticism are flying, what we don't always realize is that the accusers must criticize and carp and put us down in order to feel good about themselves.

The only way we can find peace is through accepting ourselves as we are today. We can work on those things that we can change and also be at peace with the fact that it will take time to unwind the skeins of karma and become the fullness of the Christ, the fullness of the Buddha that we desire to be.

Be at peace. Peace is the acceptance of what is and the total diligence to pursue what is with all of the spiritual laws and tools.

RECEIVE THE DIVINE MOTHER

Those who have come as false prophets and false teachers have been the instruments of the fallen ones. They have infused in every religion a false consciousness of the Father and a false consciousness of the Mother by telling us that we are sinners, that we are worthless, that we are guilty and that we are not able to do those greater works that Jesus promised.

The Mother energy of God is locked in Matter as the serpentine force of the Kundalini in the base-of-the-spine chakra until it is awakened. Once awakened, it comes forth as a fountain of light, rising along the spinal column, nourishing the chakras, quickening the dormant aspects of Christhood within. Thus it is the Mother light that frees the God-potential, the Father principle, within man and woman for the realization of Buddhic consciousness in the crown.

As noted in chapter 8, sons and daughters of God have been deprived of direct contact with the culture of the Divine Mother since the fall of the ancient Motherland of Lemuria through the desecration of the feminine ray. And so for thousands of years it has been the masculine avatars, embodying primarily the Father principle, who have set forth and demonstrated the discipline of cosmic law.

Yet many of these avatars, including Gautama Buddha and Jesus Christ, also embodied the Divine Feminine and taught the path of compassionate regard for one another and for all life. This is the way the Mother would have us relate to one another—as God, as Christ, as Buddha.

There is one God, one Christ, one Buddha, and yet that one flame burns on the altar of the heart within each of us. How can this be? It is simply that here in this transitory world, there is the appearance of separation, the appearance of loneliness. We believe that we are separate and therefore we suffer that separation from the flame of one another and from the flame of God.

The Aquarian age brings the opportunity for the integration of Father and Mother. It brings opportunity for God Self-awareness in and as the Mother. Until we can become the Mother, the Mother flame will be missing from our government, our economy, our educational systems. Without the Mother flame as the center of every area of life, that life crumbles, that life decays, because it has not the cohesive power of the Mother flame to endure.

Representatives of the Divine Mother are found in many traditions and faiths, yet they do not belong solely to those traditions and faiths. Two such representatives are the bodhisattva Kuan Yin and the Blessed Virgin Mary.

Mary, for example, has long been associated primarily with Catholicism, stuck in the doctrine and dogma of a religion that is limited to only some among the world's vast population. In truth, she is an archetype of the Divine Feminine, or Mother principle. The Mother cares for each and every one of us and leads us to the Father, the Divine Masculine, regardless of the name we attribute to that masculine principle.

On a fall morning in 1972, Mother Mary appeared to me and said:

> I want to give you a ritual of the rosary.... It is to be used as a universal adoration of the Mother flame by people of all faiths. For, you see, the salutation "Hail Mary" simply means "Hail, Mother ray" and is an affirmation of praise to the Mother flame in every part of life. Each time it is spoken, it evokes the action of the Mother's light in the hearts of all mankind.[8]

By reciting this rosary, we can contact the Divine Mother and thereby raise that Mother light within us. And as we raise the Mother light, we cannot help but positively influence the planet as a whole.[9] (An explanation of the rosary is included in Part 5.)

CONTACT THE INNER FIRE

One way the fallen angels keep us from manifesting our inner divinity is by keeping us distracted and responding to outer stimuli. This is especially so in Western society, where we are naturally more extroverted and are conditioned from birth to respond to externals. And so we are programmed to run here and there and to respond to this and that. And by the end of the day we are spent and we haven't once made contact with the inner flame. Instead, we have been distracted by every aspect of worldly ambition (and even spiritual ambition), by money making, pleasure seeking and a constant bombardment of noise that tears down the delicate balance of the flow of light in the chakras.

The fallen ones know that as more sons of God make contact with the fire of the Real Self, the greater will be the potential of the lightbearers as a whole to turn around the entire course of civilization. The permanent contact with the Real Self that Jesus the Christ and Gautama the Buddha achieved testifies to the impact that Self-realized beings can have on the world.

Each time a Son of God contacts that fire and becomes one with his God Self, the impact on this solar system and cosmos is greater than the splitting of the atom. Such is the potential power of the release of spiritual fire within you.

Therefore it behooves us as lightbearers to accept that sacred fire as our divine reality and to become one with it once again. This is the age that we have been waiting for, for thousands of embodiments. This point of cycles turning, this moment of the coming of freedom in the Aquarian age, is our time. Our time has come and we are in the right space: We are at the point of contact with our inner divinity.

Saint Germain teaches us to place our attention upon the heart chakra as a means of strengthening our contact with the inner fire:

> Your heart is indeed one of the choicest gifts of God. Within it there is a central chamber surrounded by such light and protection as that which we call a cosmic interval. It is a chamber separated from Matter, and no probing could ever discover it. It occupies simultaneously not only the third and fourth dimensions but also other dimensions unknown to man. It is thus the connecting point of the mighty silver cord of light that descends from your divine God Presence to sustain the beating of your physical heart, giving you life, purpose and cosmic integration.

I urge all men to treasure this point of contact that they have with life by paying conscious recognition to it. You do not need to understand by sophisticated language or scientific postulation the how, why and wherefore of this activity.

Be content to know that God is there and that there is within you a point of contact with the Divine, a spark of fire from the Creator's own heart, which is called the threefold flame of life. There it burns as the triune essence of love, wisdom and power.

Each acknowledgment paid daily to the flame within your heart will amplify the power and illumination of love within your being. Each such attention will produce a new sense of dimension for you, if not outwardly apparent then subconsciously manifest within the folds of your inner thoughts.

Neglect not, then, your heart as the altar of God. Neglect it not as the sun of your manifest being. Draw from God the power of love and amplify it within your heart. Then send it out into the world at large as the bulwark of that which shall overcome the darkness of the planet.[10]

Through the white-hot heat of meditation and prayer, we too can release the imprisoned lightning of our heart. Our meditations in the secret chamber are very private experiences. They start with removing our attention from what's happening around us and going within—"all the gates closed, the mind confined in the heart,"[11] as the Bhagavad Gita says. Christian tradition calls it recollection, withdrawing the mind from external affairs and placing our attention on the Presence of God within.

When we go within by devotion and love, we contact the inner flame and commune with the energy that is God. "The little spirit spark of our personal identity is the key that connects us with the Universal," Mark Prophet once said. "[God's] Spirit is the fabric of our world. His energy, his pattern is the only saving grace. We ourselves have to reidentify, reintegrate, repolarize ourselves with that light—and it's got to be done consciously."

Through prayer and meditation we turn our attention back to the Inner Light, which is the real source of our being. We become drenched with light—renewed, refreshed and replenished—so we can give more of the light to those who need it. We build up our reservoir of love. As we commune with our Higher Self, who sits on the throne in our heart, we can also access the wisdom of the heart to find solutions to knotty problems.

The mystics advise us to combine our meditations with spoken prayer that comes from a heart on fire with love. For instance, the Zohar instructs, "Whatever a man thinks or whatever he meditates in his heart cannot be realized in fact until he enunciates it with his lips."[12] The spoken word activates the fruit of our meditation upon the Divine and coalesces it in the physical.

Every spiritual tradition has its own beautiful methods for entering the heart through prayer and meditation—from the quiet recitation of sacred words to the dynamic repetition of mantras to the inspired singing of devotional songs, such as bhajans.

Part 5 introduces several prayers and decrees that can be given to expand the light of the heart and to contact the inner fire.

STEP OUT OF DUALITY

Mark Prophet taught how we can step out of the world of duality:

> We are living in a dual world. We must recognize that we live in heaven and we live in Hades all at the same time....
>
> When one finally achieves union with God, he is neither in heaven nor in Hades. He is out of it all. In other words, he steps out of the universe of dualities into the universe of Oneness....
>
> But so long as we are functioning in the level of the ego, we have problems to contend with, because the ego is oriented the wrong way....
>
> So, recognize that Heaven and Hades are in you...and that they are dual because they deal with the same equation as the fruit of the tree of the knowledge of good and evil.
>
> The Tree of Life (the I AM Presence) is distinct and apart from that, and it is supreme. In order to use the leaves of the Tree of Life for the healing of

the nations, you have to learn to cast aside the dual consciousness of good and evil, as brought out in the story of Adam and Eve in the Garden. This means that you need to be able to directly apprehend the Father and the unity of the Father's expression. Therefore, we understand the nature of the Deity a great deal more when we realize that he dwells in the purity of perfection and that the duality is only made in the fashion of a man....

So if we see our life as evil, it will become so. If we see our life as good, it will become so. As we think in our hearts, so we are. So let us then recognize this and no longer be a victim of our mental states. When mental states come, recognize that the tempter uses many forms. We are not concerned with the tempter; we are concerned with God and God-liberation.[13]

Slay the Appearance of Evil

When faced with the challenging realities, possibilities and prophecies of our time, it helps to remember these two things: First, one with God is a majority. Second, with God all things are possible.

If we look back to the story of Sodom and Gomorrah, we can learn many lessons. Sodom was a city so caught up in fleshly pursuits that its inhabitants even tried to seduce two angels who were sent to warn Lot to flee the impending destruction of the city.

When Abraham learned that God intended to

destroy the corrupt city, he bargained with God to spare Sodom and its inhabitants. God agreed to save the city if Abraham could find fifty righteous men among its population. Abraham continued bargaining until God finally agreed to spare the city if Abraham could find just ten righteous men.[14]

This ancient account shows us the mercy, love and kindness of God. It does not please God to allow the full impact of our karma to descend upon us. But because he sees that we are jeopardizing our own souls and because he respects our free will, God may, in extraordinary circumstances, do this so that we can quickly learn our lessons and progress spiritually.

Unfortunately, even though Abraham was successful in his negotiation with God, he could not find even ten righteous men. Consequently, the cities of Sodom and Gomorrah were destroyed when God rained "brimstone and fire" out of heaven upon them.[15]

What we learn from this drama is that each one of us, like Abraham, can make a supreme difference when it comes to saving our world. If God was prepared to save the wicked city of Sodom for ten righteous men when Abraham asked him to, just think what we can do through our good works and prayers when we ask God to work miracles with the violet flame and other decrees. (These decrees will be presented in Part 5).

When we pray and give dynamic decrees, we become mediators between mankind and the oncoming returning karma. By regularly imploring God and invoking his intercession, we can form a body of light that manifests as the all-consuming flame of God that transmutes karma.

Saint Germain assured us that the power of God is sufficient to overcome the evil that we see appearing in the world:

> The power of God in you is greater than all of the many things you see on a grand scale appearing. They *appear* to surround the earth and to loom large and heavy and powerful. It is the *appearance* that must be slain by the sword, which is the sacred Word of the alchemist. For it is the *appearance* of evil that takes on power in the mind of the beholder. And when the beholder is the potential alchemist, he endows the unreal with the power of permanence— and thus, it has taken place.
>
> Who will dare to challenge the destroyers in the earth?—knowing they are but specters in the night and have no power except that which the anointed ones and the people have given to them by their attention, by their fear, by their adulation, by their cursings. Whatever the attention, it does give power to the enemies of mankind.
>
> Withdraw the attention and see how their systems crumble and how the new age and the golden age shall appear right within you as the golden man of the heart steps through the veil in you![16]

All that the fallen ones have brought about is maya, or illusion, for they do not have access to the living Word. Therefore we need not fear and tremble before the fallen ones. We can place our faith in the living Word and trust in the promise of scripture: "Ye are of God, little children, and have overcome them: because greater is he that is in you, than he that is in the world"[17] (the worldly consciousness). By the grace of God, we can defeat the enemy of our Christhood.

CHAPTER 14

GOD'S JUDGMENT
OF MEN AND ANGELS

In each age we witness the coming of the One Sent, the avatar, or Christed one, who seeks to separate us from our misconceptions and to show the blind the way to see. This God-man also preaches to the seed of the wicked to give them the opportunity to see the errors in their consciousness and to choose to abandon their fallen state and once again embrace the living God. This avatar is the great separator who comes to show us the difference between Reality and unreality.

Jesus challenged the moneychangers in the temple, those who sought to make a profit because of their greed and desire—a symptom of their lack of wholeness. And so the avatars have always come to challenge us and restore us to wholeness. Sometimes it takes the strong rebuke of the embodied Christ to separate us from our illusion.

The challenge of Jesus Christ to the fallen angels as well as to the children of light has never been by human condemnation or human self-righteousness, but always by the sacred fire of the Word of the LORD, which in every age delivers the mandate "Choose you this day whom ye will serve."[1]

Lifetime after lifetime, the soul is given renewed opportunity to serve the light. There comes a time, however, when opportunity ends and that soul is weighed in the balance. It is not for us to know the times or the seasons; these are known only to the Father.[2] But we know from the Book of Revelation that when an individual's offenses against life are so great that no light remains (and thus no possibility of redemption), the Great Law calls an end to opportunity:

> And I saw a great white throne, and him that sat on it, from whose face the earth and the heaven fled away; and there was found no place for them.
>
> And I saw the dead, small and great, stand before God; and the books were opened: and another book was opened, which is the book of life: and the dead were judged out of those things which were written in the books, according to their works.[3]

Jesus often taught in parables. In the parable of the householder who planted a vineyard, Jesus speaks of the evil ways of the Watchers and the Nephilim and alludes to the consequences of their commitment to evil. He is addressing this teaching to the chief priests and elders of the people in the temple on Palm Sunday:

There was a certain householder, which planted a vineyard and hedged it round about and digged a winepress in it, and built a tower and let it out to husbandmen and went into a far country.

And when the time of the fruit drew near, he sent his servants to the husbandmen, that they might receive the fruits of it. And the husbandmen took his servants, and beat one and killed another and stoned another.

Again, he sent other servants more than the first: and they did unto them likewise. But last of all he sent unto them his son, saying, They will reverence my son.

But when the husbandmen saw the son, they said among themselves, This is the heir; come, let us kill him, and let us seize on his inheritance. And they caught him, and cast him out of the vineyard and slew him.

When the lord therefore of the vineyard cometh, what will he do unto those husbandmen?

They say unto him, He will miserably destroy those wicked men and will let out his vineyard unto other husbandmen which shall render him the fruits in their seasons.[4]

Jesus is referring here to those who have murdered the Christ (the Son of man) in the prophets, in the avatars, in the saints East and West for tens of thousands of years. These incarnate fallen angels would murder the Christ within the heart of every child of

God, within every soul in whom there is the potential to become the Christ.

Through this parable we understand that when there is the murder of life which is God, when there is the hatred of the Christ light and when Christ is murdered by the disinherited and the disenfranchised, then sooner or later, in accordance with God's timetables, the perpetrators of those crimes against God and humanity will receive the final judgment that is written in the Book of Enoch.

Because the sins of the Watchers were so great, the LORD told them, "Never therefore shall you obtain peace."[5] According to the text of the Book of Enoch, the LORD's judgment against the Watchers prevails—then and now. The author of the book writes of his instruction from the archangels regarding the awesome judgment of the fallen ones before God's throne. He delivers three heavenly parables (or similitudes) describing the glories of the kingdom and the ineffable Ancient of Days and the Son of man, who, it is said, shall bring the final judgment upon "the wicked" of the earth.[6]

THE MEANING OF JUDGMENT

Whoever the perpetrators of evil are (and we ourselves need not know), when the time comes for their judgment, the hosts of the LORD will bind and render inactive the core of absolute evil within them and all that is aligned with it. This is the true and righteous judgment that separates the Real from the unreal, thereby opening the door to salvation for millions of oppressed peoples worldwide and saving the world from the ultimate revenge of the false gods: planetary holocaust.

God has given his sons and daughters dominion over the earth. Therefore it is up to us to challenge evil when we see it. Silence is consent. When we remain silent concerning world conditions, we are in effect saying "I agree." But when, as sons and daughters of God, we challenge these conditions by the fire of Christ in our hearts, calling for that judgment by the authority of Jesus Christ, who is one with our Holy Christ Self, the LORD will send the angelic hosts to perform the work of the judgment. It is the rightness of heart, not a sense of self-righteousness, that will deliver the world.

Jesus gave us a dynamic decree to use to call for the judgment of the fallen angels who have sworn enmity against the children of God: "The Judgment Call, 'They Shall Not Pass!'" It is our empowerment to deal with evil. The apostle Paul spoke of this empowerment when he told the Christians at Corinth: "Know ye not that we shall judge [the fallen] angels?"[7]

Jesus spoke of this two thousand years ago when he told Peter, "I will give unto thee the keys of the kingdom of heaven: and whatsoever thou shalt bind on earth shall be bound in heaven: and whatsoever thou shalt loose on earth shall be loosed in heaven."[8] Today, through the Science of the Spoken Word and the Judgment Call, Jesus has given us these keys for the binding of the fallen angels.

Having Jesus as our mediator and advocate guarantees that every time we give this call in his name—in the name of his Christ and our Christ—our prayer is weighed in his heart, aligned with the Father's will and answered accordingly. For Jesus has promised: "Verily, verily, I say unto you, Whatsoever ye shall ask the Father in my name, he will give it you.... Ask, and ye shall receive, that your joy may be full."[9]

Trusting that God is the ultimate Judge, we can then do our part and act relentlessly to deal with those who seek to perpetrate their evil deeds—the entrenched forces of Antichrist within individuals, organizations, banking houses, industry, governments, et cetera. We can use the Judgment Call to go after those conditions on the planet that are anti-Buddha, anti-Christ, anti-the little children, anti-the Great White Brotherhood and anti-truth. We can use that call to go after every opposition to the absolute God-freedom of every living soul to pursue the path of freedom.

JUDGMENT AS OPPORTUNITY

I believe that there are some fallen ones who can still apply for mercy, bend the knee and bow before the Christ light. The rendering of the final judgment is quite complex, especially since there has been an intermeshing of the seed of light and the seed of darkness among the evolutions of earth.

It is our earnest prayer that those whose ungodly deeds are challenged by our call, even those who are allied with nefarious practices, might be liberated from the strong delusions of the dweller and make an about-face to serve the living God. In giving the Judgment Call, we are the champions of the soul and the defenders of the right of the individual to be free from the sinister strategies of the carnal mind and the fallen angels—to be free to manifest the Real Self.

This call is Jesus' *sword,* which sons and daughters of God invoke through the sacred *Word.* In answer to our call, Jesus and the angels go forth to save those souls of light who have fallen into the cult of success, status, hedonism and excessive materialism. With all our heart's love, we can pray without ceasing for those who cannot see that they are enslaved by their own indulgence in the not-self. We can make the commitment to help increase the Christ consciousness on earth.

JUDGMENT AS LOVE

Those who are willing to face absolute evil with the authority and power of Christ can become a part of the vanguard of lightbearers who use dynamic decrees and the power of the spoken Word to call for the judgment of the fallen angels. When we do our part by making the call and surrendering the outcome and timetable to the will of God, we can be assured that God will answer our prayer in the best possible way.

I have seen, sadly, that when some individuals become aware of evil, they become bitter and gravitate toward the extreme right or left in politics and religion. Those who are fanatical, those who are extremists, do not have the equipoise of the flame of the heart. Instead of recognizing that there are forces of evil working through individuals, they personify evil and mistakenly believe they must destroy flesh and blood. We have all seen the ultimate result of such extremism in acts of horrific destruction—the perpetuation of wars, assassinations and terrorism.

The propensity of human nature is to rise up in indignation, in hate and hate creation, or in revenge against the oppressors. This has often happened in revolutions and wars in which the children of light, manipulated by the fallen ones, have moved against their very own, believing them to be the enemy. Heads from all sides have rolled on the battlefields of life. Children of light, side by side with the mechanical creation, have fought for the causes of the fallen angels because they have been brainwashed into aligning themselves with absolute evil while believing they were defending absolute good.

The power of the people is not gained through more revolutions of the kind we have witnessed on earth but by the enlightenment of the indwelling God Presence. Within the heart of fire in the breast is the power to overthrow tyrants, to displace them by the Christ consciousness. Unless we direct that light to challenge the consciousness behind evil, the energy of evil will live on, even if the bodies of the evildoers are destroyed. Therefore, the lawful means for dealing with the fallen ones is through the use of the Science of the Spoken Word, which challenges the forces behind the evildoers by the power of transmutation. In this way, one cannot mistake the enemy.

When giving the Judgment Call, the call for the binding of the dweller-on-the-threshold, calls to the violet flame or any decrees or prayers, it is essential to do so without any sense of vendetta or a personal need to exact retribution from the forces of evil, for a vengeful attitude of mind or heart will only bind a person to these fallen ones. Therefore, a purified heart is necessary. And if at any time or in any space you are tempted to react humanly to the forces of evil, remember that this is the most dangerous state of consciousness that you can entertain, because you will become instantly bound to those against whom you direct your vengeance.

By calling upon the LORD with perfect love (and without anger, animosity, revenge or any vibration that is less than Christ truth), we will see God's justice, not our own, prevail on earth as it does in heaven.

Over the last two thousand years and more, the great avatars have left us a legacy that we are intended to embody in our confrontation with evil. It is the attainment of the flame of peace as it manifested in the heart of Jesus Christ and Gautama Buddha. Therefore, the only state of mind that is acceptable is one of non-attachment, desirelessness, absolute love and absolute awareness that God himself, as the universal light, will, in his own time and space, separate the tares and the wheat and then burn the tares and draw the wheat into his garner.

Therefore, when we call for the judgment of the fallen ones, we are not in any way demanding their death or sending hatred to them in any form. We are calling to the angels to intercede, to expose to the people what the truth is. When the people have the truth, they will no longer give the fallen ones their money or their votes. They will no longer give them their lives in support of their wars and their causes.

Without the support of the people, the power elite will have to stand alone, and they will no longer be the dominating force on earth. Instead, the sons and daughters of God and the Christed ones will be the good shepherds, the teachers, the deliverers, the healers, and so forth.

JUDGMENT AS BLESSING

The Book of Revelation reveals a path of initiation that each soul in her season must pass through if she would ascend to God. It is a study in the psychology of the soul and the testings she must master on her path to reunion with the Father-Mother God.

At any point in time and space in any century, the soul on the homeward path may experience in sequence, one after the other, the initiations encoded in the twenty-two chapters of Revelation. Lightbearers of the world, according to their soul pattern, evolution and attainment, are experiencing all of the leaves of Revelation; and each of those leaves is tumbling in time and space, though not necessarily in the same dimension, for we are multidimensional beings.

Revelation juxtaposes the soul and the collective planetary evolution with the forces of light and darkness engaged in Armageddon. The outcome of this warfare of the Spirit will be either the soul's resurrection unto eternal life or her final judgment. By free will, the soul makes choices that take her either on the path homeward to God or on the path of Lucifer and the fallen angels in rebellion against the LORD God and his Christ.

In Revelation we find an outline of these two paths and a prophecy of the outcome of freewill choices made—to be or not to be—each step of the way.

Therefore, the judgment is an ongoing, personal event in our lives. Should you choose to give invocations for the judgment, you must be prepared for whatever you send forth to also activate the light (for the exposure of darkness) in your own world. The judgment of the Son of God is the greatest blessing that anyone who loves the LORD could ever receive. It is like a pre-exam or a midterm before the final exam that lets us know where we stand vis-à-vis God's laws. When we know where we stand, what we know and what we don't know, what is pleasing and what is not pleasing to God, we can then study, correct and perfect our understanding and our actions so that when the final examination comes, we will pass.

I ask God to judge my soul daily and for his angels to rebuke my errors, to teach me and to show me the way to do better. I implore the Holy Spirit to analyze all constructive criticism from friend and foe alike and to set before me the will of God for necessary change and progress in my soul.

When we call for the judgment of the fallen ones in every nation on earth, it is important to understand that God's answer to our calls can precipitate into the physical plane at any moment and in any way he chooses. We must be prepared. Therefore, if we do not want to suffer when that karma descends, it is wise not to be tied to the fallen ones.

The lesson we need to take with us is that when we are fortified and not depending upon the forces of the world to carry us, we are not vulnerable to the machinations of the fallen ones. Thus, the more independent and separated out we become from the international institutions, the monopolies and the multinational corporations, the more secure we will find ourselves and the less affected we will be when the judgment descends upon the seed of the wicked. That judgment has been prophesied. And the masters tell us that it must descend before the golden age can come.

PART 5

THE ALCHEMICAL KEY TO WORLD TRANSFORMATION

Those in embodiment must take accountability for planet earth as their alchemical experiment....

Your thought, mind you, impresses itself on every grain of sand....

Earth is burdened. An unconscious use of alchemy has put the planet out of kilter... with the cosmic blueprint....

If you think that some spot upon the earth will not respond to your call or that you are not responsible to assist in alleviating the darkness there, then you have not understood that the whole earth is the responsibility of every lightbearer.

—Saint Germain

The Key Ingredient in All Alchemy

One of Saint Germain's most important gifts to us is his teaching on the Science of the Spoken Word, the science of invoking the light of God to produce constructive change in ourselves and in the world.

The hope of heaven is that the lightbearers' use of the Science of the Spoken Word, especially their invocation of the violet flame, will be the key to bringing in the everlasting golden ages that God has held in his heart as the divine plan for earth and her evolutions. For it is the violet flame, when invoked by people of all faiths, that will result in the transmutation of their personal karma and the planetary karma made by lightbearers and fallen angels alike.

The more swiftly and fully we balance that karma, the more likely it will be that we can avert a period of intense suffering and upheaval in the earth and that we will instead make a more gentle transition to a new age of freedom.

The spoken Word is the Word of the LORD God released in the original fiats of creation. Thus, the Science of the Spoken Word is the essential and key ingredient in all alchemy. Without the Word spoken, there is no alchemy, no creation, no change in any part of life.

It is written in the Gospel of Matthew, "By thy words thou shalt be justified, and by thy words thou shalt be condemned."[1] When sons and daughters of God focus the powerful energies inherent in the throat chakra to affirm the Word of God, they become God's agents, instruments of his commandments. Through this action, they recreate themselves after the image of the Son of God.

Using the power of the spoken Word in dynamic decrees, affirmations, prayers and mantras, lightbearers access divine energy and direct the essence of the sacred fire from the I AM Presence, the Christ Self and heavenly beings into spiritual, mental and physical conditions. The masters have given us the tools to accomplish this mighty work of the ages; we just need to use them.

It bears repeating here that the only lawful means for overcoming the fallen angels and their agenda is through transmutation. And transmutation (transforming the negative energies behind these individuals) comes about by intoning the sacred Word.

Beginning with the Word, the sacred Aum,[2] we can draw forth the light and accelerate our own vibrations until our very bodies, atoms, cells and molecules begin to contain more and more light of the creative Word itself. In this way, we will become lighter and can start living in higher planes of consciousness even while we are yet moving about in physical bodies.

This self-transcending process through the liberating power of the Word has been taught by the Gurus of East and West. And it is essential to our spiritual practice if we hope to overcome the fallen angels. The regular practice of the Science of the Spoken Word is the means whereby we, as an evolution of lightbearers, can accelerate out of the dimensions of the fallen ones who are the living dead and the mechanical creation.

The following chapters introduce this scientific and highly effective way to give prayers, affirmations and decrees. Also included are visualizations and short meditations. This material is presented to give you practical spiritual tools with which to balance your personal karma, accelerate your individual path to reunion with God, and bring forth the necessary spiritual solutions for the prophesied challenges of our time.

CHAPTER 15

THE CREATIVE POWER OF SOUND

Scientific advances and studies have pointed to what healers and sages knew thousands of years ago: Sound is a key to physical, emotional and spiritual vitality. Today, the high-pitched sound waves of ultrasound technology are being used for everything from cleaning wounds to diagnosing tumors to pulverizing kidney stones. Someday sound may even be used to inject drugs into the body, making needles obsolete.

Alternative health practitioners have been experimenting with the use of specific tones to heal the organs. And certain kinds of classical music, by composers like Bach, Mozart and Beethoven, have been shown to accelerate learning, temporarily raise IQ and expand memory.

The creative power of sound is also at the heart of the world's spiritual traditions, whether as the Jewish Shema and Amidah, the Christian Our Father, the

Muslim Shahadah, the Hindu Gayatri or the Buddhist Om Mani Padme Hum.

Hindu writings contain powerful accounts of yogis who have used mantras for protection and wisdom, to enhance their concentration and meditation, and to help them achieve enlightenment and oneness with God. In Jewish mystical tradition, Kabbalists teach that by calling upon and meditating on the names of God, we can tap into an infinite source of power to restore peace and harmony to this world.

The Zohar, the foundational text of Jewish mysticism, emphasizes that prayer is not effective unless it is spoken aloud. Kabbalist Rabbi Aryeh Kaplan points out that "in later Kabbalistic schools, it appears that biblical verses or selections from the Talmud or Zohar would be used as mantras." For example, in the famed Palestinian community of Safed, Kabbalists would repeat a verse from the Bible like a mantra. By repeating the words of sacred works as a mantra, Kaplan said that meditators would gain deep insights into the meaning of those works.[1]

Catholic tradition tells us that Saint Clare of Assisi saved her convent during an attack by Saracens when she held up the Eucharist and prayed aloud. These and numerous other examples show us that sound can create matter and change matter. And therefore it can create spiritual and material changes in our lives, including the mitigation of physical cataclysm and the evil intent of the fallen angels.

We know that sound can be a dramatic destructive force: A high-pitched note can shatter crystal, a sonic boom can crack plaster, a gunshot can set off an avalanche. Hindu and Buddhist mystics believe that mantras[2] can unleash forces that can create or destroy. Yogis have used mantras along with visualizations to light fires, materialize physical objects (like food), bring rain and even influence the outcome of battles.

Some of the best lessons on the transforming effect of sound and the scientific use of the spoken Word come from the Bible itself. In the case of Jericho, when the Israelites "shouted with a great shout" in unison, the wall of the city came tumbling down.

God had directed Joshua to have the Israelites circle the city of Jericho once a day for six days. On the seventh day they were to circle it seven times. Joshua told the people: "Ye shall not shout, nor make any noise with your voice, neither shall any word proceed out of your mouth, until the day I bid you shout; then shall ye shout."

On the seventh day, on the seventh pass around the city, Joshua gave the command: "Shout; for the LORD hath given you the city." The priests blew their trumpets and the people gave a mighty shout. The wall of Jericho fell flat, and the Israelites took the city.[3] Jericho was a city of the Nephilim, and the Israelites conquered it by directing God's power through the spoken word.

It is no longer possible or effective to fight the Nephilim hand to hand, for they have beaten our plowshares into tanks and our pruning hooks[4] into nuclear weapons. But as Joshua demonstrated at Jericho, the power of the Word is greater than the might of armies.

THE SPOKEN WORD INTENSIFIES PRAYER

The prayers and affirmations included in this book are meant to be given aloud as a dynamic prayer form known as decrees. Decrees, like other prayers, are spoken petitions to God. When we meditate, we commune with God. When we pray, we communicate with God and request his help. And when we decree, we are commanding God's light to enter our world or the world at large. Meditation, prayer and dynamic decrees are all vital to a balanced spiritual practice. However, decrees spoken aloud have a commanding effect upon the flow of energy from Spirit to Matter.

Through the prophet Isaiah, God said, "Ask me of things to come concerning my sons, and concerning the work of my hands *command ye me.*" And through Job he said: "Thou shalt make thy prayer unto him [the Almighty], and he shall hear thee.... Thou shalt also *decree* a thing, and it shall be established unto thee."[5] When you use the creative power of sound through spoken prayers or decrees, you are not just "asking" for help; you are entering into a partnership and an interactive relationship with God.

Some people question whether it is really necessary to even *ask* God to help us. If he is omniscient, why wouldn't he just automatically take care of our problems and our needs?

The answer to that question is twofold. Because God gave us free will, heavenly beings intervene in our affairs only when we invite them into our lives. There are many people on earth, though, who are suffering but do not pray, or perhaps they do not know how to pray. For some, their pain is so great that they cannot articulate their feelings of frustration, anger and so many hurts and disappointments, yet in the depths of their souls they are crying out for help.

God's promise through Isaiah addresses this situation: "And it shall come to pass, that before they call, I will answer; and while they are yet speaking, I will hear."[6] And so the angels and the masters listen not only to prayers that are clearly formed but also to the unspoken expressions of the soul, for these, too, are a form of prayer.

Prayer and decrees are direct ways of contacting God to ask for his intercession in our lives. There is a time and place to practice each type of devotion. The accelerated prayer form of decrees combines prayer, meditation, affirmation and visualization, which devotees from many traditions find greatly enhances their own spiritual practice.

The Science of the Spoken Word restores to mankind in this age the lost art of decreeing that was employed by sons and daughters of God in the early golden ages of earth's history that antedate the fall of both Atlantis and Lemuria.

Before the decline of Lemuria, invocations offered in the power of the spoken Word were given according to the science of the Logos. The perversion of this science through the practice of black magic occurred later, in the last days of Lemuria, and this misuse of God's power contributed to the destruction of that continent.

Today, the correct practice of the Science of the Spoken Word provides a way for lightbearers to return to their original perfection (i.e., oneness with God) before their expulsion from paradise, before having taken into themselves the serpentine consciousness of duality.

The great release that comes from the giving of decrees enables mankind to possess a more than ordinary power here and now for their service to the greater light of God and for the bringing in of his kingdom on earth.

THE POWER OF THE WORD OF GOD

The sound that we can use to transform our spiritual and material worlds isn't just any sound. It is the Word of God. In the ancient Hindu Vedas we read, "In the beginning was Brahman with whom was Vac, or the Word, and the Word is Brahman." Similarly, the apostle John wrote, "In the beginning was the Word, and the Word was with God, and the Word was God." And Genesis tells us that when God *spoke* the words "Let there be light," the process of creation began.[7]

Archangel Gabriel explained why invoking the Word is an indispensable tool for freeing ourselves from the fallen ones:

The reason that the spoken Word of God spoken by the Son of God within you is so viciously and so violently opposed by the fallen ones is that they have known from the beginning of their descent that all that they have created as a perversion of God has manifested through the perversion of the Word of the Son.

They have known from the beginning that when the sons of God, the Christs of God, would once more walk the earth, knowing who "I AM" and who I AM *THAT I AM,* that they would intone the Word, that the real and living sacred fire would proceed out of their mouth as out of the mouth of God,[8] and that all things would be restored to cosmic reality by that spoken Word....

Yes, your dynamic decrees are the vibration of the One Sent.... That vibration is the Word that neutralizes all programming and deprogramming of the fallen ones, all negative projections of outer and inner space, all currents of manipulation and mechanization, whatever their source, known or unknown.[9]

JESUS TAUGHT THE SCIENCE OF THE SPOKEN WORD

The Book of Hebrews tells us that Jesus upheld "all things by the word of his power," or as the Jerusalem Bible puts it, he sustained "the universe by his powerful command."[10]

For instance, Jesus healed the man who sought wholeness at the pool of Bethesda when he gave the command "Rise, take up thy bed, and walk!" When Jesus "rebuked the wind" and commanded the sea, "Peace, be still," the wind ceased "and there was a great calm."[11] And when he raised Lazarus from the dead, Jesus "cried with a loud voice, 'Lazarus, come forth!'"[12] In each case, Jesus was using the Science of the Spoken Word.

Jesus taught us to use this same method of dynamic prayer when he gave us the Lord's Prayer. Before giving us this prayer, he said, *"After this manner* therefore pray ye."[13]

This prayer is actually a decree, a series of seven commands that follow the initial address to the Father ("Our Father which art in heaven"):

> (1) Hallowed be thy name!
> (2) Thy kingdom come!
> (3) Thy will be done on earth as it is in heaven!
> (4) Give us this day our daily bread!
> (5) And forgive us our debts as we forgive our debtors!
> (6) And lead us not into temptation!
> (7) But deliver us from evil!

What we learn from Jesus' instruction is that as sons and daughters of God, we do not need to beg our Father for our daily needs. We need only ask—in the form of the command—and he will release his light, energy and consciousness to us in the form we specify.

EMPOWERMENT THROUGH THE NAME OF GOD

When God revealed his name I AM THAT I AM to Moses, he said, "This is my name forever, and this is my memorial unto all generations." The Jerusalem Bible translates that passage as "This is my name for all time; by this name I shall be invoked for all generations to come." This tells us that God is directing us to use his name to invoke his intercession. Therefore in our decrees we use "I AM THAT I AM" or "I AM" to access God's unlimited power.

I AM is more than a sacred name. It is an empowerment. It is a scientific formula. When you recite God's name with faith and love, God releases his energy as a stupendous waterfall of light to heal mind and soul and heart.

What does I AM THAT I AM mean? To me it means simply, but profoundly, "as Above, so below." God is affirming, "I am here below that which I AM above." When you say "I AM THAT I AM," you are affirming that God is where you are. In effect, you are saying: "As God is in heaven, so God is on earth within me. Right where I stand, God is. I am that I AM."

Sometimes we say to ourselves, "Where is God? Why isn't he helping me? Everything is going wrong in my household, in my business." I suggest that you try calling to God and literally commanding him: "In the name of the I AM THAT I AM, enter my life, O God! I can't do this without you! Send your angels to take command of this situation right now!"

Or you can say, "In the name of God I AM THAT
I AM, in the name of Jesus Christ and Saint Germain,
take command of _____," naming the specific
problem burdening you or a loved one.

Simple, quick prayers like this will bring the angels
right into your home. Do not be meek when you make
these calls. Give them as dynamic commands. The
greater the fervor and intensity of your heart, the
greater the response from heaven.

You can also use God's name I AM to create short,
powerful affirmations. They are powerful because
each time you say "I am _____," you are really
saying "God in me is _____." And whatever you
affirm following the words "I am" will become a reality in your world, for the light of God flowing through
you will obey that command. This is the deeper meaning of the so-called mind-body connection. The state of
your body is influenced by what you think and by what
you say. Your words are a self-fulfilling prophecy.

Many have lost their reverence for life, a reverence
for the energy of God that flows through them at every
moment, a reverence for the God that lives within them.
Reflect on the power of God within you. Do you have
a sense of awe? Do you say to yourself: "Here is God's
energy; what will I do with it today? Will I use God's
energy to reinforce the positive side of life? Will I use
it to affirm something beautiful, something real, something that matters to my spiritual progress?"

If you catch yourself saying, "I am tired" or "I am just not good enough," stop and try redirecting the power of God within you to affirm, "I AM whole!" or "I AM the victory over this habit!" or "I AM the victory over these fallen ones!"

Jesus showed us how to tap into the power of God's name when he made statements like "I AM the resurrection and the life," "I AM the Light of the world," "I AM come that they might have life and that they might have it more abundantly," and "I AM the way, the truth and the life."[14]

You can take any of these I AM affirmations and make them your own, and you can create your own I AM affirmations. Many decrees are made up of I AM affirmations. Remember, every time you say "I am _____," you are affirming "God in me is _____." And when you give a decree, it is God who is speaking that decree through you.

As you give the following affirmations, feel the power of God within you affirming your oneness with the Source of all life, for God can bring you the spiritual and material resources you need.

Transfiguring Affirmations

I AM THAT I AM
I AM the Open Door which no man can shut
I AM the Light which lighteth every man
    that cometh into the world
I AM the Way

I AM the Truth
I AM the Life
I AM the resurrection
I AM the ascension in the light
I AM the fulfillment of all my needs
   and requirements of the hour
I AM abundant supply poured out upon all life
I AM perfect sight and hearing
I AM the manifest perfection of being
I AM the illimitable light of God
   made manifest everywhere
I AM the light of the Holy of Holies
I AM a son of God
I AM the light in the holy mountain of God

WHY WE REPEAT DECREES

Decrees, like prayers and mantras, are meant to be repeated, just as Catholics repeat the Hail Mary and Buddhists their sacred chants. People often wonder why we should have to ask God more than once for something. Repeating a prayer or decree is not simply making a request over and over. It is an energy equation. Each time you repeat it, you are building a momentum. You are invoking more and more spiritual light into the situation to bring greater assistance to meet that need.

Both mystics and scientists have demonstrated the benefits of repetitive prayer. Over the centuries, mystics of the Eastern Orthodox Church reported extraordinary mystical experiences through their tradition of repeating the simple prayer "Lord Jesus Christ, have mercy on me."

Dr. Herbert Benson, president and founder of the Mind/Body Medical Institute in Boston, discovered that those who repeated Sanskrit mantras for as little as ten minutes a day experienced physiological changes—reduced heart rate, lower stress levels and slower metabolism. Subsequent studies showed that repeating mantras can benefit the immune system, relieve insomnia, reduce visits to the doctor and even increase self-esteem. When Benson and his colleagues tested other prayers, including "Lord Jesus Christ, have mercy on me," they found that they had the same positive effect.[15] In short, repetitive prayer energizes.

The prayers and decrees in this book are taken from the words of the saints and masters of East and West. Because these enlightened ones have reached the highest levels of intimate communion with God, their words are like ropes that we can use to sustain a strong spiritual connection. They are sacred formulas for the release of God's power.

THE MASTERS MULTIPLY OUR GOOD WORDS AND GOOD WORKS

When we use the Science of the Spoken Word, we can ask that our dynamic decrees be given "in the name of" any of the angels, archangels or ascended masters. In this way, our decrees are empowered by their light and attainment. The names of the masters and heavenly beings are keys by which we can access the portion of their being that they can lawfully offer to us. When we say that name in the preamble of a decree, we automatically access that portion of God's light and power for which that name is a chalice.

Saint Germain's attainment is vast. So when you decree "in the name of Saint Germain," instantaneously you have behind your call a portion of the power and light that he has garnered over many thousands of years.[16] The fire of his heart multiplies the power of your heart, and it is as though Saint Germain and you were one. In fact, you *are* one.

Therefore, when you confront the adversary within or without, you can be confident that you are meeting him with the power of Saint Germain, whose power is equivalent to or greater than the power of any fallen angel at the time of that one's fall. And therefore Saint Germain is able to fulfill the decree of the Word through you, even if your own externalized light is not adequate to the encounter with Antichrist.

The same is true of Jesus. When you desire with all your heart to do some good for life and you call upon him, he will combine his momentum and his Presence with your Christ Self and multiply your good works and words. His prophecy is thereby fulfilled that we shall do greater works than he did two thousand years ago.

Jesus has been expanding ever since he ascended, as all saints in heaven have. Their auras, their magnificence, their beauty and their love have also increased beyond any dimensions we can imagine in our present state. So when we make the call in their names, we have their light behind us.

In this way, we walk the earth hand in hand with the immortals. That universal One, that Christ, is personified for you and for me and yet always remains the eternal One—your Christ, my Christ, one only begotten Son of God.

This understanding is absolutely fundamental if we wish to solve the desperate problems with our economy, with nuclear proliferation and with the pollution of our environment and if we hope to free ourselves from those fallen angels who fooled us back in the Garden of Eden. But they cannot fool us any longer because now we know who we are. We know that I AM THAT I AM!

This is why we use the Science of the Spoken Word. We realize that the I AM Presence, the Holy Christ Self and the threefold flame in our hearts, multiplied by the living Christ in Jesus and all the saints in heaven, can move through us and in us.

VISUALIZATION ENHANCES THE POWER OF DECREES

As you experiment with the decrees and visualizations in the following chapters, understand that visualization can enhance the benefits of your decrees. That's because whatever you put your attention on, you are "plugging into" and charging with energy—it is over the flow of your attention that the energies of your Presence travel to fulfill the spoken Word.

The image you hold in your mind's eye is like a blueprint, and your attention is the magnet that attracts the creative energies of Spirit to fill it in. "We are what we think," taught Gautama Buddha, "having become what we thought."[17]

Therefore, what we think about while praying or decreeing will make a big difference in how effective these prayers and decrees will be. When we are dealing with matters related to fallen angels and prophecies in our spiritual work, it is essential that we keep our focus on a positive outcome and visualize the highest good we can imagine. For what we together focus on, we will create.

Visualize the desired outcome as if it were already taking place in the present. See it as if it were happening on a movie screen in front of you. If you don't have a specific outcome in mind, then concentrate on the words of the prayer and see the action they describe taking place before you.

The masters teach us to use the spiritual power of our vision when calling for a specific quality to manifest. For example, if you are calling for protection, you can visualize Archangel Michael and his angels surrounding and shielding you with their protective power.

If your power of vision and artistry is somewhat lacking, ask your Christ Self to teach you how to construct mental patterns of light that will form a mold into which you can pour the energies of your words. Through repetition, you will form a strong magnet, a thought-form charged with intense feeling that will magnetize from the higher octaves the light-energy that will help you to manifest the quality or action you desire.

Many decrees are easy to memorize by repeating them over time. Once you have memorized a decree, you can close your eyes as you repeat it and strengthen your concentration on your visualization.

Begin by focusing on your I AM Presence, which you can see as a blazing sun of light overhead. Concentrate on the divine spark in your heart, imagining it as a dazzling sphere of light as brilliant as the sun at noon-day. As you decree, see thousands of sunbeams going forth from your heart to heal and comfort every child of God on earth.

To help you with your visualizations, before you begin decreeing ask yourself what you would like to achieve with your decrees. Make a list of your spiritual and practical goals, and update them periodically. If your attention is riveted on a specific goal as you decree, your decrees will be infinitely more effective in producing the desired results than if your mind wanders, you are distracted and your eyes gaze randomly around the room. If you do become distracted, don't condemn yourself. Instead, gently return your mind to your focus. The more you practice, the better you will become at focusing your attention.

DECREEING WITH DEVOTION

Your center of attention should be in the heart flame at all times while you decree because it is here that your own individual focus of God's power, wisdom and love resides. Concentration at its best is a quality of the heart combined with the mind.

Decreeing must come from a place of devotion. The intellect, which has for far too long ruled the heart in most people, must be reeducated to obey the heart's call and to be obedient to the intuitive power of the heart, which most often does reflect the inner voice of the Christ Self. The fire of your heart and your love is what compels the angels and masters to answer your calls. Love is what gives shape to our desires and what should guide our visualizations. So the more heartfelt your prayers and decrees are, the more charged they will be with spiritual purpose.

To increase your devotion while decreeing, you might wish to look at a picture of your favorite saint or ascended master, a natural or man-made symmetrical pattern that represents the perfection of God (like a star, galaxy, rose or geometric form), a beautiful scene from nature or a great work of art.

WHEN, WHERE AND HOW TO DECREE

One of the best times to give your decrees is in the early morning when the angels circle the planet, clearing the atmosphere and bringing blessings to life. You will find that if you decree first thing in the morning, your day will unfold more effortlessly than if you start your day without offering your devotion and giving a few decrees.

When I take time first thing in the morning to connect with God through heartfelt prayer at my altar, I find that my day is transformed. It goes much more smoothly. I don't get caught up in needless distractions and emergencies that pull me away from my goals.

Decrees can be given anywhere, even while you are cleaning the house, doing errands, going for a walk, driving to work or taking a shower. It helps, though, when you can set aside some uninterrupted quiet time to decree before your own personal altar.

Your altar is your special place, the sacred space that helps you connect to your heart. It is the place you can go when you want to "alter"—to create change and transformation. You can create your own altar, even if it is in a corner of your bedroom or living room.

You can adorn this altar with whatever inspires you and helps you make a connection with God and with your Higher Self. You can place candles, flowers or plants on the altar. You can add pictures or statues of saints or masters as well as photographs of those for whom you regularly pray. Beautiful crystals and a crystal bowl or goblet can serve as chalices to focus God's light in your home. Above your altar or on it, you can place the Chart of Your Divine Self to help you attune with the Presence of God within.

It is best to give your decrees aloud. But if you

can't decree aloud because you are in a public place, for instance, you can repeat the decrees in your mind. Keeping your spine erect and feet flat on the floor creates a clear channel for light to flow through you unimpeded. You can also sit in the lotus posture if you choose. Breathe deeply and regularly as you decree, using the power of the breath of God to project his light through your chakras.

When you are ready to decree, first give a prayer naming where you want to direct the light you will be calling forth. Always ask for your requests to be adjusted by your Higher Self according to whatever is best for your soul and the souls of those for whom you are decreeing—in other words, always ask for the will of God to be done.

Then choose a decree. Speak the words with devotion and feeling. Endow each word with intense love for God, holding in mind your chosen visualization. Begin slowly and at the pitch of your normal speaking voice.

Speaking the decree slowly allows you to achieve a deep, heartfelt communion with God. As you repeat the decree, you can gradually increase the speed and raise the pitch. Although speeding up is not essential, the acceleration will increase the ability of your decrees to dissolve negative thoughts or energies that have attached themselves to you. You should consciously increase the speed of your decrees only if you feel the need; the decree should almost speed itself up.

Decrees are often given three times or in multiples

of three. As I have mentioned, repeating a decree is not simply making a request over and over again. Repetition intensifies the power of the decree as you qualify it with more and more of God's energy. When you are first beginning to decree, try repeating the decree three or nine times and then increase your repetitions over time.

As you repeat a decree, you will feel it take on a natural rhythm. The rhythm is one of the things that gives a decree its power. Just as the rhythm of an army marching in step can collapse a bridge, so the rhythm of decrees can create a strong spiritual force that breaks down accumulations of negative energy, habit patterns and karma. The rhythm also sets up a vibratory pattern that sends the light you have invoked across the planet.

THE ANATOMY OF A DECREE

You can think of a decree as a letter to God. It is generally composed of three parts—the preamble, the body and the closing.

1. *The preamble.* The preamble is like the salutation of a letter. In it we address the ascended masters and angelic hosts and ask them for assistance. We give them the authority to take command of any person, place, condition or circumstance.

The preamble to the decree is an appeal that compels the masters and angelic hosts to answer you, as long as you give it with love and your request is in keeping with God's will and law. The masters could no more refuse to answer this summons than could the firemen in your hometown refuse to answer your call for help.

To command the energies of God in a decree is the prerogative of our Higher Self—the part of us that came from God. The lower self, being imperfect and incomplete, does not have this authority.

Therefore we begin our decrees by saying, "In the name of the Presence of God, I AM in me, and my Holy Christ Self...." By so doing we are acknowledging that we are the agents of God, his instruments on earth, and that we are asking only for that which is the will of God.

Preambles are optional. At times it is preferable to give only the body of a decree. This is especially the case with short mantras, affirmations and commands, called fiats.

2. *The body.* The body of a decree is a statement of your desires—things you are requesting take place for yourself, others, your nation or the planet.

3. *The closing.* In the closing, you seal your decree in the heart of God for his disposition. You have proposed; now God will dispose. You also accept that God will answer your requests. If you don't consciously accept the answer to your decree, the light of God you have invoked may remain in the realm of Spirit instead of manifesting physically.

WHAT TO EXPECT FROM DECREES

There are many aspects to decreeing that have to be mastered before we can put the whole picture together—using visualization, putting feeling into the words, keeping our attention on what we are doing, and developing rhythm. Decreeing is a science[18] and it takes practice and experimentation. When you begin decreeing, you will most likely master one aspect and then another and then another until you finally put the whole thing together. It's like learning to ride a bike. When you master it, you will feel the full results.

Don't be disappointed if your decrees don't seem to bring results right away or in the way you expected. When you use the Science of the Spoken Word, you are decreeing by God's authority, and God will answer you in the way that is best for your soul. Your Higher Self may be trying to lead you in another direction, one that ultimately will bring greater soul growth.

Each of us needs faith in something, and we can have that faith in God, the masters and the angels. For people may fail us, but God and the beings of heaven will not. God always keeps his promises to us, even if we don't immediately see the answers to our prayers. They will come. The answers will surely come.

Even if you are able to decree for just a few minutes a day, it can make a difference in your outlook, your relationship with God, and the salvation of the planet. Try the Science of the Spoken Word—and see what the light can do for you and what you can do for a world in need!

CHAPTER 16

INVOKING SPIRITUAL PROTECTION

Whatever prayers and meditations you give, it is good to begin by asking for spiritual protection for yourself and your loved ones. When you pray for yourself or someone in need, you can maximize your prayer by including all those with a like need. In this section you will be introduced to a number of prayers and decrees for protection, including two short decrees that are easy to memorize: "Tube of Light" (below) and "Traveling Protection" (page 303).

STEP ONE: YOUR TUBE OF LIGHT

As you give the "Tube of Light" affirmation, a cylinder of white light will descend from Spirit in answer to your call. The saints and mystics of the world's religions have seen this white light in their meditations and prayers. The Israelites experienced the tube of light as a "pillar of a cloud" by day and "a pillar of fire" by night as they journeyed through the wilderness.[1]

A representation of the tube of light is shown in the Chart of Your Divine Self (opposite page 207). This cylinder of energy is about nine feet in diameter. It comes from the I AM THAT I AM above you and extends beneath your feet.

The white light can help you stay centered and at peace. It can guard you from the malintent of the fallen angels and from negative energies such as anger, condemnation, hatred or jealousy, whether from these individuals or from others. When you are unprotected, you become physically, mentally and spiritually vulnerable to the aggressive energies and projections of unseen forces of malintent.

The white light can also protect you from the pull of the mass consciousness. If you feel exhausted after being in a crowded public place or in a city, it may be that your physical _and_ spiritual reserves have literally been drained.

Many find it helpful to give the "Tube of Light" decree before the hustle and bustle of the day begins. During the day, if you feel de-energized, depleted or vulnerable, withdraw for a few minutes and repeat this decree.

Tube of Light

Beloved I AM Presence bright,
Round me seal your tube of light
From ascended master flame
Called forth now in God's own name.

> Let it keep my temple free
> From all discord sent to me.
>
> I AM calling forth violet fire
> To blaze and transmute all desire,
> Keeping on in freedom's name
> Till I AM one with the violet flame.

ARCHANGEL MICHAEL, THE ULTIMATE GUARDIAN

Archangel Michael is the greatest and most revered of angels in Jewish, Christian and Islamic scriptures and tradition. In the Old Testament he figures as the guardian of Israel. He appeared to Joshua as he prepared to lead the Israelites into battle at Jericho and revealed himself as "captain of the hosts of the LORD."

In Catholic tradition, he is the patron and protector of the Church. Archangel Michael was among the three heavenly visitors who revealed to the young peasant girl Joan of Arc her mission to deliver France. Called Mika'il in Muslim lore, he is the angel of nature, providing both food and knowledge to man.

The prophet Daniel spoke of Archangel Michael's role in these end times of this two-thousand-year cycle. Daniel writes:

> And at that time shall Michael stand up, the great prince which standeth for the children of thy people: and there shall be a time of trouble, such as never was since there was a nation even to that

same time: and at that time thy people shall be delivered, every one that shall be found written in the book.[2]

Signs of this time of trouble abound. If you read between the lines of the nations' news reports, you can see clear evidence that the fallen ones are among us, doing their utmost to wreak havoc in our lives and in our world.

Our hope for deliverance comes to us through the hand of Archangel Michael. To increase his presence with us, we give calls to him in the name of our I AM Presence and Christ Self.

Archangel Michael is the archangel of the first ray and he embodies the qualities of that ray—faith, protection, perfection and the will of God. He has numberless legions of angels in his command whose job it is to protect the children of God from physical and spiritual dangers.

People sometimes think that specific angels can only do certain things. But archangels and angels have a great cosmic consciousness. Though they have specialties, they can extend themselves beyond just one area of influence. So even though Michael manifests power and protection, he also brings healing for our bodies and souls. Indeed, he was revered in the early Church as the heavenly physician.

As a healing angel, he frees us from forces within and without that intensify our ailments, our burdens and our karma. He assists us in overcoming the thought processes that conceive and amplify disease, disintegration and death.

So whatever you desire to be delivered of—if you really want to be free—pray fervently and daily to Archangel Michael and he will deliver you. If you want to quit smoking or drinking or overeating, if you want to get your life in order so you can serve God better, just make the call to Archangel Michael.

Archangel Michael has personally saved my life a dozen times that I know of and probably thousands of times that I am not aware of. I am sure the same is true for you.

BATTLING THE FALLEN ANGELS ON EARTH

The age-old war of light and darkness on the planet is one in which Archangel Michael has been doing battle for aeons. When it comes to terrorism and war being waged across the globe, the only way I can see to deal with these situations is to call upon the LORD and upon Archangel Michael, the great deliverer of Moses and Joshua and the one who fights the battles on behalf of the LORD and his children. His intercession is vital.

The fallen angels, in their determination to destroy the children of God, have entangled many among mankind in their schemes. When someone commits a crime against life, it is because the soul, rather than heeding the voice of the Higher Self, has somehow been caught between the not-self and the reasoning mind and is swayed to perform certain actions that are not of the light. We can enlist Archangel Michael's help in quickening the consciousness of those who would do better if they knew better.

Another important reason to give decrees to Archangel Michael daily is because he can help you to stay focused on the goal of reunion with your Christ Self and I AM Presence.

PRAYER FOR OUR DEFENSE IN ARMAGEDDON

One way we can invoke the intercession of Archangel Michael is by giving the prayer that Pope Leo XIII wrote to him. One day after Pope Leo finished Mass, he stopped at the altar as if in a trance. Later he explained that he had overheard Satan speaking to Jesus.

In a guttural, prideful voice, Satan boasted that he could destroy the Church but he needed seventy-five years to do it. The Lord replied, "You have the time; you have the power. Do what you will." The pope understood that through prayer, sacrifice and living good lives, we could offset the power of the devil and his human agents. He recognized that Archangel Michael had a great role to play in the outcome of this conflict.

So the pope composed a prayer to invoke Archangel Michael's intercession to overcome the wiles of Satan.[3] Catholics recited this prayer at the conclusion of Mass starting in 1886, but this practice was discontinued in 1964, seventy-eight years later, when Vatican II revised the liturgy.

An adaptation of Pope Leo's prayer for students of the masters follows. It is titled "Saint Michael the Archangel, Defend Us in Armageddon." You can give this short prayer in any situation where Michael's intercession is needed.

There is a blank line in the middle of this prayer where you can state the burdens on your heart as well as the situations that you want Archangel Michael to address. Turn them over to Archangel Michael. I promise you, he *will* help you.

Saint Michael the Archangel, Defend Us in Armageddon

Saint Michael the Archangel, defend us in Armageddon, be our protection against the wickedness and snares of the devil; may God rebuke him, we humbly pray; and do thou, O Prince of the heavenly host, by the power of God, bind the forces of Death and Hell, the seed of Satan, the false hierarchy of Antichrist, and all evil spirits who wander through the world for the ruin of souls, and remand them to the Court of the Sacred Fire for their final judgment [including: insert your personal prayer here].

Cast out the dark ones and their darkness, the evildoers and their evil words and works, cause, effect, record and memory, into the lake of sacred fire "prepared for the devil and his angels."

In the name of the Father, the Son, the Holy Spirit and the Mother, Amen.

DECREES FOR PROTECTION

We all need heaven's help to protect us from seen and unseen forces. When you maintain a momentum of prayers and decrees on a regular basis, you give Archangel Michael and his legions the best opportunity to answer your calls for help when you need it. This will build a reservoir of light, sealed in your heart, for when challenges arise suddenly.

Following are decrees and fiats that you can give to call Archangel Michael into your life. These decrees are for your protection as you move about during the day and to protect you at night while your soul travels out of your body during sleep. You can use them any time you become aware of a situation anywhere in the world that has the mark of the fallen angels' consciousness behind it. With these calls, you can invite the angels of light to deal with problems of any magnitude.

Throughout the day, whenever you feel a need to reinforce protection around yourself or whenever you can take a moment to invoke protection for the children, the teens and all who are beleaguered by the tactics and influence of the fallen angels, stop and summon this magnificent archangel through a short and powerful fiat (see page 307).

Give these decrees and fiats with gusto and know that when you call to Archangel Michael and his legions, they will immediately be at your side.

Visualization:

See Archangel Michael as a beautiful, powerful, majestic archangel arrayed in shining armour with a brilliant sapphire-blue cape and aura. Visualize him standing before you, behind you, to your left, to your right, beneath, above and in the center of your form, accompanied by limitless numbers of angels who will protect and escort you wherever you go. You may also visualize Archangel Michael wielding his spiritual sword of blue flame to deliver you from all negative conditions that work against your soul's progress on the spiritual path.

The sword of blue flame of Archangel Michael creates an action of spiritual fire. In response to your call, Michael and his angels will use this sword of sacred fire to cut around your form to free you from negative energies or to deal with any condition of danger and darkness.

While you are traveling, see Archangel Michael surrounding every vehicle on the highway. You can also imagine yourself wearing a helmet and armour of blue fire that will prevent any physical or spiritual danger from reaching your body or mind.

After you give the "Tube of Light Decree" (page 294), you can give the invocation below with decrees to Archangel Michael or with any decree or prayer. You can also use it as a basis for creating your own invocations.

Invocation:

In the name of the I AM THAT I AM, I call to you, beloved Archangel Michael, and your legions of blue-flame angels to enfold me, my family, community and nation with your majestic Presence. Guide, guard and protect all who are serving the light on planet earth today.

Archangel Michael, let this earth be purged of the seed of the wicked this day! Let the entire Matter cosmos be purged of them and their evildoings, their manipulations and their genetic engineering.

O God, let the battle be fought in the earth as it was fought in heaven. Archangel Michael, we call to you in God's name to cast the Nephilim, the Watchers and all fallen ones out of the earth! For the earth is the LORD's and the fullness thereof and all they that dwell therein.[4] Therefore we claim this earth for Almighty God and all sons and daughters of light worlds without end.

We accept it done this hour in full power, O God. We accept thy sacred fire purging our minds, our souls, our bodies and purging the earth of the fallen ones who have gone forth to destroy the souls of thy children.

Instruction:

Following is a brief preamble you can give before any of your decrees. You can also use it as a template for creating your own preambles. After giving the preamble, proceed to give one or more of the protection decrees on the following pages. Give any of these decrees three or nine times or however many times you feel necessary to reinforce Archangel Michael's protection. You can refer to Part 2 of this book to invoke Archangel Michael's assistance in battling the evils of the fallen angels that are discussed there.

Preamble:

In the name of my mighty I AM Presence and Holy Christ Self, in the name of Jesus Christ, Archangel Michael and the seven archangels, I decree:

Decree:

Traveling Protection

Lord Michael before, Lord Michael behind,
Lord Michael to the right,
Lord Michael to the left,
Lord Michael above, Lord Michael below,
Lord Michael, Lord Michael wherever I go!

I AM his love protecting here!
I AM his love protecting here!
I AM his love protecting here!

Decree:

Guard, Guard, Guard Us!

Guard, guard, guard us!
　By the lightning of thy love!
Guard, guard, guard us!
　By thy Great Self above!
Guard, guard, guard us!
　By thy secret power of light!
Guard, guard, guard us!
　By thy great and glorious might!
And seal us safe forever
　In thy diamond heart of light!

I AM Michael, Michael, Michael

Visualization:

When we give this decree, Archangel Michael places his Presence over us. It is as if we are inside of him. When you are Archangel Michael where you stand, nothing can get by you, because nothing can get by the power of Archangel Michael. See this powerful, mighty archangel with his spiritual sword of blue flame "cutting you free" from addictions, burdens, limiting habits and the influence of the fallen angels.

I AM Michael, Michael, Michael!
　I stand within his flame
I AM Michael, Michael, Michael!
　By God's own I AM name

I AM Michael, Michael, Michael!
His faith ablazing here
I AM Michael, Michael, Michael!
His power and love so dear!

I AM Michael, Michael, Michael!
To light and love I bow
I AM Michael, Michael, Michael!
To defend the faith I vow
I AM Michael, Michael, Michael!
I enlist the light of men
I AM Michael, Michael, Michael!
America defend.

I AM Michael, Michael, Michael!
His shield of faith I wear
I AM Michael, Michael, Michael!
His circle and sword I bear
I AM Michael, Michael, Michael!
Enarmored by his love
I AM Michael, Michael, Michael!
Blue lightning from above!

I AM Michael, Michael, Michael!
Protected by his word
I AM Michael, Michael, Michael!
The Captain of the LORD
I AM Michael, Michael, Michael!
His legions now descend
I AM Michael, Michael, Michael!
Each child of the light defend!

Closing:

> And in full faith I consciously accept this manifest, manifest, manifest! *(give three times)* right here and now with full power, eternally sustained, all-powerfully active, ever expanding, and world enfolding until all are wholly ascended in the light and free! Beloved I AM! Beloved I AM! Beloved I AM!

Decree:

Lord Michael

[Repeat the refrain after each verse.]

1. Lord[5] Michael, Lord Michael,
     I call unto thee—
   Wield thy sword of blue flame
     And now cut me free!

Refrain: Blaze God-power, protection
     Now into my world,
   Thy banner of faith
     Above me unfurl!
   Transcendent blue lightning
     Now flash through my soul,
   I AM by God's mercy
     Made radiant and whole!

2. Lord Michael, Lord Michael,
     I love thee, I do—
   With all thy great faith
     My being imbue!

3. Lord Michael, Lord Michael
    And legions of blue—
    Come seal me, now keep me
    Faithful and true!

Coda: I AM with thy blue flame
       Now full-charged and blest,
       I AM now in Michael's
       Blue-flame armor dressed! *(3x)**

*Repeat the coda three times after each recitation
of the entire decree.

And in full faith...

FIATS TO INVOKE IMMEDIATE ASSISTANCE

Angels don't travel, not even by the speed of light. They materialize. You say their name and they are present. To call forth the immediate Presence of Archangel Michael, whether for yourself or to invoke divine intervention into a serious national or global incident, such as an earthquake or a terrorist attack, give one of the following fiats:

**Archangel Michael,
Help Me! Help Me! Help Me!**

Archangel Michael, take command of this situation!

CHAPTER 17

SAINT GERMAIN:
SPONSOR OF THE AQUARIAN AGE

Alchemist and teacher of masters and men, Saint Germain is a master of freedom who teaches us how to liberate our souls and be free from the bondage of the human condition. Saint Germain is also known in the heaven-world as a diplomat, expressing the godly qualities of dignity, grace, gentility, poise and true statesmanship. His name comes from the Latin *Sanctus Germanus,* meaning "Holy Brother."

Saint Germain holds a significant position in this age. Each of the ages is associated with one of the seven rays, or qualities, of God. During the Piscean dispensation, which is associated with the sixth ray of service and ministration, Jesus held the position in heaven's hierarchy as lord of the sixth ray and age.[1] In the Aquarian dispensation, associated with the seventh ray of freedom, Saint Germain holds the position of lord of the seventh ray and age.

Through many of his lifetimes on earth, Saint Germain served to help mankind reclaim their freedom. From the ascended state, he teaches us the science and ritual of alchemy and the art of transmutation through the violet flame by the power of the spoken Word.

THE MASTER OF FREEDOM

Saint Germain is known in heaven as the master alchemist. Alchemy is the "all-chemistry of God," which shows how each facet of creation is brought into manifestation in the material world. It deals with consciously controlling transmutations in matter and energy so that man becomes a co-creator with God.

Alchemy is the science that enables us to access the universal light that is our true heritage. Jesus demonstrated this science at the marriage in Cana of Galilee with his first miracle, when he changed the water into wine.[2] Saint Germain similarly demonstrated his mastery of alchemy when, in his embodiment as le Comte de Saint Germain in the courts of eighteenth- and nineteenth-century Europe, he removed the flaws from diamonds. For both Jesus and Saint Germain, the highest alchemy is the science of *self*-transformation, which leads to the precipitation of the Christ consciousness.

Throughout Saint Germain's incarnations—as ruler, priest, prophet, defender of the Christ, scientist and discoverer—he was engaged in a relentless effort to return souls of light to the worship of their Great God Source and hence to their eternal freedom.

Saint Germain's embodiments[3] span ages of earth's known and forgotten history, going back beyond Lemuria and Atlantis to still older civilizations. He once spoke of the most important choice that he made while incarnated on earth—a choice he urges us to make today:

> I am an ascended being, but it has not ever been thus. Not once or twice but for many incarnations I walked the earth as you now do.... I have seen civilizations rise and fall. I have seen the undulations of consciousness as mankind have cycled from golden ages to primitive societies. I have seen the choices, and I have seen mankind by wrong choices squander the energies of a hundred thousand years of scientific advancement and even degrees of cosmic consciousness that transcend that which is attained by members of the most advanced religions of the day.
>
> Yes, I have seen the choices, and I have chosen. By choosing to be free in the magnificent will of God, I won my freedom from that mortal round of incarnations and justifications of an existence outside the One. I won my freedom by that flame, that keynote of the Aquarian cycle traced by alchemists of old, that purple elixir the saints do hold....
>
> You are mortal. I am immortal. The only difference between us is that I have chosen to be free,

and you have yet to make the choice. We have the same potential, the same resources, the same connection to the One. I have taken mine to forge a God-identity....

I am Saint Germain, and I have come to claim your soul and the fires of your heart for the victory of the Aquarian age....

I have a message.... It is a message of freedom, of opportunity to rise to be what in fact you, as the stars, are ordained to be. I will assist you to implement the divine plan of your life. I will come to you, and I will speak within your heart....

I am on the path of freedom. Take that path, and you will find me there. I am your teacher if you will have me.[4]

THE POWER OF REGENERATION

Just as Jesus stood as the open door to the attainment of the Christ consciousness in the Piscean age, the Aquarian master Saint Germain comes today to initiate us on the path of soul liberation through the sacred fire of the Holy Spirit.

The prayers and practices passed down through the world's many spiritual traditions are sacred formulas for calling forth the light of Spirit. The descent of that Spirit carries a tremendous force of love—a love-action that is transmutative. In other words, when this energy flows through us, it is able to re-create us after the image of the Real Self.

This Spirit, referred to in the scriptures as the Holy Spirit, has the power of regeneration and renewal. The Holy Spirit is the ingredient of life that is the fire of cosmos, the germinal power in nature; it is the power that beats the heart and infuses every form of life with the essence of the Father-Mother God. The Holy Spirit is indigenous to every life manifestation, and without the Holy Spirit there can be no manifestation of life.

The renewing action of the Holy Spirit is a purifying process, a refining action, which must take place if the not-self is to be replaced by the Real Self. As the soul is infilled with the fire of the Holy Spirit, it identifies more and more with the Real Self and hence with all life, thereby coming into that oneness to which Jesus referred when he prayed, "Father, make them one even as we are one."

SOLVING OUR KARMIC DILEMMA

Karma is the great x factor in our spiritual progress. Over many lifetimes, the weight of both personal and planetary karma has taken its toll on mankind and on the earth body. The karma that burdens us and the planet is a complex mixture. On the one hand are the deeds of the fallen angels and those who are committed to evil. On the other are the deeds of the children of God, some of whom have accepted the lies and imitated the lifestyle and ways of the evil ones. Saint Germain is poised to help us solve our karmic dilemmas so we can realize our highest potential. To this end, he has released to us the understanding of the scientific use of the violet flame.

When we invoke the violet flame into our being and world, we transmute energies that we and the fallen angels have collectively misqualified for thousands of years. As that energy is restored, portion by portion, to its native state of purity, we free ourselves and others to walk in the light as God-free beings, and we also cleanse the earth.

The concept of the violet flame may be new to us, but throughout the ages people in deep meditation have seen the violet light and the violet fire. I meet students of the masters who tell me that they saw the violet flame in their inner eye while meditating before they ever heard the teaching on the violet flame. When they learned the teaching, their experience was confirmed.

It wasn't until Saint Germain revealed the violet flame to us in the twentieth century and taught us how to use it for the transmutation of karma that many more have been able to once again tap into its power in a scientific way.

Saint Germain originally released the dispensation of the violet flame through Guy and Edna Ballard, who founded the I AM Activity in 1932. Through that movement, Saint Germain gave to mankind at large the secret of the inner mystery of the Holy Spirit, which before that century had only been taught in the retreats of the Great White Brotherhood.

Saint Germain's hope in releasing the teaching on the violet flame was to provide the people of earth with the necessary impetus and acceleration to bring in the golden age of Aquarius. To this end, his intent is to deliver to all children of light the outer knowledge of the violet flame and its specific application for the transmutation of world karma, including the entire consciousness behind the fallen angels.

With regular use, the violet flame can bring positive change into our lives and transmute the karma that could otherwise result in the darkness prophesied for our time.

Truly, my gift of the violet flame to humanity is the alchemical key to world transformation! Nothing else can compare with it. And I say this unequivocally. For it is indeed the philosopher's stone. And you may use it liberally.... Your application of the violet flame in everything you do can make the difference as to the very survival of the human race.

—Saint Germain

CHAPTER 18

TRANSFORM THE WORLD
WITH VIOLET FLAME

Early alchemists pored over minutely ciphered texts in search of the philosopher's stone, which symbolized the transmutation of the lower animal nature into the highest and divine. Theosophical alchemists held the vision of this "Stone which is no stone," not as a physical object but as a "secret flame," a spiritual fire capable of regenerating mankind spiritually.

Thanks to Saint Germain's sponsorship of the violet flame in our age, the elusive philosopher's stone is within our reach. The violet flame is the key to individual and world transmutation. When it is invoked into action, it brings about change in whatever it contacts.

The violet flame is the aspect of the Holy Spirit that dissolves the delusions of the not-self. It is the fulfillment of the prophecy of God's own law of transmutation: "Though your sins be as scarlet, they shall be as white as snow; though they be red like crimson, they shall be as wool."[1]

Just as a ray of sunlight passing through a prism is refracted into the seven colors of the rainbow, so spiritual light manifests as seven rays, or flames. Each of the seven rays is a concentrated action of the light of God with a specific color and frequency that results in a specific action in body, mind and soul. The energy of the violet flame has the qualities of freedom, mercy, forgiveness and transmutation.

In our physical world, violet light has the shortest wavelength and therefore the highest frequency in the visible spectrum. Thus, in one sense of the word, the violet light can be seen as a point of transition from the visible to the invisible, from one plane of being to the next.

Since frequency is directly proportional to energy, and violet light has the highest frequency in the visible spectrum, the violet light also has the most energy. That means that it also has the greatest ability to change matter at the atomic level.

When you invoke any one of the seven rays in the name of God, it manifests as a nonphysical, or spiritual, flame. (You could compare this to a ray of sunlight that passes through a magnifying glass and creates a flame.) The violet flame is the seventh of these flames.

The function of fire is purification. Physical fire is

merely a stepping down of the sacred fire. That which is achieved by physical fire on the physical plane is achieved by the sacred fire on the emotional, mental and etheric planes.

HOW DOES THE VIOLET FLAME WORK?

Man is a microcosm—a miniature representation of the cosmos. Just as there is vast space between the planets and the sun, so there is vast space between the electrons and the nucleus inside every cell and atom of your body consciousness.

The space between the electron and the fiery nucleus is known as 'virgin' or 'hallowed' space. It is filled with the pulsating energy of the Holy Spirit. This Spirit is the life-essence, the essence of God.

We are constantly using this vital essence that is between the electrons and the nucleus of the atom. And therefore we are constantly qualifying that energy, stamping it with the impressions of our minds and hearts.

Imagine filling that space between the electrons with a sticky molasses-like substance that blocks the flow of light from the Macrocosm of God to the microcosm of man. What happens to the electrons? They slow down, and the light cannot pass through.

That, in effect, is what we have been doing for hundreds of thousands of years. We have been filling the space between the electrons with discord, with negative emotions such as anger, fear, hatred and frustration. Thus, the dense vibrations of misqualified energy collect and clog the very pores of life with that sticky substance, or debris. Essentially, any manifestation of imperfection fills that hallowed space with density—causing mental recalcitrance, hardness of heart and a lack of sensitivity to the needs of others; and creating a dense mass that prevents the soul from receiving the delicate impartations of the Spirit.

That is the basic concept behind where we find ourselves today. The dilemma is, how do we speed up our electrons? This can be done by removing the effluvia in those wide-open spaces. There is only one way to do this, and that is by using the same energies that we have misused—the energies of the Holy Spirit.

When we invoke the violet flame, this accelerated energy envelops each atom individually. Instantaneously, a polarity is set up between the white-fire core of the atom (which, being matter, assumes the negative pole) and the white-fire core of the flame (which, being Spirit, assumes the positive pole). This dual action of the sacred fire in the center of the atom and in the violet flame without establishes a forcefield that causes the untransmuted densities to be dislodged from between the electrons.

As this substance is loosened, the electrons begin to spin more rapidly in their orbits, and by centrifugal force the debris is thrown into the violet flame. On contact with this fiery essence, the misqualified energy is transmuted into its native purity, and we become lighter and lighter in the truest sense of the word. The greater the amount of misqualified substance thrown into the sacred fire, the greater the acceleration of the whirling electrons.

The violet flame does not destroy, for the law is precise: God's energy is neither created nor destroyed. The violet flame *changes* the water into wine. It strips atoms and molecules of the dense overlay of human imperfection and restores the natural divine perfection of the atoms, cells and electrons of the soul.

When we regularly invoke the flame of the Holy Spirit, passing it through our four lower bodies on the command of the Christ Self, things start moving. We become quickened. Light starts flowing through our pores, through our blood; our very organs are transformed; the mental body is quickened; the emotions become the reflecting agents for the energies of God, the desire of God. Our memory may even improve as the etheric body is cleansed of the records of our descent since the Fall. We find that there is an overall step-up in our being.

This is the ascension process that goes on each time the disciple invokes the sacred fire until his whole body is "full of light." But, as Jesus said, the eye must be "single."[2] This means that in order to retain the light he invokes, a person must shed the consciousness of duality, the consciousness of an existence apart from God.

MITIGATING PROPHECY
WITH THE VIOLET FLAME

Since prophecy predicts returning karma, and the violet flame can transmute karma, it follows that the violet flame can alter, mitigate or even entirely turn back prophecy.

You may think that this is impossible, but Jesus said, and I believe it: "With men it is impossible, but not with God: for with God all things are possible."[3] With God we can turn back the unformed before it crystallizes into the formed. Just so, with God we can turn back returning karma before it hits us as tornado, flood or fire; we can invoke the violet fire of the Holy Spirit and direct it through our chakras into vortices of misqualified energy to transmute that returning karma before it manifests.

Therefore it behooves us to act in time and invoke the violet flame to meet the returning karma of prophecy with the all-consuming fire of God and the command to the seven archangels so that God's people might be delivered in this time of trouble.

The astrology for the coming years—the signature of mankind's karma—shows that we can expect momentous changes. The masters tell us that the outcome is up to us: If we do our part, we can see to it that those changes usher in a golden age of peace and enlightenment.

VIOLET-FLAME DECREES

I invite you now to experiment with the violet-flame decrees on the pages that follow, applying the principles of the Science of the Spoken Word that we have discussed.

I AM a Being of Violet Fire!

The affirmation Saint Germain has given us for the Aquarian age is "I AM a being of violet fire! I AM the purity God desires!" Remember, this really means "God in me is a being of violet fire! God in me is the purity God desires!"

You can repeat this affirmation over and over again as a mantra that sings in your heart. As you give it, visualize dancing violet flames saturating the earth body—the cities and their people, the oceans and the forests—and see it consuming negative karma and habit patterns that hinder you or those you pray for. You can create your own variations on this theme wherever you perceive a need, such as:

> I AM a being of violet fire!
> I AM the purity God desires!
>
> My heart is alive with violet fire!
> My heart is the purity God desires!
>
> My family is enfolded in violet fire!
> My family is the purity God desires!
>
> Earth is a planet of violet fire!
> Earth is the purity God desires!

A variation of this short mantra can also be given to help you experience the fullness of the energy of your decrees. Sometimes we may not immediately feel the action of the light that we invoke. This is because our spiritual centers, or chakras, are clogged.

Your chakras are receiving and sending stations for the energy of God that flows to and from you each day. Situated along the spinal column on the etheric level of being, they are invisible to the physical eye, yet your very life and spiritual progress depend on their vitality.

Chakra is a Sanskrit term meaning "wheel" or "disc." Each chakra has a unique function and frequency and represents a different level of consciousness. Unfortunately, throughout our many incarnations we have taken on the energies of the fallen ones through our interactions with them as well as with others, and karmic debris has accumulated around our chakras. This debris is like the leaves that clog up a drain after it has rained. In order for the water to run through the drain properly, you need to clear away the leaves.

In order for God's light to flow through your chakras, you need to clear the effluvia clinging to those sacred centers. When your chakras and the circuits of energy that connect them are clear, you will feel more energetic, positive, joyful and giving. When they are clogged, you will feel sluggish, pessimistic or sick without even knowing why.

Give this simple mantra while visualizing your chakras bathed in violet flame to help purify them:

My chakras are centers of violet fire!
My chakras are the purity God desires!

I AM the Violet Flame

"I AM the Violet Flame" is a powerful mantra. It is short and you can repeat it many times to build a strong momentum of violet flame.

Visualization:

Visualize yourself surrounded by the violet flame as you see it in the Chart of Your Divine Self enfolding the lower figure (shown opposite page 207). See the violet flame come to life as if you were looking at a movie. The flames rise and pulsate around you in different shades and gradations of purple, pink and violet. See these flames pass through your body, caressing each organ and chakra and restoring wholeness. See them saturating your mind and your emotions, relieving all burdens.

One of my favorite visualizations for this decree is to see the seven seas filled with violet flame. Meditate on the power of the seven seas and then translate that thoughtform to a giant, peaceful violet-flame sea that envelops the entire planet. Imagine the weight of it, the power of it, the energy of it! The violet flame has the capacity to totally transform the planetary body.

You can use either of the following preambles before giving violet-flame decrees or use them as the basis for creating your own preambles:

Preamble 1:

In the name of God, I AM THAT I AM, and my own Holy Christ Self, I call to Saint Germain and the violet-flame angels for your divine intercession into the situation of [name any personal or planetary condition]. Release the sacred fire of the violet flame into the cause and core of this condition and the consciousness behind it.

Preamble 2:

In the name of my mighty I AM Presence and Holy Christ Self, I call to Saint Germain and the violet-flame angels for the transmutation of the entire conglomerate of energy behind the fallen angels who refuse to bend the knee and come into alignment with the holy will of God. I call you now to saturate the earth with the violet flame for the awakening of the children of light everywhere, nation by nation. Awaken the hearts where the threefold flame does burn. Awaken them to the manipulation of the fallen angels and the threat to their God-given freedoms.

I ask that these calls be adjusted to the holy will of God.

Decree:

> I AM the violet flame
> In action in me now
> I AM the violet flame
> To light alone I bow
> I AM the violet flame
> In mighty cosmic power
> I AM the light of God
> Shining every hour
> I AM the violet flame
> Blazing like a sun
> I AM God's sacred power
> Freeing every one

More Violet Fire

Visualization:

The decree "More Violet Fire" is known for its rhythm and for the spiraling action of the violet flame that follows the rhythm.

As you give this decree, commune with your I AM Presence. Feel the love of your "lovely God Presence" enfolding you completely as you let go of all anger, worries, concerns and fears.

Visualize a waterfall of light descending from your I AM Presence. See this light being released through your chakras as streams of glistening energy going forth to bless and comfort those for whom you are praying.

See the violet flame dissolving the cause, effect, record and memory of personal and planetary karma. Remember that no problem is too insignificant or too big to tackle with the violet flame.

Decree:

> Lovely God Presence, I AM in me,
> Hear me now I do decree:
> Bring to pass each blessing for which I call
> Upon the Holy Christ Self of each and all!
>
> Let violet fire of freedom roll
> Round the world to make all whole
> Saturate the earth and its people, too,
> With increasing Christ radiance shining through!
>
> I AM this action from God above
> Sustained by the hand of heaven's love,
> Transmuting the causes of discord here,
> Removing the cores so that none do fear.
>
> I AM, I AM, I AM
> The full power of freedom's love
> Raising all earth to heaven above
> Violet fire now blazing bright
> In living beauty is God's own light
>
> Which right now and forever
> Sets the world, myself, and all life
> Eternally free in ascended master perfection!
> Almighty I AM! Almighty I AM! Almighty I AM!

FORGIVENESS DECREES

Practicing forgiveness is an important part of our spiritual path. Since forgiveness is an aspect of the violet flame, we can use violet-flame decrees to help us with this process, which begins with self-forgiveness.

Forgiveness of Self

Understand that if you do not first forgive yourself, you cannot forgive others. And unless you forgive yourself, you cannot be free from the condemnation of the fallen ones. Therefore, you must forgive yourself for accepting their condemnation and internalizing it as self-belittlement, self-condemnation and self-pity. Realize that these are not of your own soul but are projections of the fallen angels and those who have been influenced by them.

Because of this self-condemnation, mankind have a great tendency to harden their hearts, condemning themselves for wrongs that they may have done to others or even to themselves, and imagining that for these reasons God has cast them out and that they are outcasts from the eternal Presence.

If you are in a state of self-condemnation, you have put yourself outside the circle of God. If you have done something that you condemn yourself for, go to your altar and confess it. If you do it again, go back to the altar and confess it again. Get counseling. Look at your psychology, your childhood, your parents, and so forth. Call on the law of forgiveness every time you condemn yourself. Then you will be able to jump right back into the circle of God. God forgives you even before you ask him for forgiveness.

Forgiveness of Others

Forgiveness of ourselves and others is not always easy, but without forgiveness we cannot make spiritual progress. When we refuse to forgive a friend or a supposed enemy who has wronged us, even if he wrongs us again and again, we tie ourselves not only to that person but to his anger or to his other negative states. Therefore, we are not truly free until we resolve that anger and resentment and balance the karma.

There may be times when we feel we cannot forgive someone because we believe the crime that one has committed against us or a loved one has been too great. It can be a very hard thing to forgive certain actions taken by people. It can be hard to forgive a child molester who has taken something of the soul of a child that may not be regained in that life. It can be hard to forgive the murderer, the rapist, the one who sets fire to a house or destroys a business, and so forth.

So what is the anatomy of forgiveness that we can truly follow in good conscience and with profound sincerity and no withholding?

In a situation like this, God has taught me that we should forgive the soul and ask God to bind the not-self, which caused the person to commit the crime. No matter how bad a person's deeds are, we should always forgive the soul, thereby avoiding a karmic entanglement. Hatred binds; love frees.

The Presence of God within us is what allows us to direct God's light through our prayers and to call to God for divine justice, mercy and forgiveness. We do this with absolute peace and God-harmony and then we submit our prayers to the will of God and let go of the matter. We don't have to know the outcome of our prayers. God knows the secrets of all hearts and he is unerring in his judgments.

The soul may be tainted and impure and have all kinds of problems, but that soul still has the potential to one day realize God. Therefore, no matter how bad an action or crime may be, we can still call on the law of forgiveness for that soul.

We can pray for the soul to be taught by God on inner levels and to be liberated from momentums of a wounded psychology and from records of the past that have caused that soul to make the decision to sin. We can give violet-flame mantras and we can call to God for forgiveness and pray for that soul to make a turnaround and to come into the service of God.

Visualization and Meditation:

As you give the "Forgiveness" decree that follows, send your love and forgiveness to all whom you have ever wronged and to all who have ever wronged you, releasing these situations into God's hands.

Decree:

Forgiveness

I AM forgiveness acting here,
Casting out all doubt and fear,
Setting men forever free
With wings of cosmic victory.

I AM calling in full power
For forgiveness every hour;
To all life in every place
I flood forth forgiving grace.

DECREES FOR WORLD FREEDOM AND MERCY

When giving decrees, you can concentrate on urgent conditions in a specific neighborhood, city or nation, an entire continent or the whole earth. You can also pray that the action of the sacred fire invoked by your decrees into a particular condition be multiplied and spread to every corner of the earth.

Keeping abreast of current world, national and local events will allow you to make your prayers specific so that you can direct God's light, according to God's will, into those situations that are most urgent.

Visualization:

Whether you direct the violet flame into a specific problem or throughout the earth, visualize the area being flooded by violet flame to erase all the problems therein.

See angels marching through the streets of the cities or other locations, establishing grids of light that replace the old grids of human karma. See the violet flame enveloping nations and peoples, freeing all from oppression. See the violet flame penetrate deeper and deeper into the earth, transmuting the records of the fallen angels' presence.

Invocation:

In the name of the Presence of God, I AM in me, and my own Holy Christ Self and Holy Christ Selves of all mankind, beloved Saint Germain and your violet-flame angels:

Take command of all terrorism and war, violent crime, child abuse and pornography, and [name urgent conditions]! Flood these situations with the violet flame. Let mercy be amplified throughout the earth. Free the earth and all mankind from oppression and from the burdens of karma. Penetrate the earth to transmute the records of the fallen angels' and their misdeeds. Let it be done according to God's will.

Decree for World Mercy

Flood, flood and flood the world by the power of the sacred fire with enough of the cosmic quality of mercy from the heart of God to saturate the earth and all thereon, including myself, with more mercy than we will ever need until all are wholly ascended and free!

Let this mercy be amplified without limit, expanding its service so as to free all from the power of every recalcitrant substance, thought and manifestation, transmuting all life and changing all into the illumined, invincible power of Christ victory over every negative condition, which automatically raises all men into their own God-given estate and the full victory of the ascension!

Melt, dissolve and transmute daily all hate and hate creation, including the entire accumulation of human discord over the large cities of the world!

Mitigate the effects of mass karma and restrain the reaction thereof by cosmic wisdom and mercy in perfect divine balance as an overcoming victory for all those whose hearts yearn for victory and recognize the power of their Presence to sustain it without limit until all the world is God victorious, illumined, ascended and forever free in the light.

Closing:

And in full faith I consciously accept this manifest, manifest, manifest! *(give three times)* right here and now with full power, eternally sustained, all-powerfully active, ever expanding and world enfolding until all are wholly ascended in the light and free! Beloved I AM! Beloved I AM! Beloved I AM!

CHAPTER 19

MORE DECREES FOR PERSONAL AND PLANETARY CONDITIONS

There are decrees to invoke divine guidance, to ask for healing and wholeness, to overcome ingrained habits, and to increase God's qualities within you. Other decrees invoke heaven's assistance to transcend the not-self, to remove blocks to personal abundance, to heal the economy, to put an end to evil and to restore brotherhood and peace on earth.

Whatever spiritual practice you may already have, you can augment it with decrees and get additional help in any area of your life.

A DECREE FOR THE ECONOMY

Any of the decrees and prayers in this book can be given for the purpose of healing the economy. However, Saint Germain has identified one mantra that we can use specifically for this purpose. "I AM the Light of the Heart" is a mantra that he has offered to us as a gift from his heart. It is easy to memorize and can be used as a perpetual mantra, which, as it flows through your heart and mind, may also flow through the arteries of commerce, business and the international banking houses. With this decree, we empower the angels to work at inner levels to heal the wounds in the economy and the body politic of the nations.

Since Saint Germain sponsors us in the use of the violet flame, we also use this decree to make contact with his heart and to celebrate the divine flame within our own hearts.

I AM the Light of the Heart
by Saint Germain

Visualization:

First, visualize light descending from your I AM Presence and Holy Christ Self over your crystal cord. (See the upper and middle figures depicted in the Chart of Your Divine Self opposite page 207.) See it flowing to your heart chakra, where it will be released according to the worded matrix of your decree.

Next, center your attention on your heart. Visualize it as a dazzling sphere of white light. Picture the brilliance of the sun at noonday and transfer that picture to the center of your chest.

Then visualize the light of God's heart shining through your heart. See thousands of sunbeams going forth from your heart as light rays to penetrate and dissolve any darkness, despair or hopelessness within you or the people of earth.

See yourself projecting your love (which is God's love) out into the cities of the world. See that love as an intense fiery-pink laser beam breaking down all barriers in your life and in the governments and economies of the nations.

Decree:

I AM the Light of the Heart

I AM the light of the heart
Shining in the darkness of being
And changing all into the golden treasury
Of the mind of Christ.

I AM projecting my love out into the world
To erase all errors
And to break down all barriers.
I AM the power of infinite love,
Amplifying itself
Until it is victorious, world without end!

A DECREE FOR JUDGMENT

As explained in chapter 14, the Judgment Call is used to deal with the forces of evil on this planet. It is important to remember that we do not give the Judgment Call to get even with individuals by wishing them harm. Two wrongs do not make a right. We give this call to check the proliferation of evil and the energy behind it and to halt injustices. We give it because without our intense supplications for divine intercession, many innocent souls could become the victims of the greed, lust or hatred of evildoers.

Instruction:

Before you give the Judgment Call, first give the "Tube of Light" decree (page 294) and decrees to Archangel Michael (chapter 16) to establish a strong force-field of protection around yourself. You may also wish to give violet-flame decrees (chapter 18).

Then say a prayer specifically naming the conditions you want halted in answer to this decree, and conclude by submitting the outcome to the will of God. You can repeat this decree over and over again for the binding of fallen angels and the liberation of all people.

The most effective posture for giving this decree is to stand and raise your right hand to shoulder height using the *abhaya mudra* (gesture of fearlessness). The palm is turned outward and the fingers pointed upward. Place your left hand at the center of your chest, where your heart chakra is located. Position your hand with the thumb and first two fingers pointing inward. Center in your heart and feel the intense love of God flowing from your heart.

JESUS THE CHRIST

The Judgment Call
"They Shall Not Pass!"

For the Judgment of the Fallen Angels Who
Have Sworn Enmity against the Children of God

In the name of the I AM THAT I AM,
I invoke the Electronic Presence[1] of Jesus Christ:
They shall not pass!
They shall not pass!
They shall not pass!
By the authority of the cosmic cross
   of white fire it shall be:
That all that is directed against the Christ
   within me, within the holy innocents,
   within our beloved messengers,
   within every son and daughter of God
Is now turned back
   by the authority of Alpha and Omega,
   by the authority of
   my Lord and Saviour Jesus Christ,
   by the authority of Saint Germain!

I AM THAT I AM
   within the center of this temple
   and I declare in the fullness of the entire
   Spirit of the Great White Brotherhood:
That those who, then, practice the black arts
   against the children of light
Are now bound by the hosts of the Lord,
Do now receive the judgment of the Lord Christ

within me, within Jesus
and within every ascended master,
Do now receive, then,
the full return—multiplied
by the energy of the Cosmic Christ—
of their nefarious deeds
which they have practiced
since the very incarnation of the Word!

Lo, I AM a Son of God!
Lo, I AM a flame of God!
Lo, I stand upon the rock of the living Word
And I declare with Jesus, the living Son of God:
They shall not pass!
They shall not pass!
They shall not pass!
Elohim. Elohim. Elohim. *(chant the last line)*

A DECREE TO BIND
THE DWELLER-ON-THE-THRESHOLD

The decree for the binding of the dweller-on-the-threshold is an alchemical formula for casting out the conglomerate of the carnal mind of ourselves and the fallen angels.

If you have not already given the "Tube of Light" decree and decrees to Archangel Michael and to the violet flame in this prayer session, give these at this point so that your aura is sealed in light. Then proceed to give the next decree.

Instruction:

Center in your heart and name those elements of the dweller-on-the-threshold that you want to bind and cast out. You can also name aspects of consciousness that have been sewn into the fabric of society through the consciousness of the fallen angels, such as pride, selfishness, greed, fear, anger, hatred and rebellion.

"I Cast Out the Dweller-on-the-Threshold!"

In the name of my beloved mighty I AM Presence and Holy Christ Self, Archangel Michael and the hosts of the LORD, in the name Jesus Christ, I challenge the personal and planetary dweller on the threshold, and I say:

You have no power over me! *You* may not threaten or mar the face of my God within my soul. *You* may not taunt or tempt me with past or present or future, for I AM hid with Christ in God. I AM his bride. I AM accepted by the LORD.

You have no power to destroy me! Therefore, be *bound!* by the LORD himself.

Your day is *done!* You may no longer inhabit this temple.

In the name I AM THAT I AM, be *bound!* you tempter of my soul. Be *bound!* you point of pride of the original fall of the fallen ones! You have no power, no reality, no worth. You occupy no time or space of my being.

You have no power in my temple. You may no

longer steal the light of my chakras. You may not steal the light of my heart flame or my I AM Presence.

Be *bound!* then, O Serpent and his seed and all implants of the sinister force, for *I AM THAT I AM!*

I AM the Son of God this day, and I occupy this temple fully and wholly until the coming of the LORD, until the New Day, until all be fulfilled, and until this generation of the seed of Serpent pass away.

Burn through, O living Word of God!

By the power of Brahma, Vishnu, and Shiva, in the name Brahman: I AM THAT I AM and I stand and I cast out the dweller.

Let him be bound by the power of the Lord's host! Let him be consigned to the flame of the sacred fire of Alpha and Omega, that that one may not go out to tempt the innocent and the babes in Christ.

Blaze the power of Elohim!

Elohim of God—Elohim of God—Elohim of God

Descend now in answer to my call. As the mandate of the LORD—as Above, so below—occupy now.

Bind the fallen self! *Bind* the synthetic self! Be *out* then!

Bind the fallen one! For there is no more remnant or residue in my life of any, or any part of that one.

Lo, I AM, in Jesus' name, the victor over Death and Hell! (2x)

Lo, *I AM THAT I AM* in me—in the name of Jesus Christ—is *here and now* the victor over Death and Hell!

Lo! it is done.

DECREES TO THE DIVINE MOTHER

In this age of Aquarius, we are meant to express more of the Mother aspect of God. We can enhance this experience by offering prayers and devotions to the Divine Mother. Drawing closer to the energy of the Divine Feminine helps to liberate the creative feminine energy within man and woman—the energy of beauty, creativity, intuition and inspiration.

When we raise the sacred fire of the Mother, we can tap into the power of the Divine Mother to go forth in defense of her children. We can invoke the Mother light to challenge and overcome every abuse and desecration of the bodies of mankind, some of which are outlined in chapter 8 of this book.

The concept of God as Mother is not new to Eastern spirituality. The Hindus who meditate upon the Mother as the Goddess Kundalini describe her as a coiled serpent whose light-energy activates levels of spiritual consciousness in each of the chakras as it rises along the spine from the base to the crown.

Whether we are male or female, we are intended to raise this sacred light of our innermost being that lies dormant within us. The key to unlocking this Kundalini energy is adoration of the Mother principle.

Mother Mary has assured me that the raising of the Kundalini is indeed a part of Western tradition, and this is why she appeared to several of the saints with the safe and sound method of raising the Mother light through the rosary. The saints have been portrayed with a white light, or halo, around their heads because they have raised the Kundalini and opened their crown chakras.[2] They have entered into the bliss of God.

We know that the great mystics East and West (including Ramakrishna, Saint John of the Cross, Saint Thérèse of Lisieux and Padre Pio) have all had this inner experience of being so filled with the divine passion, the bliss of the Beloved, as to defy comprehension.

We can begin to heal the afflictions of this age by cleaving to the Divine Mother through prayer and service. To increase the effectiveness of our prayers, it is helpful to establish a strong tie of devotion to those who have personified the Divine Mother through the centuries—great lights such as Mary the Mother; Kuan Yin, the Bodhisattva of Compassion; and the Hindu goddesses Parvati, Lakshmi, Kali and Durga.

A Miraculous Escape— The Power of the Rosary

In her many appearances throughout the world, the Blessed Mother has stressed over and over again that the rosary is key to bringing about world peace.

One of the most stunning examples of the miraculous power of the rosary is from World War II. When the atomic bomb was dropped on Hiroshima in 1945, about eighty thousand people died instantly. Everyone within a mile radius perished from the searing blast— except eight men who were living near the center of the blinding nuclear flash. Others living farther away continued to die from the lethal effects of the radiation, but not these men.

Since then, some two hundred scientists have examined the eight men, trying in vain to determine what could have saved them from incineration. One of the survivors, Father H. Shiffner, S.J., gave the dramatic answer on American TV: "In that house the rosary was prayed every day. In that house we were living the message of Fátima."[3]

If enough people would give the rosary daily, Mother Mary said, it would "give strength to every heart" and "prevent a great deal of destruction of human life during the days that are ahead." When we give Mary's rosary, we are taking part in step one of her plan to help bring peace to the world.[4]

A New-Age Rosary

In Mary's new-age scriptural rosary, the Hail Mary prayer is different from the traditional Catholic version. She replaced the word "sinners" with "sons and daughters of God" and replaced the words "now and at the hour of our death" with "now and at the hour of our victory over sin, disease and death." She said it was important that we not continually accept the label of "sinner" but affirm our true identity as victorious sons and daughters of God.

Following is the Hail Mary in the new rosary:

Hail Mary

**Hail, Mary, full of grace
the Lord is with thee.
Blessed art thou among women
and blessed is the fruit of thy womb, Jesus.**

**Holy Mary, Mother of God,
Pray for us, sons and daughters of God,
Now and at the hour of our victory
Over sin, disease and death.**

Mother Mary has taught that when we say "Hail, Mary," we are not giving our worship to an image or a person in an idolatrous way; we are saluting the Mother ray, the Ma-ray, which is what the name Mary means. We are giving devotion to the principle of God that is Mother. This principle is universal in all cultures and religions. The acknowledgment of the Mother principle, whether in primitive cultures as a goddess of fertility or in any of her other guises, is fundamental to life, to birth, to crops, and so forth.

So we salute the Mother ray in God, in the universe, in Mother Mary and all lightbearers. We give adoration to the light within each of the saints—the one light that is God—rather than to the personality. Through giving the Hail Mary regularly, we can safely and gently raise the energies of the Kundalini for the unfolding of our soul's full potential. And we can invoke the light of the Mother to defeat the strategies and evil intent of the fallen angels and to defend the people of God on earth.

Prayers for Surrender, Attunement and Peace

Letting your spiritual self do the work is an attitude, a way of life. If something in your life seems too hard to do or you feel yourself dwelling on the past, feeling burdened by world events or worrying about the future, take a step back, consciously turn over the problem to your Higher Self, and let go. Say one of the simple prayers that follow: "Prayer of Surrender," "Prayer for Attunement" or "Affirmations for Peace."

Prayer of Surrender

Beloved Christ Self, enter into my being and act through me this day for the highest good in this situation. Cut me free from all self-limitation, spiritual blindness and unhealthy habits that do not enable me to see you and your will clearly. Amen.

Prayer for Attunement

Beloved mighty I AM Presence, Father of all Life—
    Act on my behalf this day:
Fill my form.
Release the light that is necessary
    For me to go forth to do thy will,
And see that at every hand the decisions I make
    Are according to thy holy will.
See that my energies are used to magnify the LORD
    In everyone whom I meet.

See to it that thy holy wisdom released to me
  Is used constructively for the expansion
  of God's kingdom.
And above all, beloved heavenly Father,
  I commend my spirit unto thee.
And I ask that as thy flame is one with my flame,
  The union of these two flames shall pulsate
To effect in my world
  The continuous alertness and attunement
Which I need with thy holy Presence,
  With the Holy Spirit, and with the World Mother.

Affirmations for Peace

I accept the gift of peace in my heart.
I accept the gift of peace in my soul.
I accept the gift of peace in my mind
  and in my emotions.
I say to all that would tempt me away
  from my center of peace:
  I shall not be moved.
  Peace, be still! Peace, be still!
  Peace, be still!
  I AM the gentle rain of peace.
  I AM a servant of peace.
  I AM sealed in the heart of peace.
  May the world abide
    in an aura of God's peace!

CHAPTER 20

THE COMING GOLDEN AGE: A VISION FOR THE FUTURE

The records of golden-age civilizations have been buried with the continents that sank beneath the Atlantic and Pacific oceans. But these records are not forever lost. They remain as impressions upon the ethers, upon that substance and dimension known as *akasha*.[1] Therefore they can still be read and studied by those with heightened soul sensitivity.

While all that remains accessible to our waking consciousness is a misty concept or dream of a golden age, these memories are impressed deep within the subconscious recesses of our mind. Historians may count as mere fairy tale, legend or mythology these soul memories of earth's early, early history before the Fall of man. But our souls know the truth, and so we yearn for that ideal which can be and should be.

Through the ages, men of extraordinary vision have tapped into the etheric recordings and have inspired us through their writings. Among these visionaries are Plato, Thomas More and Francis Bacon, who dreamed that a more perfect society was possible.

The commandment of Jesus "Be ye therefore perfect, even as your Father which is in heaven is perfect"[2] applies to nations as well as to individuals. The attainment of God-perfection is possible because perfection is the natural estate of man toward which the soul gravitates and because it has been attained before.

As has been stated earlier, the Fall of man was the descent in mankind of the feminine principle. Prior to the descent of that energy, before the subjugation of the feminine aspect of man and woman, there existed a fusion of the Macrocosm of God and the microcosm of mankind, a fusion of the Divine Masculine and the Divine Feminine principles in mankind. And because this state of oneness and harmony existed during prior periods of man's history, we have the continuing dream and the striving for its realization once again.

The members of the first three root races were the first to walk upon the virgin soil of earth. They never knew the feeling of limitation or struggle or even the burden of a dense, physical form such as we now wear. The powers they wielded would be considered miraculous by those whose memory scans only the relatively short period in which earth has been immersed in a synthetic civilization and consciousness.

Those early souls came forth from God having transparent bodies of light, and they sustained life in one body for as long as a thousand years. When they reembodied, they retained the memory, faculties and mastery they had attained in former lives.

Mark Prophet read the akashic record of those early golden ages and shared his vision. It is a vision of what can take place again on earth:

The entire planet was a veritable Garden of Eden, and man ate every fruit and herb that was charged by Nature's helpers with the essence of the immortal Spirit to energize and revivify his mind and form. The ground was transparent like crystal, and the rays from the sun in the center of the earth glowed softly beneath man's feet.

The total absence of evil within these early golden-age civilizations did not lessen the variety and spice of life. On the contrary, the activities and creative opportunities of these evolutions were heightened by the infinite manifestations of Truth and the unlimited potential for its expression in science, art, architecture, devotional worship of the Godhead, and sacred communion between man and nature—all inherent within the divine consciousness to which all had direct access.

During the period of rest, when the souls of men, together with their lower vehicles, were recharged for another round of service, there was an ever-present radiance from the white-fire core like an aurora borealis. Thus, total darkness was unknown, and evil as the energy veil was no more real than a fairy tale. To the Almighty, man gave the glory for each accomplishment.

The focus of man's adoration was the Sun behind the sun that ruled the day, the symbol of the unfoldment of the only begotten Son of God, whose promise would be fulfilled in each one. The stars defined intervals of time and space and were the giant reflectors of man's blissful adoration of the One Supreme Being. These crystal coordinates marked man's courses—past, present and future— and magnified his mystical feelings of heavenly joy, which rippled across the web of life, the *antahkarana* of cosmos.[3]

A NEW HEAVEN AND A NEW EARTH

A golden age on earth is indeed a present possibility, but a prerequisite for its coming is the final judgment of the fallen ones. This requirement that the Watchers come to naught and that the Nephilim be judged, along with their offspring and their giants, is made clear in the pronouncements of the LORD God recorded in the annals of Enoch and in the Bible.

Saint John's vision of "a new heaven and a new earth" to come after the final judgment of the seed of the wicked is recorded in Chapter 21 of the Book of Revelation:

And I John saw the holy city, new Jerusalem, coming down from God out of heaven, prepared as a bride adorned for her husband.

And I heard a great voice out of heaven saying, Behold, the tabernacle of God is with men, and he will dwell with them, and they shall be his people, and God himself shall be with them, and be their God.

And God shall wipe away all tears from their eyes; and there shall be no more death, neither sorrow, nor crying, neither shall there be any more pain: for the former things are passed away.

And he that sat upon the throne said, Behold, I make all things new. And he said unto me, Write: for these words are true and faithful.

And he said unto me, It is done. I am Alpha and Omega, the beginning and the end. I will give unto him that is athirst of the fountain of the water of life freely.

He that overcometh shall inherit all things; and I will be his God, and he shall be my son....

John described a jeweled, golden city, where only the light of God prevails:

And there came unto me one of the seven angels....

And he carried me away in the spirit to a great and high mountain, and shewed me that great city, the holy Jerusalem, descending out of heaven from God,

Having the glory of God: and her light was like unto a stone most precious, even like a jasper stone, clear as crystal;...

And the building of the wall of it was of jasper: and the city was pure gold, like unto clear glass.

And the foundations of the wall of the city were garnished with all manner of precious stones. The first foundation was jasper; the second, sapphire; the third, a chalcedony; the fourth, an emerald;

The fifth, sardonyx; the sixth, sardius; the seventh, chrysolyte; the eighth, beryl; the ninth, a topaz; the tenth, a chrysoprasus; the eleventh, a jacinth; the twelfth, an amethyst.

And the twelve gates were twelve pearls: every several gate was of one pearl: and the street of the city was pure gold, as it were transparent glass.

And I saw no temple therein: for the Lord God Almighty and the Lamb [the Christ] are the temple of it.

And the city had no need of the sun, neither of the moon, to shine in it: for the glory of God did lighten it, and the Lamb [the Christ] is the light thereof.

And the nations of them which are saved shall walk in the light of it: and the kings of the earth do bring their glory and honour into it.

And the gates of it shall not be shut at all by day: for there shall be no night there.

And they shall bring the glory and honour of the nations into it.

And there shall in no wise enter into [the city] any thing that defileth, neither whatsoever worketh abomination, or maketh a lie: but they which are written in the Lamb's book of life.[4]

Thus Saint John assures us that to see the end of the era of the seed of the wicked is to behold the dawn of a golden age.

ACCELERATION IS THE REQUIREMENT

Moving into a golden age will require an acceleration of consciousness in the people and therefore the elimination of the consciousness of the fallen angels. Archangel Uriel, the servant of the LORD who leads the seed of the wicked to the judgment seat, explains:

When the fallen angels are brought to the judgment, even as the tares are separated from the wheat…, there is the hand of God…lowered, symbolically, and there is the acceleration of the very vibrations of the earth. And there is the catching up of the children of God in a mighty rapture, for they are rapturous in the new wave of light and the new vibration of the light.

The rapture is the descent of the Christ into the temple of his people, thereby accelerating their vibration [so] that they no longer see death[5] because they no longer wear bodies subject unto the laws of mortality and death. And there is a planetary

ARCHANGEL URIEL WITH THE FALLEN SATAN

raising by the power of the resurrection, even by
the mighty power of the archangels who stand as
coordinates in the earth.... And there is a sacred
fire. And you will see that all of the pollutions of
the earth and the rivers and the waters and the atmosphere and the earth body are accelerated and
purity is restored.

And therefore the golden age...will come in the wavelength and vibration that is not in this dense plane but accelerated from it. All those who are of the light will be found together in that rapture of union with the beloved Christ Self. And all who have received him as the God of very gods within the temple are fused by the Holy Spirit and know themselves forever and forever as one [in the Christ consciousness]....

...There is the period before the judgment of the angels who fell and the period after the judgment of the fallen angels. These periods are known in heaven as the dark ages preceding the great golden age, which cannot manifest upon earth except the judgment come.

Therefore understand the meaning of the acceleration of light. Understand the new light within your body and soul. Understand that this people must rise unto the holy mountain of God and... come apart from the world that is yet controlled by the fallen angels.[6]

THE OPPORTUNITY AT HAND

Consider the principle of the mist and the crystal. The mist is the unformed, the uncongealed. It is the energy of returning karma that is not yet clothed with physical form. Before it crystallizes, the mist can be read and known as a karmic record of nonresolution whose time has not yet run its course. When all the sand has fallen in the hourglass and the resolution does come, we say the mist has become the crystal.

Therefore, time and space grant us the option to balance karma before that karma falls due—to pay off the mortgage, so to speak, before the bill collector takes our farm, our business or our house. And that is precisely what being in embodiment on planet earth is all about. We have a window of opportunity to undo the unrighteous deeds we have done and the records of unrighteousness in the planet, an opportunity to do righteous deeds in their place and to implore the merciful intercession of the Almighty.

Oneness with God is the key to the victory of an age. If billions of people upon earth could understand this and know just how near and dear God is to us and we are to him, there would not be the threatening of cataclysm and of great planetary upheaval and terrible things coming upon us at the end of this age.

In meditation one day I was looking at the problems of the earth and I saw the soul of humanity as being on a clipper ship. Very clearly I saw this ship passing through a narrow channel with high mountains on both sides, like a fjord. The waters were choppy and the sides of the ship had to be carefully guided to avoid a crash on either side. (I took this to symbolize the extremes of left and right in the world scene.) I saw the ship guided by the hand of God. Responsible individuals took the helm and I saw the ship pass safely through that narrow way. And finally I saw, at the very far, far end, miles down, the opening and the great light of the sun shining on the golden sea.

I share this vision with you and I invite you to pray. I invite you to use prayer as the great guiding force in your life. I believe that if we will invoke the violet flame for the transmutation of the negative records in the earth and in our souls and subconscious, then God will mitigate the dark prophecies.

I am supremely confident that God has placed within us the natural resources and the spiritual resources to meet all of these problems. I believe that the very prophecy I bring is this: If we the people of God have the truth about what we are facing on planet earth today, and if we embrace our ability and opportunity to contact God through the Science of the Spoken Word and heartfelt prayer, then and only then, by God's grace, we *can* change the course of history.

NOTES

Prelude *One of Those Great Moments…*

1. Lemuria, or Mu, was the lost continent of the Pacific which, according to the findings of James Churchward, archaeologist and author of *The Lost Continent of Mu,* extended from north of Hawaii three thousand miles south to Easter Island and the Fijis and was made up of three areas of land stretching more than five thousand miles from east to west. Churchward's history of the ancient Motherland is based on records inscribed on sacred tablets he claims to have discovered in India. With the help of the high priest of an Indian temple he deciphered the tablets, and during fifty years of research confirmed their contents in further writings, inscriptions and legends he came upon in Southeast Asia, the Yucatan, Central America, the Pacific Islands, Mexico, North America, ancient Egypt and other civilizations. He estimates that Mu was destroyed

Unless otherwise noted, books and other products cited in these notes are published by or available from Summit University Press.

approximately 12,000 years ago by the collapse of the gas chambers which upheld the continent.

Atlantis was the island continent that existed where the Atlantic Ocean now is and that sank in cataclysm (the Flood of Noah) approximately 11,600 years ago as calculated by Churchward. The lost continent was vividly depicted by Plato, "seen" and described by Edgar Cayce in his readings, recalled in scenes from Taylor Caldwell's *Romance of Atlantis,* and scientifically explored and authenticated by the late German scientist Otto Muck. In his dialogues, Plato recounts that on "the island of Atlantis there was a great and wonderful empire" that ruled Africa as far as Egypt, Europe as far as Italy, and "parts of the continent" (thought to be a reference to America, specifically Central America, Peru and the Valley of the Mississippi). It has been postulated that Atlantis and the small islands to its east and west formed a continuous bridge of land from America to Europe and Africa.

See James Churchward, *The Lost Continent of Mu* (1931; reprint, New York: Paperback Library Edition, 1968); Otto Muck, *The Secret of Atlantis* (New York: Pocket Books, 1979); Ignatius Donnelly, *Atlantis: The Antediluvian World* (New York: Dover Publications, 1976); Phylos the Thibetan, *A Dweller on Two Planets* (Los Angeles: Borden Publishing Co., 1952).

2. See *The Opus Majus of Roger Bacon,* trans. Robert Belle Burke, vol. 1 (Philadelphia: University of

Pennsylvania Press, 1928), pp. 400–401.

3. George Santayana, *Reason in Common Sense,* vol. 1 of The Life of Reason (1905; reprint, New York: Dover Publications, 1980), p. 284.

Chapter 1   THE FORBIDDEN MYSTERIES OF ENOCH:
The Untold Story of Men and Angels

1. Isa. 14:12–15; Luke 10:18; Rev. 12:7–9.

2. Gen. 32:24–26; Hos. 12:4.

3. Gen. 19:1–11.

4. Judg. 13:2–21.

5. Franz Delitzsch, *A New Commentary on Genesis,* trans. Sophia Taylor, 2 vols. (Edinburgh: T. & T. Clark, 1888), 1:225.

6. Filastrius, *Liber de Haeresibus,* no. 108.

7. Delitzsch, *New Commentary on Genesis,* p. 223.

8. Dr. Laurence's translation (1883 edition), updated with new explanatory footnotes, was reprinted in Elizabeth Clare Prophet's *Fallen Angels and the Origins of Evil.*

9. En. 10:15. I believe that the seventy generations have long passed and that this is the era of judgment. The offspring of the Watchers are unbound and have been loosed on the earth for the final testing of the souls of light.

10. R. H. Charles, ed. and trans., *The Book of Enoch* (Oxford: Clarendon Press, 1893), pp. 148–50.

11. En. 15:8.

12. Zohar 1:55a–55b.

13. See "Concealed References to the Watchers (and Nephilim) in Scripture," p. 297 in Elizabeth Clare Prophet's *Fallen Angels and the Origins of Evil.*

14. Matt. 5:5.

15. Matt. 26:24.

16. En. 38:2.

17. Luke 6:24.

18. En. 93:7.

19. Jude 4, 12, 13.

20. Jude 14, 15.

21. Eph. 3:16; Col. 1:27.

22. From the Greek *ho eklelegmenos,* lit., "the elect one."

23. Charles Francis Potter, *The Lost Years of Jesus Revealed,* rev. ed. (Greenwich, Conn.: Fawcett, 1962), p. 97.

24. Sons of Belial: the seed of the fallen angel Belial who sought to supplant the seed of Christ at every hand. In the Old Testament, *belial* is usually interpreted as a common noun meaning worthlessness, ungodliness, or wickedness. In II Cor. 6:15, Belial is used as a proper name for a prince of demons. Some Jewish apocryphal works make Belial synonymous with Satan and he is described in Milton's *Paradise Lost* as one of the fallen angels.

25. En. 54:5.

26. John 12:31. See *The Scofield Reference Bible* (New York: Oxford University Press, 1945), p. 1133, marginal notation d.

27. Matt. 5:28.

28. We each have four lower bodies that are envelopes of our soul. The soul uses these bodies as vehicles to progress spiritually: (1) the physical body, which we can see and touch; (2) the desire, or astral, body, which contains our emotions; (3) the mental body, which is our conscious mind; and (4) the etheric, or memory, body, which contains the memories of all of our past lives.

29. Isa. 14:16–19.

30. Unless it is uncovered that etymologically the term "man" was applied in certain instances to other than earthlings (i.e., to extraterrestrials or the Nephilim) the application of "man" to Lucifer gives strong indication that Isaiah believed that the "cast down one" was embodied as a mortal man.

31. Cyprian, "The Treatises of Cyprian," *Ante-Nicene Fathers,* 5:556; Aphrahat, "Select Demonstrations," in *Gregory the Great, Ephraim Syrus, Aphrahat,* ed. James Barmby and John Gwynn, *A Select Library of Nicene and Post-Nicene Fathers of the Christian Church,* ed. Philip Schaff and Henry Wace, 2d ser., 14 vols. to date (1890–1899; reprint ed., Grand Rapids, Mich.: Wm. B. Eerdmans, 1979–), 13 (1898): 353.

32. Some copies of the Greek Septuagint translated the Hebrew words "sons of God" (Gen. 6:2) as "angels of God." See Charles, *Book of Enoch,* p. 62.

33. Bernard Jacob Bamberger, *Fallen Angels* (Philadelphia: Jewish Publication Society of America, 1962), pp. 78–79; Julius Africanus, "The Extant Fragments…of the Chronography of Julius Africanus," *Ante-Nicene Fathers,* 6:131.

34. Jude 6.

35. J. H. Kurtz, *History of the Old Covenant* (Edinburgh: T. & T. Clark, 1859), 1:98. See also Job 1:6; 2:1; and the commentaries on 1:6 in the *Jerusalem Bible* and the *Ryrie Study Bible.* Cp. Pss. 29:1; 82:1; 89:6. The "sons of God" in Deut. 32:8 *(Jerusalem Bible)* are in most cases understood by scholars to be angels—specifically, the guardian angels assigned to the nations. One theory has it that the Massoretic scribes of the sixth to tenth centuries thought that this idea might lead to the worship of these guardian angels, and therefore they changed the original Hebrew words "sons of God" (which they knew to mean "angels") to "children of Israel"— which then found its way into the King James Version of the Bible. Pre-Massoretic manuscripts recently discovered prove that "sons of God" was the original term in the Hebrew Scripture.

It ought to be considered that the term "sons of God" might have originally referred to sons of God in heaven, Christed ones of whom Jesus was one. Some of these sons of God might have fallen, out of the misplaced ambition to create on earth by their Christic seed a super race who could lead mere earthlings or the creation of the Nephilim on the paths of righteousness and to ultimate reunion with God. Though well-intended in their desire to upgrade the evolutions of the planet, these sons of God might not have had the divine approbation. Therefore the Watchers, once fallen and judged as unworthy of the ascent to God, having lost the sacred fire of their original anointing, would have determined in any case to dominate the scene of earth life with their superior intellect and overwhelming presence yet residual from their lost estate. If in fact the Watchers were the fallen sons of God and the Nephilim the fallen angels, we can understand both the difference of their modus operandi and reason for being and the dissimilarity of their natures which remains observable to the present.

The doctrine of the only begotten Son of God having been misconstrued to designate one son only, namely Jesus, the Anointed, would of course make this theory preposterous to today's Christian. However, when correctly understood, the Christ, "the only begotten Son of God," is revealed to the soul by the Holy Spirit to be the true Self of every son of God, "the Light which lighteth [ignites the divine spark in] every man that cometh into the world." Christ, the Light, the Word, is therefore an office and a mantle which the son of God by the Father's grace may 'put on' and 'become', fully integrating with and assimilating the only begotten of God until he does embody or incarnate that Christ—i.e., that Christ flame or Christ consciousness which Jesus as the embodiment of the Son of God had the power to ignite, as John writes: "As many as received him, to them gave he power to become the sons* of God, even to them that believe on his name: which were born, not of blood, nor of the will of the flesh, nor of the will of man, but of God" (John 1:12–13).

I believe that John and Paul both received this teaching from Jesus. For John also says, "Beloved, now are we the sons* of God, and it doth not yet appear what we shall be: but we know that, when he shall appear, we shall be like him; for we shall see him as he is. And every man that hath this hope in him purifieth himself, even as he is pure" (I John 3:2–3).

Paul, who was taught directly by Jesus Christ from higher planes, mentions the oneness of Christ as well as the "inner man" in several key passages: "To be strengthened with might by his Spirit in the inner man; that Christ may dwell in your hearts" (Eph. 3:16–17). "Because ye are sons, God hath sent forth the Spirit of his Son into your hearts, crying, Abba, Father. Wherefore thou art no more a servant, but a son; and if a son, then an heir of God through Christ" (Gal. 4:6–7). "I live; yet not I, but Christ liveth in me" (Gal. 2:20). "God would make

---

*Gk *tekna*, "children" or "offspring."

known what is the riches of the glory of this mystery among the Gentiles; which is Christ in you, the hope of glory" (Col. 1:27). "For as many as are led by the Spirit of God, they are the sons of God. For ye have not received the spirit of bondage again to fear; but ye have received the Spirit of adoption, whereby we cry, Abba, Father. The Spirit itself beareth witness with our spirit, that we are the children of God: and if children, then heirs; heirs of God, and joint heirs with Christ; if so be that we suffer with him, that we may be also glorified together.... For the earnest expectation of the creature waiteth for the manifestation of the sons of God" (Rom. 8:14–17, 19). "That ye may be blameless and harmless, the sons* of God, without rebuke, in the midst of a crooked and perverse nation, among whom ye shine as lights in the world" (Phil. 2:15).

Although the Bible speaks distinctly of sons of God in heaven and angels in heaven, it seems that the distinction between these two types of spiritual beings holding two distinct types of heavenly offices has been lost to the understanding of the children of God on earth. It seems that the term "son of God" designates one of greater light and attainment, who had been crowned with more glory and honor than that bestowed upon the angels, but who must yet grow into the fullness of the stature of the one Jesus Christ chosen by the Father to be the incarnate Word, nourisher of our souls.

---

*Gk. *tekna*, "children" or "offspring."

36. Bamberger, *Fallen Angels,* p. 79.

37. J. T. Milik, ed. and trans., *The Books of Enoch: Aramaic Fragments of Qumran Cave 4* (Oxford: Clarendon Press, 1976).

38. Ibid., p. 31.

39. Ibid.

40. Julian Morgenstern, "The Mythological Background of Psalm 82," *Hebrew Union College Annual* 14 (1939): 106.

41. Ibid., pp. 106–7.

42. *Jerusalem Bible.*

43. Morgenstern, "Mythological Background of Psalm 82," p. 107.

44. Ibid., p. 82.

45. Paul D. Hanson, "Rebellion in Heaven, Azazel, and Euhemeristic Heroes in 1 Enoch 6–11," *Journal of Biblical Literature* 96, no. 2 (1977): 218.

Chapter 2   THE FALL OF LUCIFER, OF MAN AND THE COMING OF THE LAGGARDS

1. Gospel of Bartholomew 4:54, in *The Apocryphal New Testament,* trans. M. R. James (Oxford: Clarendon Press, 1924), at www.gnosis.org/library/gosbart.htm

2. See Heb. 9:23.

3. Gen. 2:17.

4. See Rev. 20:14; 21:8. See also Ezek. 18:4, 20.

5. Gen. 4:2–8.

6. Gen. 4:22.

7. Gen. 4:26.

8. The Second Book of Adam and Eve, chaps. 19–22, in *The Lost Books of the Bible and the Forgotten Books of Eden* (New York: New American Library, Meridian Book, 1974). Also published in Elizabeth Clare Prophet's *Fallen Angels and the Origins of Evil*, pp. 395–407.

9. Sons of God, men or angels. See notes to chapter 1, n. 35.

10. Deut. 7:1–3.

11. Prior to the sinking of Atlantis, while Noah was yet building his ark and warning the people of the great Flood to come, the Master R (the R signifying Rakoczy) called Saint Germain and a few faithful priests to transport the flame of freedom to a place of safety in the Carpathian foothills in what is now Romania. Here they carried on the sacred ritual of expanding the fires of freedom even while mankind's karma was being exacted by divine decree. In succeeding embodiments, Saint Germain and his followers, under the guidance of the Master R, continued to guard the shrine. Later, the Master R, assisted by Saint Germain, established a spiritual retreat at the site of the flame and founded the royal House of Rakoczy. The retreat, once physical, is now in the etheric plane.

12. Mark L. Prophet, *The Soulless One: Cloning a Counterfeit Creation*, pp. 95–96, 99.

13. Matt. 13:24–30, 36–43.

14. John 8:44.

15. Eph. 6:12.

16. Mark L. Prophet, *Soulless One,* pp. 96, 98.

Chapter 3 STRATEGIES, TACTICS AND
              LIES OF THE FALLEN ANGELS

1. Matt. 10:16.

2. The term 'Son of man' (with a capital *S*), which
   Jesus used in reference to his own mission, defines
   the soul who has descended from the I AM Presence as the Son of God (see pp. 205–7). Integrated
   with the Christ Self, this soul is now archetypically
   the presence of the universal soul of humanity. As
   in the life of Jesus, the Christ (Light) of the one
   becomes the Christ (Light) for all. And the Son of
   man is perpetually one with and representing the
   Holy Christ Self of all souls evolving on earth.

       The term 'son of man' (with a lowercase *s*) is
   applied to all souls who embody with the mission of
   bearing the Light, balancing their karma, fulfilling
   their divine plan, and returning to God in the ritual
   of the ascension. The term 'son of man' indicates
   that the potential exists for Divine Sonship through
   the path of personal Christhood—putting on day
   by day the garment of one's Lord.

3. Rev. 12:12.

4. I Sam. 17:4–50.

5. Gen. 11:1–9.

6. Gen. 11:8.

7. Rev. 12:14; Dan. 7:25; 12:7.

8. John 1:9.

9. Quoted in Mark L. Prophet and Elizabeth Clare Prophet, *The Path of the Higher Self,* pp. 105–6.

10. Rev. 12:10.

11. John 14:12.

12. Sons and Daughters of God. Until we become the Christ, we are sons and daughters of God with a lowercase *s* and a lowercase *d*. As we increase in Christhood, so we may come to the point where we can be called a Son or a Daughter of God with a capital *S* or a capital *D*. Sons and Daughters of God with a capital S and a capital D have become the Christ. Jesus is the Son of God with a capital S and he is the full incarnation of the Christ, the full incarnation of the Word. We are not equal to Jesus Christ because we do not have the full attainment that he has. But we have the potential and the seed of light within us whereby God expects us to follow in the footsteps of Jesus Christ.

13. John 1:9.

14. See John 14:23.

15. The nine gifts of the Spirit are (1) the word of wisdom, (2) the word of knowledge, (3) faith, (4) healing, (5) the working of miracles, (6) prophecy, (7) the discerning of spirits, (8) divers kinds of tongues, (9) the interpretation of tongues. (See I Cor. 12:1, 4–11.)

16. Saint Augustine (A.D. 354–430), bishop and early Church Father. Early theologians had toyed with the idea that man's wretched state of affairs is somehow related to the Fall of Adam and Eve in the Garden. But it was Saint Augustine who fashioned this notion into what remains a cornerstone of Christian theology—original sin. Augustine argued that bad things happen to good people because all people are bad by nature, and the only chance for them to overcome this natural wickedness is to access God's grace through the Church. As Augustine wrote, "No one will be good who was not first of all wicked" (*City of God* 15.1, in *Nicene and Post-Nicene Fathers,* 1st ser., 2:285.).

17. Ps. 51:5.

18. Rom. 8:17.

Chapter 4   THE TARES AMONG THE WHEAT

1. The archives of the Great White Brotherhood are housed in the heaven-world. These records contain the true history of the earth, of the solar system, of the galaxy, and of the universe. Events that are unknown and unchronicled in the annals of men, but which must be known, are recorded so that the children of God can fulfill their destiny in this age.

2. John 3:3.

3. John 3:13.

4. John 8:23.

5. En. 14:4; 12:7; 13:1.

6. Matt. 23:27.

7. Erich Fromm, *The Heart of Man* (New York: Harper and Row, 1964), p. 40.

8. Matt. 13:24–30.

9. Matt. 7:1; Luke 6:37.

10. I John 4:1.

11. The Real Self is also known as the Higher Self, the part of us that is identified with God. It is the immortal Spirit that is the animating principle of all manifestation. See also chapter 11.

12. Mark 4:25; Matt. 13:12; 25:29; Luke 8:18; 19:26.

13. Ps. 94:3.

14. John 9:39.

PART 2 INTRODUCTION: *Amassing Power and Control*

1. Chakra: (Sanskrit, "wheel," "disc," "circle.") The chakras are the spiritual energy centers in man. The seven major chakras are positioned along the spinal column from the base of the spine to the crown (see pp. 324–25). They are internal step-down transformers that regulate God's energy according to the needs of our four lower bodies.

Chapter 5 GLOBAL ECONOMIC MANIPULATION

1. William Rees-Mogg, *The Reigning Error: The Crisis of World Inflation* (n.p.: Hamilton, 1974), p. 66. See also David Hackett Fischer, *The Great Wave: Price Revolutions and the Rhythm of History* (New York: Oxford University Press, 1999).

2. *Pearls of Wisdom,* vol. 23, no. 7. Although Saint Germain gave this dictation in 1980 and was referring to the United States, his words are equally relevant to the economic conditions in many nations today, thirty years later. All quotations from Saint Germain in this chapter are from this source.

3. Sacred labor. That particular calling, livelihood or profession whereby one establishes his soul's worth both to himself and to his fellowman. One perfects his sacred labor by developing his God-given talents as well as the gifts and graces of the Holy Spirit and using them in service to humanity. The sacred labor is not only one's contribution to one's community but it is also an indispensable component of the path to reunion with God through the giving of oneself in practical living for God.

4. Gal. 6:7, 8.

5. *Pearls of Wisdom,* vol. 31, no. 3.

6. Encyclopaedia Britannica, Macropaedia, 15th ed., s.v. "Fugger Family."

7. The embedding of subliminal messages in advertising has been analyzed in three books by Wilson Bryan Key: *Subliminal Seduction: Ad Media's Manipulation of a Not So Innocent America, Media Sexploitation* and *The Clam-Plate Orgy* (New York: New American Library, 1973, 1976, 1980).

8. Gen. 3:4.

Chapter 6   INTERNATIONAL TERRORISM AND ANARCHY

1. Rom. 3:8.

Chapter 7   GENETIC MANIPULATION

1. Akashic records. The impressions of all that has ever transpired in the physical universe is recorded in a substance and dimension known as akasha (Sanskrit, from the root *kās* "to be visible, appear," "to shine brightly," "to see clearly"). Akasha is primary substance, the subtlest, ethereal essence that fills the whole of space; "etheric" energy vibrating at a certain frequency so as to absorb, or record, all of the impressions of life. These records can be read by adepts and those whose soul (psychic) faculties are developed.

2. Edgar Evans Cayce, *Edgar Cayce on Atlantis,* ed. Hugh Lynn Cayce (New York: Warner Books, 1968), pp. 71–72.

3. Ibid., pp. 60, 69.

4. Brad Steiger, *Atlantis Rising* (New York: Dell Publishing Co., 1973), p. 63.

5. Gen. 1:11, 12.

6. Gen. 6:4.

7. Golem (Hebrew for embryonic or incompletely developed substance, shapeless matter): In Jewish folklore, a robotlike servant made of clay and brought to life by pronouncing the sacred name of God over its form, writing God's name on a piece of paper

and putting it in the golem's mouth, or inscribing the word for truth *(emeth)* on its forehead. If the paper or inscription were removed, the golem would be reduced to a pile of clay. In medieval times, the belief in the creation of golems was common and was attributed to various rabbis throughout Europe.

The most famous golem legend, which has several different variations and has inspired novelists and playwrights, is that of Rabbi Judah Loew (or Löw) of Prague (c. 1520–1609), a historical figure who was a practitioner of the Kabbalah and a Talmudic scholar. He is said to have created a clay man and endowed him with life in order to defend the Jews of Prague from superstitious Christians who accused them of using the blood of Christian babies to bake their matzohs (unleavened bread). The golem served as the rabbi's agent and successfully apprehended those who were spreading the false rumor. He would perform tasks for Rabbi Loew during the week, and every Friday evening the rabbi would turn him back into a heap of clay by removing the inscription from his forehead, because all creatures are supposed to rest on the Sabbath (or, as another version of the legend goes, because the rabbi feared that the golem would profane the Sabbath).

One Friday, however, the rabbi forgot to do this and the golem turned into a dangerous wildman just before the Sabbath began. Rabbi Loew pursued and finally caught up to his golem run amok, tore from his forehead the sacred name of God, and never brought him back to life again. Rabbi Loew's story was the basis for Gustav Meyrink's famous novel *Der Golem* (1915); a German silent film based on Meyrink's novel (1920), which served as an archetype for later films on the Frankenstein theme; and the play by H. Leivick, *The Golem: A Dramatic Poem in Eight Scenes* (1921). See Isaac Bashevis Singer, "The Golem Is a Myth for Our Time," *New York Times*, 12 August 1984; Arnold L. Goldsmith, *The Golem Remembered, 1909–1980: Variations of a Jewish Legend* (Detroit: Wayne State University Press, 1981), pp. 15–20; Gershom Scholem, *On the Kabbalah and Its Symbolism*, trans. Ralph Manheim (New York: Schocken Books, 1969), pp. 180, 199, 202–3; The Universal Jewish Encyclopedia, s.v. "Golem."

Chapter 8   DESECRATION OF THE CULTURE OF THE MOTHER

1. I Cor. 3:16.

2. Kabir, quoted in Swami Prabhavananda and Christopher Isherwood, trans., *How to Know God* (Hollywood, Calif.: Vedanta Press, 1981), p. 158.

3. Rev. 12:3–6, 13, 15–17.

4. *Pearls of Wisdom,* vol. 17, no. 5.

5. The Lords of Karma dispense justice to earth, adjudicating karma, mercy and judgment on behalf of every soul. All souls must pass before the Karmic Board before and after each incarnation, receiving their assignment and karmic allotment for each life-

time beforehand and the review of their performance at its conclusion. The Lords of Karma have access to the complete records of every soul's incarnations on earth. They determine who shall embody, as well as when and where. They assign souls to families and communities, taking into consideration the karma that must be balanced. The Karmic Board, acting in consonance with the individual's Higher Self, determines when the soul has earned the right to be free from the wheel of karma and the round of rebirth.

6. As recorded in *The Forgotten Books of Eden,* the children of Jared (descendants of Seth) were lured down the Holy Mountain of God by the children of Cain, who committed all manner of abominations and serenaded them with sensual music from the valley below. See Elizabeth Clare Prophet, "Prologue on the Sons of Jared Taken from the Second Book of Adam and Eve," *Fallen Angels and the Origins of Evil,* pp. 395–407.

7. Prov. 14:12.

8. *Pearls of Wisdom,* vol. 27, no. 32.

9. About 4.5 million American children under the age of 18 have been diagnosed with Attention-Deficit/ Hyperactivity Disorder (ADHD), according to 2006 statistics from the Centers for Disease Control and Prevention (CDC).

   Doctors often treat these conditions with behavior-modifying drugs to enable the child to calm down and focus on learning tasks. Ritalin, the most frequently prescribed drug, contains a powerful psychostimulant that is in the same class of drugs as cocaine but with effects described as even more potent and potentially addictive. Other drugs used to treat children with ADHD may carry warnings about hallucinations, increased aggressive behavior, suicidal thoughts and behavior, stroke and heart attack. The long-term effects of these drugs on children are unknown.

A major concern is that of misdiagnosis, as there is no specific test for the condition, only subjective evaluation. About one million children may have been improperly diagnosed with ADHD for reasons that include inadequate observation before diagnosis, pressure to rush treatment, and assessment of immature behavior for the child's grade level. (This last reason is, in some cases, attributable to the child being younger than his classmates.)

Today, 90 percent of Ritalin's sales are based in the U.S. There are reports that children as young as two years of age have received Ritalin even though the drug is approved only for those age six and older.

For additional information, including possible causes and natural therapies, see http://search.mercola.com/Results.aspx?k=ritalin. See also "Ritalin and ADHD—Recent Developments," by J. Huber, http://webhost.bridgew.edu/jhuber/readings/ritalin_and_adhd_recent_developments.html (viewed on the Web 9/1/10).

10. See David Gutierrez, "Prescription Drugs Kill 300 Percent More Americans Than Illegal Drugs," *Natural News,* November 10, 2008, http://www.truthout.org/ 111208HA

11. Richard Martin, "Prescription Drug Epidemic Spreads to Babies," *St. Petersburg Times,* July 16, 2010, http://www.tampabay.com/news/health/prescription-drug-epidemic-spreads-to-babies/1109348

12. In the U.S. alone, more than 440,000 deaths per year are linked to smoking. About 49,000 tobacco-related deaths each year are related to secondhand smoke exposure. Worldwide, tobacco use currently causes over five million deaths annually, and that number is expected to increase to over eight million deaths per year by 2030. Smokers die an average of thirteen to fourteen years earlier than nonsmokers. See http://www.cdc.gov/tobacco/data_statistics/fact_sheets/fast_facts/index.htm

13. See Helen Wambach, *Life before Life* (New York: Bantam Books, 1979), p. 26.

14. In *Life before Life,* Dr. Wambach presents findings on topics such as "choosing to live again," "when the soul enters the fetus," and "adopted children, premature births and caesarians."

15. Hypnosis, even when done with the best of intentions, can make us spiritually vulnerable. It can open us to elements of the subconscious and uncon-

scious of the practitioner. Through hypnosis we may also prematurely uncover records of events from past lives that we are not ready to deal with.

16. Wambach, *Life before Life,* p. 164.

PART 3 INTRODUCTION: *Recalling Enoch's Prophecy*
1. Jude 14, 15.

Chapter 9 UNDERSTANDING PROPHECY
1. Matt. 24:6–8.

2. Jon. 3:7–9.

3. *Pearls of Wisdom,* vol. 29, no. 75.

4. *Pearls of Wisdom,* vol. 30, no. 46.

5. *Pearls of Wisdom,* vol. 39, no. 12.

6. Street children. Saint Germain gave this message in Brazil in 1996. In urban areas and developing nations around the world, homeless children, called street children, live and work in public. They sleep in empty buildings, parks, even cardboard boxes and find food in garbage or refuse heaps. Commonly, the children turn to begging, crime—stealing, drug running and prostitution—or working for street vendors. In some cities, in an effort to "clean up" urban areas, police and citizen groups are known to target the street children, beating and, in extreme cases, murdering them.

7. *Pearls of Wisdom,* vol. 39, no. 12.

PART 4   INTRODUCTION: *In the Twinkling of an Eye*

1. Matt. 3:10; 7:17–20; Luke 3:9; 6:43.

2. I Cor. 15:52.

Chapter 11   ACCEPT YOUR DIVINE IDENTITY

1. Gen. 1:26, 27.

2. Ps. 82:6, 7. See also John 10:34.

3. Exod. 33:16; Lev. 20:24, 26; II Cor. 6:14–18.

4. Exod. 3:13–15.

5. I John 3:1, 2.

6. Sidney Spencer, *Mysticism in World Religion* (1963; reprint, Gloucester, Mass.: Peter Smith, 1971), p. 250.

7. From 303 to 311, Christians suffered their most severe persecution under the Roman emperor Diocletian. His edicts, continued by his successor, Galerius, brought the destruction of churches and sacred books, the enslavement of Christian household servants, torture, and death to some 1,500 believers. The obstinance of the Christians, who refused to sacrifice to the gods or pay homage to the Roman emperor, as well as the astounding growth of their religion, was a threat to the established order. But the persecutions failed to suppress the spread of Christianity, and the hopelessly ill Galerius issued an edict of toleration in 311 shortly before his death, asking for the prayers of the Christians in return for "our most gentle clemency." In what is considered a turning point for Christianity, Constantine, competing

for control of the Roman empire, won a decisive battle in 312 after seeing a vision of a cross in the sky bearing the words "in this sign conquer" and then ordering his soldiers to paint the cross on their shields as he was directed to do in a dream. Constantine became sole emperor in 324, and while declaring himself a Christian he continued to support both paganism and Christianity.

Although Constantine became an ever-stronger defender of the Christian cause and was baptized on his deathbed, some historians claim that he shrewdly used religion as a means to further his own political ends. In 325, when the bitter Arian controversy threatened schism in the Church, Constantine himself called the first ecumenical council of over 300 bishops in Nicaea, presided over the opening session, and took part in its debates; for "in the Arian controversy lay a great obstacle to the realization of Constantine's idea of a universal empire which was to be attained by aid of uniformity of divine worship" (The New Schaff-Herzog Encyclopedia of Religious Knowledge, s.v. "Nicaea [Nice], Councils of").

Arius taught that Christ was not equal or eternal with the Creator but as the Logos was the first and highest of created beings, whereas his opponents said the Son was "of one substance with the Father." As historian Will Durant observes, "If Christ was not God, the whole structure of Christian doctrine would begin to crack; and if division were permitted on this question, chaos of belief might destroy the unity and authority of the Church, and therefore its value as an aide to the state." The council rejected Arius' position and adopted the Nicene Creed, which read in part: "We believe in one God, the Father Almighty,... and in one Lord Jesus Christ, the Son of God, the only-begotten of his Father,... God of God, Light of Light, very God of very God."

Athanasius, who became the chief proponent of Nicene orthodoxy, explained that the intent of the creed was to show that "the resemblance of the Son to the Father, and his immutability, are different from ours: for in us they are something acquired, and arise from our fulfilling the divine commands" (*A Select Library of Nicene and Post-Nicene Fathers of the Christian Church* [Grand Rapids, Mich.: Wm. B. Eerdmans Publishing Company, 1979], 2d. ser., 14:3–4).

Arius, anathematized by the council, was exiled by edict of Constantine, who also ordered all his books to be burned upon penalty of death. Some of the bishops who assented in the presence of Constantine to the wording of the creed later expressed their remorse. "Only on returning home," says Wilson, "did Eusebius of Nicomedia, Maris of Chalcedon and Theognis of Nicaea summon the courage to express to Constantine in writing how much they regretted having put their signatures to the Nicene formula: 'We committed an impious act, O Prince,' wrote Eusebius of Nicomedia, 'by subscribing to a blasphemy from fear of you.'... Although no gospel regarded Jesus as God, and not even Paul had done so, the Jewish teacher had been declared Very God through all eternity, and a whole new theology would flow from this.... Even in the John gospel, the one most inclined to make Jesus divine, he is reported as stating quite categorically, 'the Father is greater than I' (John 14:28)."

Furthermore, the emperor's involvement in Church affairs created a precedent for civil leadership in Church councils. Nicaea "marked the replacement of paganism with Christianity as the religious expression and support of the Roman Empire," says Durant. "By [Constantine's] aid Christianity became a state as well as a church, and the mold, for fourteen centuries, of European life and thought." See Ian Wilson, *Jesus: The Evidence* (San Francisco: Harper and Row, 1984), pp. 162, 168, 176; and Will Durant, *Caesar and Christ,* vol. 3 of *The Story of Civilization* (New York: Simon and Schuster, 1944), pp. 652, 659, 661, 664.

8. Hans Jonas, *The Gnostic Religion* (Boston: Beacon Press, 1963), p. 34.

9. Gospel of Philip 67:26, 27; 61:29–35, in James M. Robinson, ed., *The Nag Hammadi Library in English* (San Francisco: Harper & Row, 1977), pp. 140, 137.

10. Exod. 33:20.

11. Exod. 3:2.

12. I Cor. 15:41.

13. Col. 2:8–10.

14. Sons and Daughters of God. See notes to chapter 3, number 12.

15. Matt. 3:17.

16. Eccles. 12:6.

17. *Ratnagotravibhāga* 1.28, in Edward Conze et al., eds., *Buddhist Texts through the Ages* (1954; reprint, New York: Harper and Row, Harper Torchbooks, 1964), p. 181.

18. *The Upanishads*, trans. Juan Mascaró (1974; reprint, Baltimore: Penguin Books, 1965), pp. 61, 60, 59.

19. Ibid., p. 66.

20. *Meister Eckhart: Sermons and Treatises*, trans. and ed. M. O'C. Walshe (Longmead, Shaftesbury, Dorset: Element Books, 1987), 3:107.

21. Joseph James, comp., *The Way of Mysticism* (New York: Harper and Brothers Publishers, n.d.), p. 64

Chapter 12 CONQUER THE ENEMY WITHIN

1. Elaine Pagels, *The Gnostic Gospels* (New York: Random House, 1979), p. 152.

2. Robinson, *Nag Hammadi Library in English*, p. 125.

3. Matt. 6:24.

4. Robinson, *Nag Hammadi Library in English*, p. 149.

5. Robert McQueen Grant, *Gnosticism and Early Christianity* (New York: Harper, 1966), p. 80.

6. G. R. S. Mead, trans., *Pistis Sophia: A Gnostic Gospel* (Blauvelt, N.Y: Spiritual Science Library, 1984), pp. 278, 279.

7. Phil. 4:7.

8. Quoted in Mark L. Prophet and Elizabeth Clare Prophet, *Paths of Light and Darkness,* pp. 206–8.

Chapter 13 RE-CREATE YOURSELF

1. John 5:30; 14:10.

2. Phil. 2:6.

3. Deut. 33:25.

4. Matt. 18:20.

5. Matt. 6:34.

6. Pss. 38:12; 64:5; 141:9; Prov. 22:5; Jer. 5:26; 18:22.

7. See Mark L. Prophet and Elizabeth Clare Prophet, *Lost Teachings on Finding God Within,* in The Lost Teachings of Jesus series, pp. 88–92.

8. Quoted in Mark L. Prophet and Elizabeth Clare Prophet, *Mary's Message for a New Day,* p. 120.

9. Mother Mary has released the Scriptural Rosary for the New Age together with messages and letters addressed to her children, published in *Mary's Message for a New Day* and *Mary's Message of Divine Love.* The thirteen rosaries in these books are for each day of the week and six evenings. Mary has released the Fourteenth Rosary (the Mystery of Surrender) as well as the 15-min. scriptural Child's Rosary, for children and adults, published in *The Age of the Divine Mother.* For rosaries in audio format, call 1-800-245-5445 or 406-848-9500.

10. *Saint Germain On Alchemy: Formulas for Self-Transformation,* pp. 350–51.

11. Bhagavad Gita, VIII:12.

12. Zohar 3:294a, quoted in *The Wisdom of the Zohar: An Anthology of Texts,* 3 vols., comp. Isaiah Tishby and Fischel Lachower, trans. David Goldstein (1989; reprint, New York: Oxford University Press for the Littman Library of Jewish Civilization, 1991), 3:952.

13. Mark L. Prophet, August 21, 1970.

14. Gen. 18:20–32.

15. Gen. 19:24.

16. *Pearls of Wisdom,* vol. 29, no. 58.

17. I John 4:4.

Chapter 14   GOD'S JUDGMENT OF MEN AND ANGELS

1. Josh. 24:15.

2. See Acts 1:7.

3. Rev. 20:11, 12.

4. Matt. 21:33–41.

5. En. 16:5.

6. See En. 37:3; 38:1; 45:1; 56:1. The Book of Enoch and all the other Enoch texts are published in Elizabeth Clare Prophet's *Fallen Angels and the Origins of Evil: Why Church Fathers Suppressed the Book of Enoch and Its Startling Revelations.*

7. I Cor. 6:2–3.

8. Matt. 16:19; 18:18.

9. John 16:23, 24. See also Matt. 21:22; John 14:13; 15:16.

PART 5   INTRODUCTION:
The Key Ingredient in All Alchemy

1. Matt. 12:37.

2. The sacred syllable Aum (or Om) has been intoned for thousands of years. The Aum releases the frequency of the Word, which went forth as the origin of creation. All that manifests comes out of the sacred Aum, and all returns to it. In the East, yogis have recognized the Aum as the mantra of mantras. In the Bible, the apostle John wrote, "In the beginning was the Word, and the Word was with God, and the Word was God" (John 1:1).

   Aum is thought to be the most abstract and yet the most concrete symbol of divinity. As a manifestation of spiritual power, it signifies the presence of the Absolute within maya, the impermanent. When we intone the Aum, we are affirming our true being. Chanting this syllable is like chanting the I AM THAT I AM, the name of God given to Moses. It attunes the soul with that energy, the fullness of the Real Self, in whose image and likeness we are made.

Chapter 15   THE CREATIVE POWER OF SOUND

1. Aryeh Kaplan, *Jewish Meditation: A Practical Guide* (New York: Schocken Books, 1985), pp. 56–57.

2. A mantra is a word or combination of words held to be sacred. Many mantras are composed of Sanskrit words. According to Hindu tradition, mantras were received by God-inspired sages who were able to listen to the fundamental tones of the universe.

3. Josh. 6:1–20.

4. Plowshares and pruning hooks. See Isa. 2:4; Joel 3:10; Micah 4:3.

5. Isa. 45:11; Job 22:27, 28.

6. Isa. 65:24.

7. John Woodroffe, *The Garland of Letters* (Pondicherry, India: Ganesh and Co., n.d.) pp. 4–5; John 1:1; Gen. 1:3.

8. Ps. 18:8; Job 41:19; Jer. 5:14; Rev. 11:5.

9. Archangel Gabriel, *Mysteries of the Holy Grail,* pp. 268–69.

10. Heb. 1:3.

11. John 5:8; Mark 4:39; Luke 8:24.

12. John 5:25; 11:43.

13. Matt. 6:9.

14. John 11:25; 8:12; 10:10; 14:6.

15. See Herbert Benson, M.D., with Miriam Z. Klipper, *The Relaxation Response,* rev. ed. (New York: HarperCollins Publishers, Quill, 2001).

16. To learn more about Saint Germain's embodiments, see Mark L. Prophet and Elizabeth Clare Prophet, *Lords of the Seven Rays: Mirror of Consciousness.*

17. Gautama Buddha, *The Dhammapada.*

18. For more teaching on the science of decreeing, see Mark L. Prophet and Elizabeth Clare Prophet, *The Science of the Spoken Word.*

Chapter 16 INVOKING SPIRITUAL PROTECTION

1. Exod. 13:21, 22; Num. 14:14; Neh. 9:12, 19; Ps. 78:14.

2. Dan. 12:1.

3. *St. Michael, Defend Us in Battle* (n.p.: Marian Press, n.d.).

4. Ps. 24:1; I Cor. 10:26, 28.

5. *Lord* is used here as a term of honor, denoting that Archangel Michael carries the power and presence of God.

Chapter 17 SAINT GERMAIN:
　　　　　　　SPONSOR OF THE AQUARIAN AGE

1. Each of the seven rays has a hierarch, called a lord, who focuses the Christ consciousness of that ray. Before being appointed to this office in the heavenly hierarchy, a candidate must have demonstrated mastery on that ray throughout numerous incarnations. Each astrological age is accompanied by a dispensation from God for the spiritual advancement of mankind. The vision for an age is held by its governing master, called the hierarch, or lord, of that age.

2. John 2:1–11.

3. Saint Germain's embodiments. See notes to chapter 15, n. 16.

4. Quoted in *Saint Germain: Master Alchemist,* pp. 13–15.

Chapter 18   TRANSFORM THE WORLD
                 WITH VIOLET FLAME

1. Isa. 1:18.

2. Matt. 6:22.

3. Mark 10:27.

Chapter 19   MORE DECREES FOR PERSONAL
                 AND PLANETARY CONDITIONS

1. Electronic Presence: a powerful replica of an ascended master, the fullness of his tangible light
   body, which can be focalized in time and space
   within the aura of a disciple. A devotee who calls to
   an ascended master (in the name of the I AM THAT
   I AM) may be blessed with his Electronic Presence.

2. Author Philip St. Romain writes: "There is nothing
   in Christian teaching comparable to the Hindu notions of chakras… and kundalini energy. Neither
   will one find in Christianity anything like the spiritualities associated with the yoga system, which are
   designed to lead one up through the various centers
   to the experience of union. Nevertheless, the chakras
   … and the awakening of kundalini can be identified
   in the experiences of many, many Christian mystics"
   (*Kundalini Energy and Christian Spirituality* [New
   York: Crossroad, 1991], pp, 74–75).

3. Francis Johnston, *Fatima: The Great Sign* (Washington, N.J.: AMI Press, 1980), p. 139. In her message
   to the children at Fátima, Mother Mary warned
   that the world is fragile, that mankind's "sins"
   (karma) have put earth in a precarious place. Her

remedy: pray and quickly make amends where you have harmed others. She outlined three specific steps to bring about world peace: recitation of the rosary, devotion to her Immaculate Heart, and penance. See "Mary's Plan for Peace," in *Saint Germain's Prophecy for the New Millennium,* chap. 10.

4. See Mary's Scriptural Rosary "The Glorious Mysteries," in *Mary's Message for a New Day,* p. 208. This rosary is especially appropriate for the topics addressed within this book.

Chapter 20   THE COMING GOLDEN AGE: A VISION FOR THE FUTURE

1. Akashic records. See notes to chapter 7, n. 1.

2. Matt. 5:48.

3. See Mark L. Prophet and Elizabeth Clare Prophet, *The Path of the Higher Self,* p. 67.

4. Rev. 21:2–7, 9–11, 18–27.

5. Gen. 5:24; Heb. 11:5.

6. *Pearls of Wisdom,* vol. 24, no. 15.

Picture Credits

Grateful acknowledgment is made for permission to reproduce the following material:

Archangel Michael (frontispiece), stained-glass window by Tiffany Studios, installed at St. Peter's Chapel, Mare Island, Vallejo, Calif.

Fallen Lucifer (p. 33): *Lucifer (le génie du mal),* by Guillaume Geefs, Cathedral of St. Paul, Liège, Belgium; photograph by Luc Viatour, www.lucnix.be

Fallen Angels and the Origins of Evil

Why Church Fathers Suppressed the Book of Enoch and Its Startling Revelations

by Elizabeth Clare Prophet

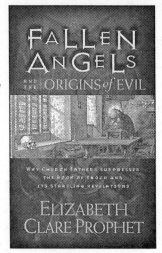

Did rebel angels take on human bodies to fulfill their lust for the "daughters of men"?

Did these fallen angels teach men to build weapons of war? That is the premise of the Book of Enoch, a text cherished by the Essenes, early Jews and Christians, but later condemned by both rabbis and Church Fathers. The book was denounced, banned and "lost" for over a thousand years—until in 1773 a Scottish explorer discovered three copies in Ethiopia.

ISBN: 978-0-922729-43-2
Pocketbook   524 pages $9.95

Elizabeth Clare Prophet examines the controversy surrounding this book and sheds new light on Enoch's forbidden mysteries. She demonstrates that Jesus and the apostles studied the book and tells why Church Fathers suppressed its teaching that angels could incarnate in human bodies.

Fallen Angels and the Origins of Evil takes you back to the primordial drama of Good and Evil, when the first hint of corruption entered a pristine world—earth.

Contains Richard Laurence's translation of the Book of Enoch, all the other Enoch texts (including the Book of the Secrets of Enoch), and biblical parallels. 12 illustrations.

SUMMIT UNIVERSITY 🌿 PRESS®

To order call 1-800-245-5445

I Am Your Guard

Terrorism. War. Earth changes. Violent crime. The threats to our families, nations and environment are enormous. Now more than ever, we need Archangel Michael. This breakthrough book will introduce you to Archangel Michael and how you can call for his protection. Revered in Jewish, Christian and Islamic traditions, Archangel Michael can protect you and your loved ones in times of trouble. All you need to know is how to ask for his help. This book shows you how.

ISBN: 978-1-932890-12-9
112 pages $8.95

Is Mother Nature Mad?

Global warming. Tsunamis. Earthquakes. Raging fires. *Is Mother Nature Mad? How to Work with Nature Spirits to Mitigate Natural Disasters* answers the age-old questions: Are natural disasters God-made or man-made? Is extreme weather a cyclic activity? What if anything has man done to bring disasters upon the earth? This book provides practical spiritual tools to help restore harmony to the environment and to mitigate extreme weather conditions. Complete with real-life stories.

ISBN: 978-1-932890-13-6
112 pages $8.95

The Story of Your Soul

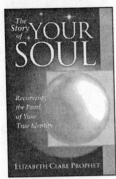

ISBN: 978-1-932890-11-2
136 pages $8.95

The soul has been likened to a pearl cast into the sea of the material universe. The goal of our life is to go after that pearl and recover our true identity. This book champions your profound worth and nobility, which only you can make a reality. Gain seven practical keys for your soul's journey, such as how to spend quality time with your soul, recognize the not-self and learn while you sleep.

How to Work with Angels

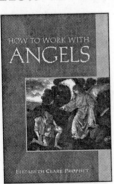

ISBN: 978-0-922729-41-8
118 pages $8.95

"Angels—and our relationship to them—are neither a trend nor a fad…. Ultimately, one's relationship with an angel is a personal one, and in *How to Work with Angels*, you'll discover how to make angels more present in your life…. Whether for love, healing, protection, guidance, or illumination, angels stand ready to help you in many practical and personal ways…. Also included here are a collection of visualizations, affirmations, prayers and decrees."

—BODHI TREE BOOK REVIEW

Saint Germain On Alchemy
Formulas for Self-Transformation

"If you think alchemy is just some archaic sleight of hand for changing lead into gold, *Saint Germain On Alchemy* will set you straight. It's about transformation: transforming yourself—first spiritually and then materially. But it doesn't stop there. Alchemy aims to transform the world itself, to guide the unfoldment of history."

—RICHARD NOLLE, author of CRITICAL ASTROLOGY

ISBN: 978-0-916766-68-9
pocketbook 540 pp. $9.95

Four books in one, including *Studies in Alchemy* and *Intermediate Studies in Alchemy* plus a section on how to experience the full potential of your heart...

"Your heart is indeed one of the choicest gifts of God. Within it there is a central chamber surrounded by a forcefield of such light and protection that we call it a 'cosmic interval.'...Be content to know that God is there and that within you there is a point of contact with the Divine, a spark of fire from the Creator's own heart, called the threefold flame of life. There it burns as the triune essence of love, wisdom and power. Each acknowledgment paid daily to the flame within your heart...will produce a new sense of dimension for you."

—SAINT GERMAIN

OTHER TITLES FROM
SUMMIT UNIVERSITY ✺ PRESS®

RELATED TITLES

Fallen Angels and the Origins of Evil

I Am Your Guard

Is Mother Nature Mad?

The Story of Your Soul

The Creative Power of Sound

*Violet Flame
to Heal Body, Mind and Soul*

*Saint Germain's Prophecy
for the New Millennium*

ADDITIONAL TITLES

ISSA: The Greatest Story Never Told

The Shakespeare Code

Saint Germain On Alchemy

The Lost Years of Jesus

Your Seven Energy Centers

Karma and Reincarnation

The Art of Practical Spirituality

How to Work with Angels

Creative Abundance

Soul Mates and Twin Flames

Alchemy of the Heart

FOR MORE INFORMATION

Summit University Press books are available at fine bookstores everywhere. A wide selection of our titles has been translated into a total of 29 languages.

To download a free catalog of Summit University Press books, eBooks, CDs and DVDs:

Go to www.SummitUniversityPress.com

or

Contact us at:

Summit University Press
63 Summit Way, Gardiner, MT 59030-9314 USA

1-800-245-5445 or 1-406-848-9500
Fax: 1-800-221-8307 or 1-406-848-9555

Email: info@SummitUniversityPress.com

SUMMIT UNIVERSITY 🔥 PRESS®

The logo of Summit University Press, the flame in the bowl, represents the spiritual essence abiding within each of us. The mission of Summit University Press is to help readers worldwide fulfill their unique spiritual potential by expanding the flame within.

MARK L. PROPHET AND ELIZABETH CLARE PROPHET have pioneered techniques in practical spirituality, including the creative power of sound for personal growth and world transformation. Among their best-selling titles are *Fallen Angels and the Origins of Evil, Saint Germain On Alchemy, The Science of the Spoken Word, The Lost Years of Jesus, The Human Aura* and *The Story of Your Soul*. A wide selection of their books has been translated into a total of 29 languages and is available worldwide.

The unpublished works of Mark L. Prophet and Elizabeth Clare Prophet continue to be published by Summit University Press.